THE PENGUIN

HISTORICAL
ATLAS OF
THE PACIFIC

Also by Colin McEvedy

The Penguin Atlas of African History

The Penguin Atlas of Ancient History

The New Penguin Atlas of Medieval History

The Penguin Atlas of Modern History

The Penguin Atlas of North American History

The Penguin Atlas of Recent History

The Atlas of World Population History
(with Richard Jones)

Century World History Factfinder

THE PENGUIN

HISTORICAL
ATLAS OF
THE PACIFIC

Colin McEvedy

PENGUIN REFERENCE

PENGUIN BOOKS

Published by the Penguin Group
Penguin Putnam Inc., 375 Hudson Street,
New York, New York 10014, U.S.A.
Penguin Books Ltd, 27 Wrights Lane,
London W8 5TZ, England
Penguin Books Australia Ltd, Ringwood,
Victoria, Australia
Penguin Books Canada Ltd, 10 Alcorn Avenue,
Toronto, Ontario, Canada M4V 3B2
Penguin Books (N.Z.) Ltd, 182–190 Wairau Road,
Auckland 10, New Zealand
Penguin India, 210 Chiranjiv Tower, 43 Nehru Place,
New Delhi 11009, India

Penguin Books Ltd, Registered Offices:
Harmondsworth, Middlesex, England

First published in Penguin Books 1998

1 3 5 7 9 10 8 6 4 2

LIBRARY OF CONGRESS CATALOGING IN PUBLICATION DATA
McEvedy, Colin.
The Penguin historical atlas of the Pacific/Colin McEvedy.
p.   cm.—(Penguin reference books)   Includes index.
ISBN 0-14-02.5428-5 (pbk.)
1. Pacific Ocean—Historical geography—Maps. 2. Pacific Ocean—Maps.
3. Islands of the Pacific—Maps. I. Title.
II. Title: Historical atlas of the Pacific. III. Series.
G 2861.S1 M3 1998   <G&M>
911'.9—DC21   98-9434   Maps

Printed in the United States of America
Set in Minion
Designed by Virginia Norey

Contents

Introduction

This is one of a series of atlases that use maps and text to tell the story of a continent or a similar-sized slice of the earth's surface. It differs from its companion volumes in the extent of the area it covers, which, the Pacific being the size it is, comes to nearly half the globe. The larger scope poses problems for both maps and text.

Take the base map first. If every element in this map were drawn strictly to scale, most of the Pacific's few features would be invisible—the islands because they are so small, the atolls (coral rings) because they are so thin. But many of these specks and wisps are essential members of the cast, so we have to get them onto the map somehow. The solution is to use a standard symbol—a small circle—to mark the position of selected islands. Not too many, because that would lead to an overly busy picture; not too few, because a minimum number is needed to define the shape of each of the various clusters. The end result may not be, in the strictest cartographic sense, a map of the Pacific, but it is a fair representation. The few oceanic islands that are larger than the symbol (which has a diameter of about 50 miles, or 80 km) appear in their correct geographical guise: this is the case, for example, with the "Big Island" of Hawaii. Atolls, with their tiny surface areas, are always represented by conventional circles.

So far, so consistent. Unfortunately, an opposite set of rules apply to the Pacific rim, where the geography is easy to read even on a map of this scale. The requirement here is not to magnify but to simplify. What we need to know about the Japanese, Philippine, and Indonesian archipelagos is their basic layout, and to attempt to show even a selection of the minor islands that clutter the channels between the major ones would be to confuse the eye to no profit. The same goes for the complicated, island-strewn coasts of South China and Korea: in the name of clarity the offshore elements have to be drastically culled. If this sounds a bit cavalier, it is worth remembering that every map selects and distorts. At the simplest level this is because it is impossible to represent a spherical surface on a plane. The modified Mercator projection used for the base map, for example, means that the horizontal scale varies with latitude. The effect is considerable: a mile at the top of the map comes out twice as long as a mile at the

equator. Siberia, Alaska, and the Canadian northwest may be vast, but they aren't quite as vast—or, for that matter, quite the same shape—as the atlas suggests.

A final cartographic point: despite the book's title, the base map does not cover all of the Pacific; the southeast corner is missing, along with South America's contribution to the rim. What you get instead is Southeast Asia. This is a good trade—the Southeast Asians were responsible for peopling the Pacific, whereas South America's role in the region's history has been negligible. In fact, it's an offer that the historical geographer can't refuse: people are the primary concern, and it is their movements that define the stage.

As regards the narrative, the effects of the enhanced scale are every bit as significant. Whereas the other atlases in the series deal with coherent groups of societies—the classical world centered on the Mediterranean, medieval Christendom and Islam, Europe in early modern times, and so on—there is little linkage between the different cultures that developed in and around the Pacific. When the first Europeans came on the scene in the sixteenth century, they found peoples at every stage of development: Paleolithic and Neolithic, imperial and feudal. About all they had in common was their total or near-total ignorance of each other. In movie terms, this is the one about strangers from entirely different walks of life who end up sharing a lifeboat. The nineteenth century brought these strangers together, and the twentieth has made traveling companions of them. But though it is now reasonable to talk of the Pacific as an economic unit, the cultural differences engendered by distance are still marked. Where the other atlases have a single story line, this one has a mix of tales that plait together only gradually.

A FEW WORDS ABOUT LIMITS AND USAGES. The map doesn't quite cover its half of the globe: there are cutoffs in the north (at 65°N, just short of the Arctic Circle) and the south (at 50°S, considerably short of both the Antarctic Circle and Antarctica). Small maps on pages 48, 56, and 64 show some of the area missing in the north (the Bering Strait region); others, on pages 34 and 46, show the entry to the Pacific via the southern tip of South America.

In general, places named in the text appear on the map opposite. When they don't, you can locate them by using the index and the index map or, on occasion, the small maps, and insets to the main maps. The names of the four major Japanese islands (Hokkaido, Honshu, Shikoku, and Kyushu) and the four most significant states on the opposite side of the ocean (British Columbia, Washington, Oregon, and California) rarely appear on any of the maps: you should know where these are, and be ashamed of yourself if you don't.

On the whole, the closer events are to the center of the map, the more notice is taken of them, but all changes registered on the map get a line or two. The only area not treated is the corner of India that appears at the left-hand margin: this belongs to another world and is in general ignored. An exception is the period of British rule, when the subcontinent provided the base for the extension of the British empire into the Far East. Consequently it gets a label, though little other attention, during the years between the British acquisition of Bengal (1763) and the end of the Raj (1947).

The chronological sequence has a similar bias, favoring modern times over the more distant past. We are into historical time by map 5 (1200 BC), and on the eve of the voyages of discovery by map 14 (AD 1415). From this point on the coverage becomes fuller: as against the single map that serves the fifteenth century, the sixteenth and subsequent centuries get at least five maps each, and the twentieth century gets twelve.

Money is expressed in Venetian ducats in the early sixteenth century, in sterling from the late sixteenth century to the late eighteenth, and in United States dollars (with sterling equivalent) after 1782. Distances are in statute miles, followed by the equivalent in kilometers. Until 1900, Japanese personal names are given in Asian order, with the family name first: in this century they are written western-style, with the family name last.

On the question of spelling, I have tried to be consistent without getting fanatical about it. Chinese names are given in the Pinyin form officially adopted by the People's Republic in 1958: exceptions have been made where a long-established English usage remains current, as in the case, for example, with Canton and Chiang Kai-shek. The common alternatives, most of them examples of the Wade-Giles system of transliteration, are given in the index and cross-referenced. Burmese place names are given in the forms laid down by the authorities in 1989, except in the case of Ava, where I have preferred the old-style spelling to the official Inwa. I have also kept the dichotomy between ethnicity and citizenship in its old form (Burman, Burmese) as against the officially favored Bamar, Myanmar. Again, most of the variants are listed and cross-referenced in the index.

IT IS OBVIOUS THAT A HISTORY of half the world—and roughly 40 percent of its population—must be a précis to end all précis, and that the atlas has to skip many interesting topics. There is very little here for the archaeologist, the anthropologist, and the cultural historian: many of the stories that they would wish to have told, and indeed are well worth telling, have had to be left out. There's nothing on Lapita pottery or cargo cults or Polynesian taboos; no mention of Melville in the Marquesas or of Gauguin on Tahiti. However, this page provides an opportunity to pull back one anecdote from the mountain of discarded tales, and, on the grounds that it makes me smile (on a good day; on bad days it makes me more anxious), I've chosen the following incident from Perry's first visit to Japan. The Japanese authorities resisted this because they were convinced that contact with the outside world would be detrimental to the existing order—indeed, would actively promote disorder. A good example of what they feared was the Taiping rebellion currently in progress in China. Anxious to bring the American around to their point of view, the Japanese asked Perry what he thought had been the root cause of the Chinese rising. "Discontent of the people with the government" was the commodore's prompt reply. The answer so astonished the Japanese interpreter that, after turning it over in his mind for some moments, he decided not to translate it at all. The plenipotentiaries assumed that Perry's few words simply acknowledged the telling nature of the point they had made, and everyone relaxed. Even as a debating point the American concept of the people as sovereign couldn't make it across the beach. East is East, as Kipling said some years later.

Things are different now, of course. The Japanese have universal suffrage and regular elections; they have even voted a government out of office on one occasion. Some neighboring countries have also taken significant steps along the road to democracy, and the hope must be that, as living standards rise, the rest of East Asia will follow. My guess—on a good day—is that we won't be too far into the twenty-first century before this hope is fulfilled.

PART 1   SETTING THE SCENE

With one-third of the earth's surface area, the Pacific Ocean is the world's biggest single feature. It is double the size of the Atlantic and could accommodate all of the five continents. Nonetheless, it is only a shadow of its former self: at its best, some 200 million years ago, it stretched over an entire hemisphere. The continents were then all on the far side of the globe, fused into a single landmass that we now call Pangaea.

The engine that maintained this lopsided distribution was the East Pacific Rise, a crack in the earth's surface that ran from the Antarctic up toward the North Pole at around 110–120° W. Cracks of this type have been present throughout the earth's history and have generated much of its geography. They appear wherever there is an upwelling of unusually hot rock in the earth's mantle. Some of this hot rock oozes out from the crack to form new strips of ocean floor; most of it creeps away sideways, carrying the strips away from the crack. Successive strips fuse to form plates, one on either side of each crack, and, as more strips are added, the plates slowly migrate over the earth's surface, in some instances carrying whole continents on their backs. Of course there has to be a balancing consumption of plate material elsewhere: this happens where the plates collide with each other. One of the two is forced under, and most of the loser's material subsequently sinks back into the mantle.

In its heyday the East Pacific Rise generated two enormous plates, one covering the western half of the Pacific hemisphere and holding Asia in place, the other covering the eastern half and pressing the Americas up against Europe and Africa. Each year the Rise added a few centimeters of rock to the inner edges of the two plates, and tens of millions of years later the same rock arrived at the plates' outer boundaries, where it was subducted under the margins of the continental plates. However, not all of it was consumed in this process; some of it bubbled back up and fueled lines of volcanoes on the plate margins. This is the reason why the rim of the Pacific has always been marked by a "ring of fire," a girdle of volcanically active islands and mountain ranges.

Some 150 million years ago the East Pacific Rise acquired a serious rival, the Mid-Atlantic Ridge. This first appeared in the form of a crack between the Americas and Africa. It proved energetic enough to create a new ocean, the Atlantic, driving the Americas westward. As they moved to the west, the Americas consumed the western half of the ocean floor generated by the East Pacific Rise. By the date of this map North America was closing up on the Rise and had actually overrun a small part of it.

The eastern half of the floor was also being encroached on, in this case by Australia, which had split off from Antarctica at the same time as the Americas had separated from Africa, and was now moving up from the south. Only Asia was still being held at arm's length by the ocean floor generated at the East Pacific Rise. In fact, the Pacific Ocean was beginning to be largely a matter of one plate, which is why geologists now reserve the term Pacific Plate for the one that corresponds to the surface geography.

The map gives a current view of how the Pacific hemisphere looked 28 million years ago. There's not much argument about the positions of the continents, though the way of showing them, by using mostly modern outlines, is a bit dodgy: the actual coastlines would have varied from these, often quite considerably. Nor is the basic shape of the major plates in dispute. Island geography is another matter. Though most of the larger islands had already been created (at plate margins, by the bubbling-back process already described), many were still far from their present positions and keeping very different company. The Philippine Sea Plate, rotating clockwise, is thought to have done most of the necessary work, bring-ing the central and southern Philippines (P) up to meet Luzon (L), and carrying a long train of bits and pieces across the top of New Guinea: Halmahera (H), which ended up just to the northeast of it; a set of fragments (NNG), which got caught by New Guinea's advance and were subsequently transformed into its northern coast; and New Britain (NB), which has retained its separate identity.[1]

Oceanic islands—islands formed on the body of the plate, rather than at its edges—certainly existed, but they are typically short-lived structures and most of those that feature on present-day maps of the Pacific weren't in existence 28 million years ago. We do know of one that was, Midway Island, which began to form about this time. More of this over.

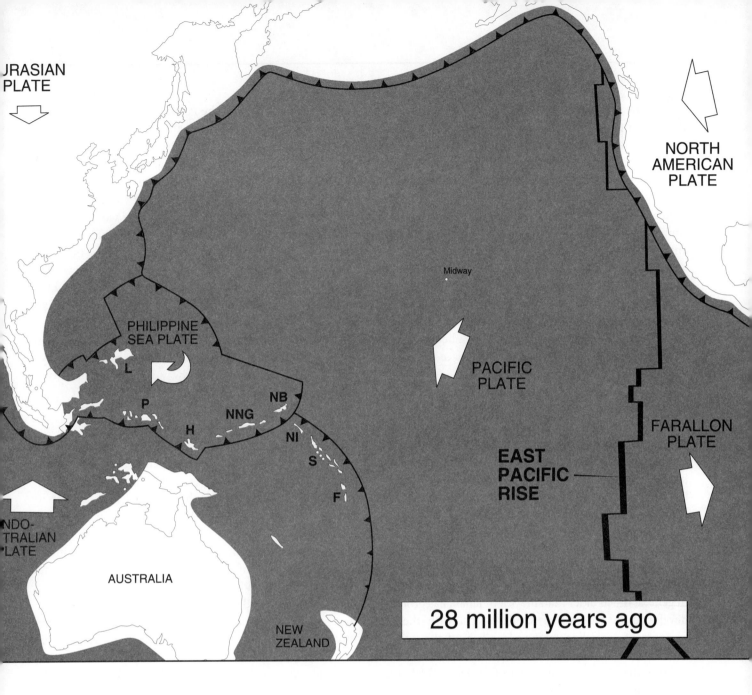

EURASIAN PLATE

NORTH AMERICAN PLATE

Midway

PACIFIC PLATE

PHILIPPINE SEA PLATE

L

P

H

NB

NNG

NI

S

F

EAST PACIFIC RISE

FARALLON PLATE

INDO-AUSTRALIAN PLATE

AUSTRALIA

NEW ZEALAND

28 million years ago

*1. The line of islands just below New Britain is made up of New Ireland (NI), the Solomons (S), and Fiji (F). The first two were moving southwest, but Fiji, which had its own microplate, was rotating counterclockwise, while otherwise staying put. The map, which is concerned with the broad picture, doesn't show the Fiji microplate or various other minor features. In particular, it omits the train of islands extending west-northwest of Midway, of which Kure is the sole survivor today. The others still exist in the form of the (submerged) Emperor Seamounts: their rise, migration, and fall are the result of the same mechanism that created the current Hawaiian archipelago, as described overleaf.

The convention for plate edges is that the sawtooth trim points toward the winning plate: for example, the North American Plate is riding over the Farallon Plate, or as geologists prefer to put it, the Farallon Plate is being subducted beneath the North American Plate.

As the continents that ringed the Pacific moved to their present-day positions—which they had done, give or take a kilometer or so, by the date of this map—the ocean's outline underwent some interesting changes. One of the best known occurred as North America moved across the northern part of the East Pacific Rise. This didn't put the fire out: the overlapped section of the Rise simply rearranged itself into an active southern segment and a northern shear zone. The southern segment proved energetic enough to split Baja California off from Mexico: the shear zone, the famous San Andreas Fault, allowed the Pacific Plate to retain control of the coastal strip of United States California. As a result this strip moves with the plate: it is sliding—juddering might be a better word—northwestward across the advancing face of North America.

Other modifications to the geography of the Pacific have been caused by "back-arc spreading." We have seen how subducted material bubbles back at the edges of a plate to form island chains. The Kurils and Aleutians, for example, mark the northern border of the Pacific Plate. back-arc spreading is caused by material that gets further back under the winning plate before bubbling back: this deeper distillation creates not islands, but extra sea floor. The Sea of Japan formed in this way, beginning sometime before the date of the last map: first it split the Japanese islands off from the mainland of Asia, then it pushed them out to their present position. The Philippine Sea, though in general much older than the Sea of Japan, has probably developed in a series of similar steps, with the last episodes of spreading taking place behind the Bonins, Volcanos, and Marianas.

From the Marianas the border of the Pacific Plate runs southwest via Yap and the Palaus toward the head of New Guinea, then east along the top of New Guinea, southeast past the Bismarcks, the Solomons, Vanuatu, and Fiji (all of which have their own miniplates), and finally southward to New Zealand.

Activity along the western edge of the Pacific Plate explains the existence of most of the larger Pacific islands, but what is the mechanism responsible for the smaller "oceanic" islands that occur on the body of the plate? We had one example on the first map, the island of Midway. This was created at a "hot spot," a place where extra-hot mantle rock was able to break through the sea floor and start building a volcano. Since Midway first raised its head above the waves, however, two things have happened: the conveyor-belt action of the Pacific Plate has moved it off its hot spot and carried it 1500 miles (2500 km) to the northwest, and the hot spot has glooped out a whole series of new islands. The result is that there is now a line of them stretching back from Midway to the one currently under construction, the "Big Island" of Hawaii. One hot spot has created an archipelago. The line would be even longer than it is if the seas didn't gradually batter the islands down. This decline sets in as soon as a new-made island is moved off the cooker, though in the warm waters of the Central and South Pacific the process is delayed by the coral reefs that form protective rings around the islands. In fact, the last state of a hot-spot island in the tropics typically takes the form of an atoll, an empty coral ring with a few sandbar islets scattered around its periphery. This is the condition of Midway today, and there are splendid examples of atolls at the northern ends of many of the island chains in the South Pacific.

If the Pacific Plate has, by and large, managed to maintain its integrity over the last 28 million years, the Indo-Australian Plate has done better than that; it has ground its way northward at the expense of both the Eurasian and the Philippine Sea plates. At the extreme left of the map it is just possible to make out India's collision with Asia, a collision responsible for the massive crustal thickening expressed in the Himalayan and associated mountain ranges, and, back of them, the Tibetan Plateau. On the central front the advance of Australia has pushed New Guinea past the end of the Indonesian archipelago, creating some odd-shaped assemblages like Sulawesi in the process. Biologically, however, Indonesia and Australasia remain separate worlds. The channels between Borneo and Sulawesi, and between Bali and Lombok, are too wide for land animals to swim and too deep to be significantly diminished even at the extremes of the ice ages, when the sea level fell by more than 100 meters. This was fortunate for the Australian fauna, much of which was not really competitive. Australia had broken off from Pangaea at a time when only the simpler sort of mammals were in existence, and simple mammals—either egg-laying monotremes or pouched marsupials—were all that Australia had. By contrast, Asia was plentifully stocked with placental mammals, an order that had evolved later and was generally more efficient.

This was not just a matter of having bigger and better herbivores or larger and more persistent carnivores—the placentals included types that had no marsupial equiva-

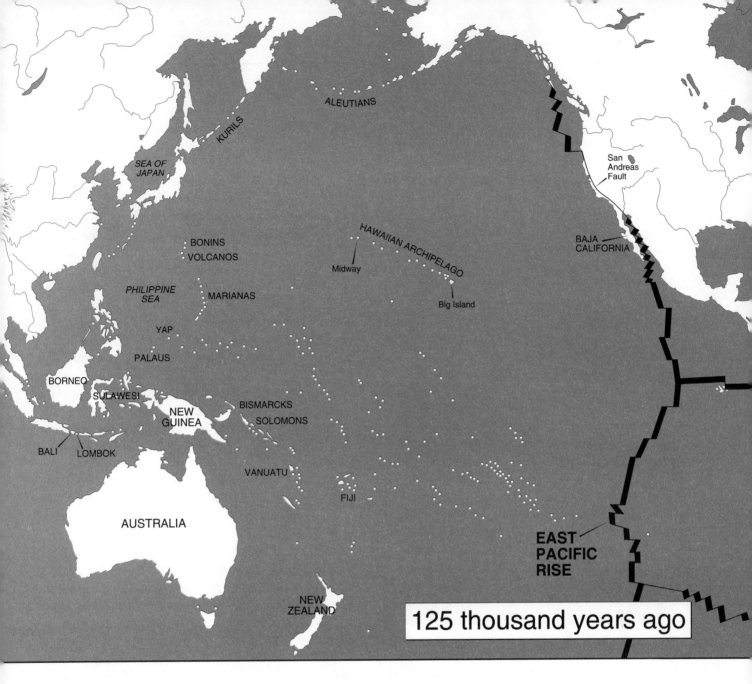

ALEUTIANS

KURILS

SEA OF
JAPAN

San
Andreas
Fault

BONINS
VOLCANOS

HAWAIIAN ARCHIPELAGO

Midway

BAJA
CALIFORNIA

PHILIPPINE
SEA

MARIANAS

Big Island

YAP

PALAUS

BORNEO

SULAWESI

NEW
GUINEA

BISMARCKS

SOLOMONS

BALI   LOMBOK

VANUATU

FIJI

AUSTRALIA

EAST
PACIFIC
RISE

NEW
ZEALAND

125 thousand years ago

lent. A good example is the primate order (lemurs, monkeys, and apes), which had brought more brain to the business of browsing. The latest primate model was particularly impressive: the genus *Homo* was quicker-witted than any of its predecessors and had emerged from Africa, where it had evolved, with a formidable range of skills. These included fire-raising, toolmaking, and rudimentary speech. Moreover, sometime around the date of this map, the existing form, *H. erectus,* was replaced by an even smarter version, *H. sapiens.* This was clearly a species to watch.

Around 50,000 BC humans succeeded in making the crossing from the eastern end of the Indonesian archipelago to Australia. The sea level was low at the time—about 100 meters lower than at present—but not low enough to expose a land bridge: the people who made the crossing, the ancestors of today's Australian Aborigines, must have had boats of a sort. Probably these boats were little different from the bark canoes used by the coastal Australian tribes when they were first observed by Europeans, rickety craft braced by irregular struts, viable only in calm seas. The rest of their equipment was equally basic: spears but not bows and arrows, no domestic animals, no cultivatable plants, baskets but not pottery. Not that they were in any way backward: this was the technological level of the era, and the hunter-gatherer communities they left behind in Asia would have had no more.

The reason the sea level was low was that much of the water normally in the oceans was locked up in the massive ice caps that covered Canada and northern Europe. For this was an ice age, a period when, for reasons which are still not entirely clear, the earth's climate got markedly colder, and, with some relatively short intermissions, stayed that way for hundreds of thousands of years. This posed great problems for the human populations living in northern latitudes. In Europe a special cold-adapted physique evolved, which helped the locals cope with the bitter weather. Another approach was to improve the equipment needed to operate in such a hostile environment, and this proved to be the superior option. By 10,000 BC the hunters of Asia had warm enough clothing and sufficiently effective weapons to operate in the far north, where herds of mammoth provided a good living for those brave enough to tackle them. Eventually this brought these early Asians to the eastern end of the land bridge that connected Siberia with Alaska. The way into America proper was still blocked by the massive North American ice cap, but the ice age was now ending (or intermitting?) and the ice caps were shrinking, a process that accelerated in the course of the tenth millennium BC. Finally the North American cap split into two halves, opening up a corridor through which a band of hunters, perhaps consisting of no more than 50 individuals, was able to make its way south to the Great Plains. Behind it, the window of opportunity was already closing, for as the ice caps continued to melt, the sea level rose and the Beringian land bridge became the Bering Strait.[1]

It seems that the first Americans made short work of the previously unhunted mammoths and mastodons of the Great Plains. The flint spearheads ("Clovis points") characteristic of this initial phase of Paleoindian culture have been found embedded in mammoth skeletons at the sites shown on the map. All of them have been radiocarbon-dated to around 9250 BC. This has been taken as the date of the map, which thus marks the point when humans completed their colonization of the major land masses.

As regards the stay-at-homes of East Asia, we can now, thanks to linguistic analysis, divide them into four stocks. The north of the continent—Siberia, Mongolia, and Manchuria—was occupied by peoples speaking Eurasiatic languages. South of them—in the northern half of China and in Tibet—were the Sino-Tibetans; and, south of them—in the southern half of China and mainland Southeast Asia—the Austrics. South again—in the island world that stretches from the Andamans across the Indonesian archipelago to New Guinea, the Bismarcks, and the Solomons—we have the Indo-Pacific peoples. These linguistic groupings coincide reasonably well with the ethnic groupings previously proposed by physical anthrolopologists, who called the Eurasiatics "archaic Caucasians," the middle two stocks "Mongoloids," and the Indo-Pacific group "Melanesians."

At one time it was thought that the Melanesians' Negroid characteristics—their black skin, broad noses, and frizzy hair—indicated a relationship with the populations of sub-Saharan Africa. Blood group studies soon showed that there was no basis for this idea, the similarities being simply an example of parallel evolution by two populations living on the equator. Melanin, the pigment that makes black people black, is present in all human stocks: its main function is to protect the skin from damage by the ultraviolet rays in sunlight, and it will obviously be selected for in the tropics. Conversely, it will be needed less in higher latitudes, and the progressive change in skin color, from the Melanesians' black through the Austrics' brown and the Sino-Tibetans' yellow to the white of the Austro-Asiatics, reflects this diminishing requirement.

The rise in sea level caused by the melting of the ice caps cut Australia off from New Guinea and Tasmania from Australia. The native Tasmanians were wiped out in the course of the European settlement of the island, but anthropologists have examined their bones and linguists have looked at what was recorded of their speech: both agree that they seem to have been closer to the Indo-

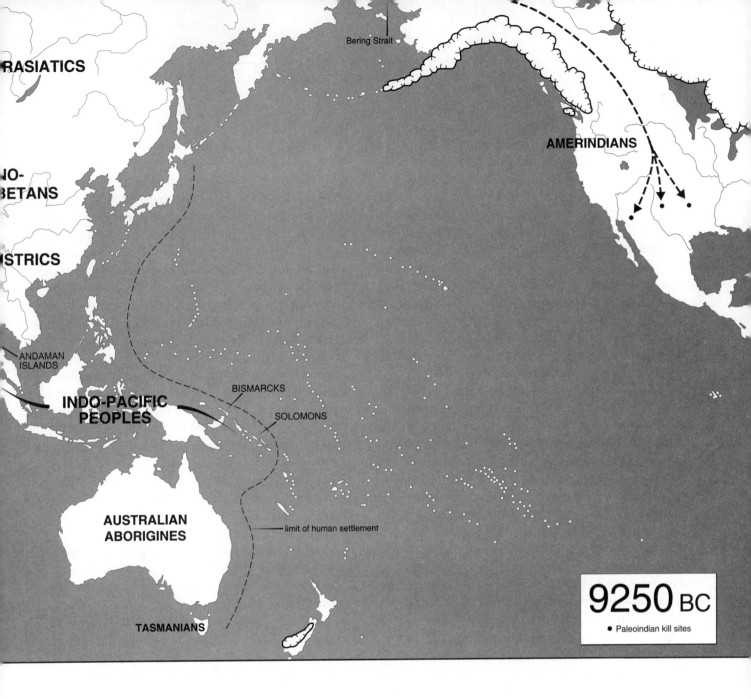

RASIATICS

NO-
BETANS

STRICS

ANDAMAN
ISLANDS

INDO-PACIFIC
PEOPLES

BISMARCKS

SOLOMONS

AUSTRALIAN
ABORIGINES

limit of human settlement

TASMANIANS

Bering Strait

AMERINDIANS

9250 BC

• Paleoindian kill sites

Pacific stock than to the Australian. It is very difficult, looking at the map, to see how this can be so. One is inclined to echo the pious lady who, on being told of Darwin's theory of evolution, said, "Let us hope that it is not true, and, if it is, that it does not become generally known."

*1. The explanation most commonly trotted out for ice ages is a variation in received sunlight caused by wobbles in the earth's rotation. But this cannot be a significant factor, because ice ages are major, irregular, and global, whereas the sunlight fluctuations defined by the Milankovitch equations are minor and periodic and have opposite consequences in the Northern and Southern Hemispheres. The phenomenon must be related to the changing configuration of the continents, but exactly how remains debatable.

Between the tenth and fifth millennia BC hunter-gatherers moved into the various peninsulas and island arcs that form the northern part of the Pacific rim. The result was the breakup of the Eurasiatic phylum into separate linguistic stocks. The far north was occupied by the Eskimo-Aleut of the Bering Strait region and the Chukchi-Kamchatkans of northeastern Siberia. The Eskimo-Aleut, who had developed a highly specialized way of life based on fishing and seal hunting, expanded into North America: the Eskimo—better known nowadays as the Inuit—following America's northern coast and eventually spreading all the way along it to Greenland; the Aleut turning south to occupy the Alaskan peninsula and Aleutian Islands. The Chukchi-Kamchatkans differentiated into the Chukchi (in the interior) and the Kamchatkans (occupying the peninsula named after them). Two different stocks competed for the Japanese islands. The Ainu moved into the archipelago from the north, via the island of Sakhalin: from Hokkaido one group continued south into Honshu, while another turned northeast, into the Kurils. The Japanese—who at this stage can hardly have differed significantly from the Koreans—entered Honshu from Korea: they occupied the southern half of Honshu, plus Kyushu and Shikoku; they also moved into the Ryukyu Islands to the south of Kyushu. The stay-at-homes in this time of Eurasiatic dispersal were the Altaic peoples, the ancestors of the present-day Turks, Mongols, and Tungus. The southern limit of their distribution is indicated by a line of circles, a convention that will be developed further in subsequent maps.

To the south of the Altaic peoples, note the division of Sino-Tibetan into Tibeto-Burman (on the Tibetan plateau) and Chinese (along the Yellow River). Further south still, the Austric linguistic phylum has split into Proto-Austro-Tai (in south China) and Austro-Asiatic (in southeast Asia). The Austro-Asiatics have been given an oblique shading to distinguish them from the Proto-Austro-Tai and Tibeto-Burmans to their north, and the Indo-Pacific peoples to their south. Overshadowing these linguistic developments, however, is the appearance of a new lifestyle. Many of the people in this region were no longer simply gathering the plants they ate—they were cultivating them. For these pioneers the Old Stone Age was over: the New Stone Age—the Neolithic, the age of agriculture—had begun.

Three Pacific peoples embraced the new lifestyle to a greater or lesser extent: the Chinese, the Proto-Austro-Tai (PAT-speakers), and, at the far end of the Indonesian archipelago, the Indo-Pacific Papuans of New Guinea. Of the three the Chinese were much the most enthusiastic. Throughout the Yellow River valley the temporary camps of the hunter-gatherers were replaced by permanent villages; the relatively indolent habits of the hunter gave way to regular hours of labor in the fields; and animals that had been the object of the hunters' chase, most notably the pig, were domesticated and brought into the agricultural cycle. By the fourth millennium BC the area had become home to a peasantry 1 million strong, and the Chinese nation had acquired the exceptional numerical strength that has been one of its leading characteristics ever since.

The Chinese staple was millet, a cereal that remains important today. Now, however, it is completely overshadowed by rice, which is the main food for literally billions of people. Yet the people who domesticated rice, the PAT-speakers, seem to have been surprisingly lukewarm about it, at least to start with. Rice became part of their diet but didn't dominate it, and the basics of their way of life continued much the same as before. As a result, their number didn't increase much: they remained almost as thin on the ground as when they had been hunters and gatherers.

Much the same could be said about the Papuans, who pioneered the development of yet another staple, taro. Taro plots were always small, more like gardens than fields; shifts of habitation remained common; and the men still spent most of their time hunting. There were more Papuans than there had been before they invented their system of horticulture, eventually perhaps ten times as many. But that was a far cry from the hundredfold increase already achieved by the Chinese.

A few minor points. The Austro-Asiatics have moved into the Nicobar Islands, separating the Indo-Pacific Andaman Islanders (A on the map) from the rest of their kin. And the PAT-speakers have colonized Taiwan. Rice cultivation subsequently began there: it was also seeping into the Austro-Asiatic zone. In North America, note the appearance of the Athapascans, who arrived from Asia about 6000 BC and made a meager living hunting caribou and moose through the subarctic regions of Canada. Linguists, who refer to them as Na-Dene (pronounced "Nahdenay"), have not, as yet, managed to work out their position in the language tree, but presumably they will turn out to be an aberrant branch of the Eurasiatic stem.

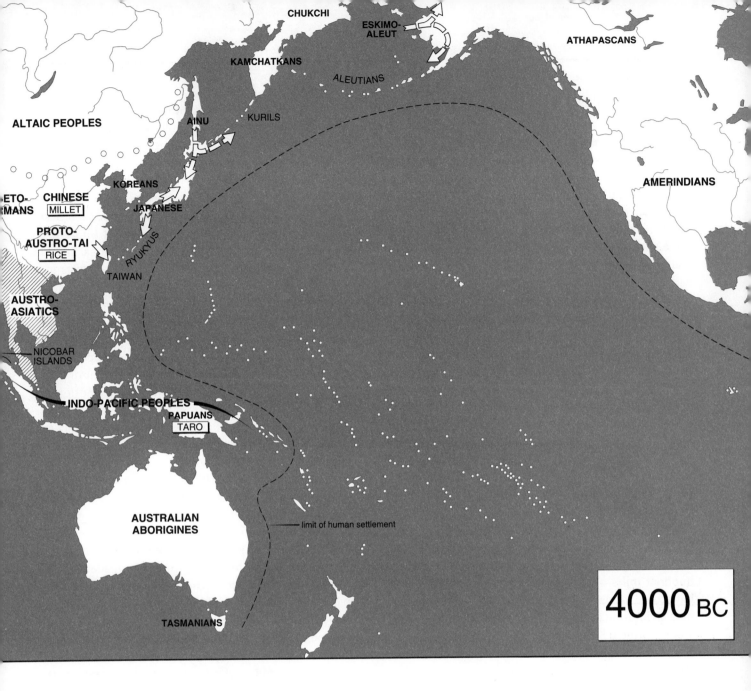

CHUKCHI

ESKIMO-
ALEUT

ATHAPASCANS

KAMCHATKANS

ALEUTIANS

KURILS

AINU

ALTAIC PEOPLES

AMERINDIANS

KOREANS

ETO-
MANS

CHINESE
MILLET

JAPANESE

PROTO-
AUSTRO-TAI
RICE

RYUKYUS

TAIWAN

AUSTRO-
ASIATICS

NICOBAR
ISLANDS

INDO-PACIFIC PEOPLES

PAPUANS
TARO

AUSTRALIAN
ABORIGINES

limit of human settlement

4000 BC

TASMANIANS

By the middle of the second millenniuum BC the Yellow River valley had been under cultivation for more than 3000 years, and its population was into the millions—5 million would be a reasonable guess. This human resource provided the basis for the first political structure we can put on our map, the Shang kingdom of North China. Later history knew of 30 Shang kings, but very little of their doings, and in modern times some scholars came to the conclusion that there was more myth than matter to the traditional list. However, in the 1930s excavations at the Shang capital, the city of Yin, confirmed that kings and kingdom really had existed. The most striking evidence came in the form of inscribed "oracle bones." These are not, alas, historical records of any directly useful sort, but annotations written on the bones used in the divination ceremonies of the Shang court. They confirm the reality of the Shang dynasty: more important, they show that the Chinese had already developed the script that was to become the hallmark of their civilization. The stereotyped questions ("Should the king make sacrifice today?") illustrate another facet of Chinese culture, the conviction that good harvests depended on correctly performed court rituals. Heaven and earth found their only safe connection through the royal person.

Of course, there was also a practical side to Shang rule. The king could raise armies several thousand strong, sufficient to impose his will on the territories within several hundred miles of the capital. Tributary embassies may have come from even farther afield. But the focus of Chinese civilization at this time was restricted to the central section of the Yellow River valley: those living beyond this horizon, whatever their nature, were regarded as "barbarians."

The barbarians were an interesting lot—not so much to the south, where the Tai peoples were stuck in their rather desulatory semiagricultural cycle (and were probably already beginning to lose territory to Chinese colonists), but to the west and north, where the Tibeto-Burmans of the Tibetan plateau and the Altaic peoples of the Mongolian grasslands had developed a pastoral style of life, herding cattle, sheep, and horses. This enabled them to multiply up to reasonable population levels: perhaps 100,000 for the Altaians south of the Siberian forests (i.e., below the gray tint), and something similar for the Tibeto-Burmans. Considering the bleakness of their environment, the achievement was remarkable.[1]

In Taiwan the PAT-speakers who had settled the island in the Neolithic era subsequently evolved a language of their own, a development that linguists mark by designating them Austronesians. As such they became the founding members of an ethnolinguistic group that was to play a leading role in Pacific history. The opening chapter in the story has the Taiwanese Austronesians discovering a route to the Philippines and colonizing the northernmost members of this island group. This may not sound like a major event—the journey is made easy by a line of stepping-stone islands, and the number of colonists involved was probably very small—but the settlers brought their rice-based agriculture with them, the environment proved appropriate for this, and the subsequent rise in numbers stimulated further expansion. As they moved through the archipelago, the migrants developed their seafaring skills: in particular they improved their dugout canoes by adding side boards and outriggers, transforming what had been unstable, easily swamped craft into reliable seagoing vessels. They emerged from the southern Philippines fully equipped for the next stage in their adventure.

This began around 2500 BC with a series of voyages that probed the major island systems south of the Philippines. It developed into a pattern of continuing exploration and colonization—the Austronesian radiation—that eventually covered 200° of longitude, more than half the globe. Initially the main thrust was probably made via the Makassar strait between Borneo and Sulawesi. It opened up these two islands to colonization and, beyond them, the smaller but more fertile islands of the next range, Java, Bali, and Lombok. The natives of this region, Indo-Pacific tribes still at the hunter-gatherer stage, were too few and too scattered to put up effective resistance: the newcomers, with their rice-based lifestyle, quickly became the dominant element in the western half of Indonesia. We know them as the Malay.[2]

A second line of advance, via Halmahera and the north coast of New Guinea, produced less in the way of immediate results. The Papuan peoples of New Guinea were at a comparable agricultural level, and their staple, taro, seems to have been better suited to the local environment than the newcomers' rice. As a result, the Papuans lost little territory to the would-be immigrants, whose passage along the north coast of New Guinea added a scattering of new tribes to the area but didn't alter the fundamentally Indo-Pacific nature of the region's population. It was only when they reached beyond the Bismarcks and Solomons

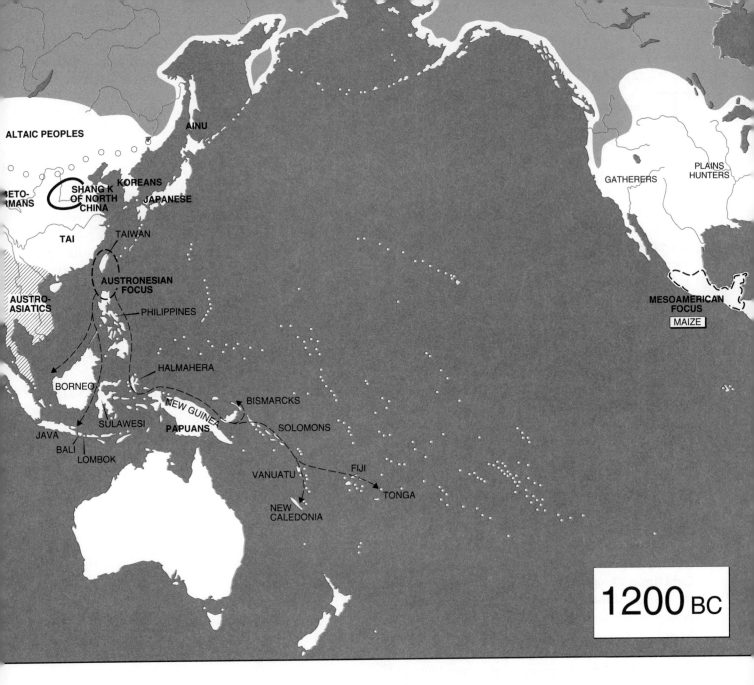

ALTAIC PEOPLES

AINU

ĿETO-
RMANS

SHANG K
OF NORTH
CHINA

KOREANS

JAPANESE

TAI

TAIWAN

AUSTRO-
ASIATICS

AUSTRONESIAN
FOCUS

PHILIPPINES

HALMAHERA

BORNEO

BISMARCKS

SULAWESI

NEW GUINEA

JAVA

PAPUANS

SOLOMONS

BALI

LOMBOK

VANUATU

FIJI

NEW
CALEDONIA

TONGA

GATHERERS

PLAINS
HUNTERS

MESOAMERICAN
FOCUS

MAIZE

1200 BC

to the previously uninhabited islands of Vanuatu, New Caledonia, Fiji, and Tonga that the migrants came into their own. Even then many aspects of this new Austronesian province were heavily modified by Papuan elements picked up en route: the staple was taro, not rice, and the people looked almost as much like Papuans as Filipinos.

America entered the Neolithic later than Asia, but agriculture was well established there by the date of this map. The staple was maize: its culture was developed in Mesoamerica (central and south Mexico plus northern Central America) with a subsequent spread to the south, particularly the Andean zone of South America.

*1. The gray tint that covers the northern latitudes of Asia and America in this and subsequent maps is saying several interrelated things: that the climate is ferociously cold and bleak, making the practice of any form of agriculture very difficult indeed, that the population is consequently extremely sparse—less than 100,000 all told at the date of this map—and that, because of this, we can ignore the whole area for a long time to come (specifically, until the seventeenth century AD).

*2. The Malay had a look at Australia's northern coast but couldn't find anywhere suitable for settlement and didn't stay long—just long enough to lose a few dingos, the dogs they carried with them partly as pets, partly as food parcels. The dingos flourished in their new home, causing some interesting changes in the local fauna: several of the more hopeless of the native herbivores became extinct (most notably the giant wombat), and so did the rather ineffective marsupial carnivores, the thylacine and the Tasmanian devil (except on Tasmania, where the dogs couldn't get at them).

The hegemony of the Shang kings of North China came to an end in the mid-eleventh century BC when invaders from the western borderlands overthrew the established order and founded a new dynastic line, the Zhou. Nominally the Zhou were in charge from about 1050 BC to 256 BC, an all-time record for a Chinese dynasty; but in practice the control the Zhou kings exercised over the country was limited in the first half of this period and nonexistent in the second. The final phase, the "era of warring states," saw half a dozen kingdoms—Zhou not included—contending for a supremacy that was finally won by the king of Qin in 221 BC. To celebrate this achievement the victor promoted himself from king (*wang*) to "first emperor" (*shi huang di,* strictly speaking "first august emperor").

The China ruled by the first emperor was a lot bigger than the China of the Shang kings. During the intervening centuries the Chinese had spilled over from the valley of the Yellow River to the valley of the Yangzi, displacing the native Tai tribes and creating the Chinese kingdom of Chu. In due course Chu fell to Qin: subsequently the first emperor dispatched an army to the far south (modern Guangdong) and annexed this region too.

Progress north was less striking, but the frontier was pushed up to the edge of the Gobi Desert, which was as far as it was sensible to go. Even this entailed the takeover of the strip of grassland along the southern border of the Gobi (Inner Mongolia, as opposed to Outer Mongolia on the far side of the Gobi), which meant subduing or expelling the Altaic pastoralists who lived there. These belonged to two confederacies—the Xiongnu, whose main base was Outer Mongolia; and the Xianbei, whose range stretched from Inner Mongolia northeastward into what is now Manchuria. Rather surprisingly in view of later events, neither the Xiongnu nor the Xianbei put up much resistance and the first emperor was able to consolidate his new northern frontier by building a first version of the Great Wall.[1]

Military matters were far from monopolizing the first emperor's attention. He imposed a single currency on all his dominions, together with a unified system of weights and measures. He built roads and issued laws about which vehicles could use them. And, in his determination to make his subjects see his empire as the only possible form of government for China, he ordered the records of all earlier states to be burned—a move that earned him the undying enmity of the scholar class. This partly explains

why he is remembered as a Stalinist tyrant, the other part of the explanation being that that is exactly what he was.[2]

The rate of spread of the Austronesians slowed down markedly after the outpouring recorded on the previous map. As far as the western branch is concerned, this is because it had nowhere obvious to go once it had completed its occupation of the Indonesian archipelago. The eastern branch notched up a couple of successes—the colonization of the Marianas (from Mindanao, via the Palaus and Yap) and the discovery of Samoa (by the Tongans, circa 1000 BC)—but these were to be the last advances for a long time to come. With them the Austonesians had reached the edge of the Pacific Plate; and the world that lay beyond, a world of small islands and vast distances, posed challenges that they were not, as yet, equipped to meet.[3]

Note that the Austro-Asiatic stock of Southeast Asia has now split into Mon, Khmer, and Viet substocks.

---

*1. Until recently the Xiongnu were termed Huns in English-language accounts, which brought a welcome touch of the familiar to what is, for most westerners, a rather intimidating series of transliterated Chinese names. Alas, that identification is now rejected. In fact, by current reckoning, the two aren't even close, the Huns being Turks and the Xiongnu Mongols.

The border of circles around the Xiongnu and Xianbei represents

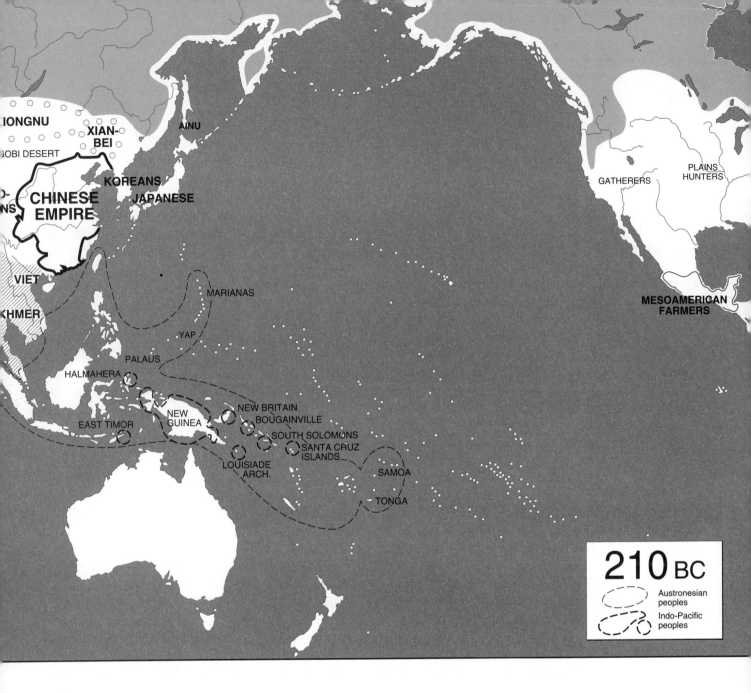

a shift in the meaning of this symbol. In the preceding map the circles showed the southern limit of the Altaic peoples: here, and in subsequent maps, their use is restricted to the tribes of the steppe, and some equally Altaic peoples to their north are left unmarked. This is simply a matter of who is important and who is not. The range indicated for the Xiongnu, incidentally, corresponds to Outer Mongolia; Inner Mongolia is the strip of territory immediately inside the northern frontier of the Chinese empire, with an extension northward into the Xianbei area (i.e., to the east of the Gobi).

No trace has ever been found of the Great Wall built by the first emperor. It certainly wasn't anything like the Wall existing today, which is a Ming construction, and it may well have been an outpost line rather than a continuous structure.

*2. The first emperor has been in the news again since the discovery, in 1974, of a "terra-cotta army" guarding his tomb: its 6000 life-size statues are an appropriate illustration of the scale on which he operated. An unexpected feature of the find is the absence of iron weapons: all the metal parts of the spears, swords, halberds, and crossbows are bronze, and this at a time when China, by all accounts, had been in the Iron Age for several hundred years. Subsequent re-examination of the archaeological data for North China suggests that bronze remained the norm for weapons until the first century AD. So much for the theory that Qin owed its success to a superior iron-based military technology.

*3. The Indo-Pacific peoples may not have done quite as badly as the map suggests, because the outlines given derive from the present-day language distribution. That there were more Indo-Pacific enclaves in existence in the third century BC is highly probable; what is less likely is that there were enough of them to affect the overall picture of Indo-Pacific retreat.

The Qin dynasty founded by the first emperor proved short-lived. Rebel armies, already active during the brief reign of the second emperor (210–207 BC), soon swept away his even more ephemeral successor (206 BC); their leaders then fought among themselves until a winner emerged in the person of Gao Zu, founder of the Han dynasty. Gao Zu made a welcome contrast to the first emperor. He mistrusted officialdom and saw no need for overmuch government: while he reigned, the people prospered. Unfortunately his successors proved less able to keep the bureaucrats in check, and as the governmental machine gathered momentum again, there was a gradual drift back to Qin values. One obvious result was a great expansion of the empire. By the reign of Wu Di, the "Martial Emperor" (141–87 BC), armies were being dispatched in all directions: to Korea, to Central Asia, to the southern borderlands of China and the north of Vietnam. All China's neighbors were to be brought within the orbit of the "son of heaven."

One of the most interesting of Wu Di's acquisitions is Gansu, the ribbonlike strip of territory bordering the northeastern quarter of the Tibetan plateau. This was used as a corridor by merchants trading to and from the oasis towns of Central Asia. Wu Di's generals thought that policing this traffic, of which the staple was Chinese silk, could be profitable, so they decided to move beyond Gansu and put garrisons into some of the oases—Turpan is an example, and there were others even further west and hence off our map. But this meant constant fighting with the Xiongnu, who fiercely defended their right to levy tolls on the "silk road" caravans. The Chinese treasury couldn't cope with the increasing demands placed on it by these campaigns, and eventually the policy of all-around expansion had to be curtailed. Gansu was retained, as were all the acquisitions in the south bar Hainan island, but the oases of the "western region" were abandoned, along with most of Korea. On the northern frontier compromises were made with the Xiongnu, some of whom were allowed back into Inner Mongolia on condition that they acknowledged imperial suzerainty.

Despite this bit of backpedaling the Han empire remained a colossal structure. It was also durable, lasting in all for some four centuries (202 BC–AD 220). With only occasional lapses it maintained peace within China during this period, much as its contemporary, the Roman empire, did in the west. And, like Rome, its cultural influence extended far beyond its borders. An achievement on

this scale goes a long way toward explaining why the Han have always had a favorable press. Another factor is that the later Han rulers put the role of the intelligensia in government on a permanent footing. As far back as the era of the warring states, Confucius had taught that affairs of state were best entrusted to men of education and gravity, not princes of the blood or men of valor. The later Han took the Confucian line as far as was practical at the time. Of course, the system had to accommodate the military and the well-connected, but wherever possible the man of letters was preferred.

While the Chinese were marshaling armies tens of thousands strong, a few boatloads of Austronesians were making history of a different sort. One group from the southern end of the Solomons discovered and colonized the atolls scattered across the ocean to their north—the Gilberts, the Marshalls, and the easternmost of the Carolines. Another group, at the far end of the Austronesian world, began an even more daring series of voyages. In fact, the people who made up this group achieved such startling results that they earned themselves a new name: they are the ancestral Polynesians.

The Polynesians evolved from islanders of mixed Melanesian and Austronesian stock (but purely Austronesian speech) who had settled Tonga and Samoa in the second half of the last millennium BC. Culturally they never got beyond a Neolithic level: indeed, because they gave up making pots, relying on baskets instead, they actually dropped a bit as regards domestic technology. But when it came to boats, they were in a class of their own. Keeping in touch was difficult in this part of Austronesia, where islands were small and far apart. The Polynesian answer was the double canoe, with a load-bearing central platform. The increased capacity of these vessels, and the strong sails they carried, enabled the Polynesians, sometime around the date of this map, to discover the Marquesas, 2000 miles (3300 km) east of Samoa. There they established a center for the further dissemination of their race and culture.[1]

Mesoamerica, though technically still at a Neolithic level, had now acquired some of the trappings of a higher culture. The most obvious expression of this is the ceremonial center, with its elaborate pyramid temples. Many of the Mesoamerican communities built complexes of this type, often decorated with frescoes and reliefs of impressive vigor. If anything were to temper one's admiration for these achievements, it would be the Mesoamer-

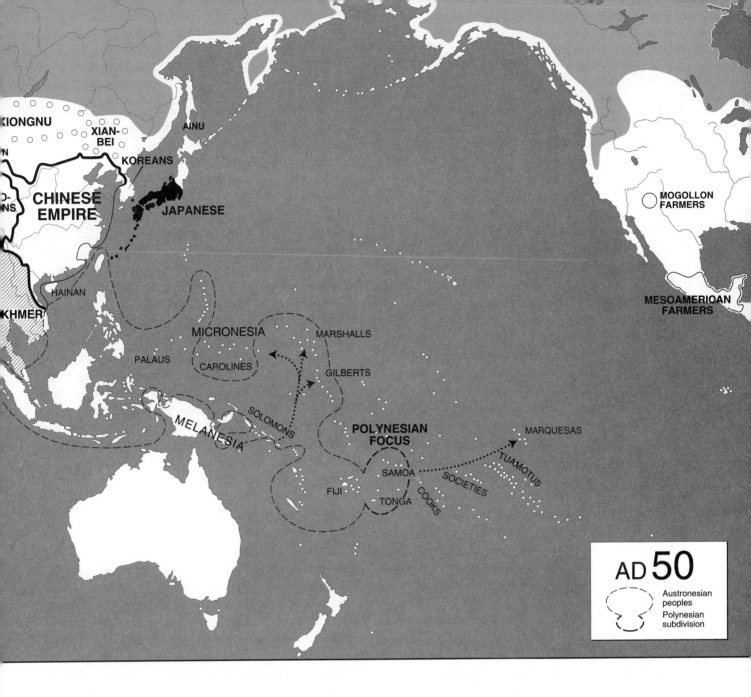

AD **50**

Austronesian peoples

Polynesian subdivision

icans' obsession with human sacrifice. That this was the essential purpose of their temples is all too plain, despite modern attempts to label individual examples as observatories or, would you believe, hospitals.

Some minor points to note on the map. The Japanese have been given a distinctive marker (solid black); the Neolithic has reached North America in the shape of the maize farmers of the Mogollon culture; Micronesia (Palau to the Gilberts) and Melanesia (New Guinea to Fiji) are contrasted with a nascent Polynesia. The distinction between the three island worlds is useful, but it is worth remembering that, in terms of human geography, both Micronesia ("world of small islands") and Melane-

sia ("islands of the blacks") are more complex units than Polynesia ("many islands"—but ethnically straightforward).

*1. It is, as yet, unclear whether the Polynesians got to the Marquesas in one hop, or, as seems more likely, as a result of a sequence of moves through the Cooks, Societies, and northern Tuamotus.

In the long run the Han decision to allow the nomads back into Inner Mongolia proved unwise. By the early fourth century the various Xiongnu and Xianbei tribes living there were doing pretty much as they pleased, and in 308 a rebel Xiongnu chieftain actually proclaimed himself emperor. In the course of the next eight years he mastered the Yellow River valley, deposed the legitimate emperor, and set up the first of a kaleidoscopic series of nomad kingdoms—no less than 16 in all—that ruled North China during the remainder of the century. In the end the region settled down under the Tuoba, a Xianbei lineage referred to by Chinese historians as the Northern Wei dynasty. Meanwhile, emperors of Chinese stock ruled the southern half of the country from Nanjing.[1]

On the map, the Tuoba empire has been given a border of half-circles. This indicates its peculiar ethnic structure: a Chinese peasant base (99 percent of the whole) with a ruling caste drawn from an Altaic pastoral minority (the other 1 percent). That it could exist in this form was a tribute to the exceptional military skill that the steppe peoples had developed by this time. Because they learned to ride as soon as they could walk, nomads made superb cavalrymen, able to run rings around the infantry armies that were the natural expression of the Chinese peasant state. To this mobility they added a vicious skill with the bow: only when an enemy force had been pricked and bled for hours—sometimes for days—did the nomads move in for the kill. By then there was usually no doubt about the outcome.

If the Chinese had great difficulty coming up with a response to the nomads' tactics, they had a cultural weapon that always enabled them to win out in the end. At first, the victors wanted only the trappings of power, the silks and subsidies, the grand titles and legitimizing princesses. Gradually they adopted Chinese ways of doing things and Chinese ways of thinking. Eventually the rulers ended up indistinguishable from the ruled.

Imitation of things Chinese was not limited to the nomads. On the basis of contacts made in the late second century BC, at the height of the Han empire's forward policy, the northern Koreans developed a Chinese-style state, the kingdom of Koguryo, which, in turn, was copied by the princes of Paekche and Silla in the south of the peninsula. Even the Japanese are reported to have sought the approval of the Chinese court. However, this is a period when very little is known about the political structure of Japan, and the little that is known is contradictory.

Chinese accounts suggest a patchwork of tribal chieftains, whereas the Japanese remember this as the era of the Yamato kings. Perhaps the Yamato hegemony was real enough but was more a matter of shamanistic ceremonial than direct control. That would fit well with what we know of Japan's later evolution.

During this period the Polynesians demonstrated their mastery of ocean voyaging by discovering, and where appropriate colonizing, most of islands and atolls of the Central and South Pacific. Perhaps the most remarkable single achievement was the settlement of the Hawaiian Islands from the Marquesas, 2200 miles (3500 km) to the south. The Marquesans have also been credited with the discovery of Easter Island, often described as the most remote place on earth; however, linguistic analysis suggests that in this case the settlers came from Raivavae in the Australs. For the Ellice Islands there is no need to look further than Samoa. Meanwhile, the Austronesians, using simpler craft, completed the occupation of the Carolines. They also achieved the almost incredible feat of colonizing Madagascar from Sumatra, the distance traveled, presumably by accident, amounting to some 3500 miles (5700 km).[2]

Mesoamerican society had now entered its classic phase (AD 300–900), in which the pyramids were cased in stone and the temples that topped them decorated with elaborate reliefs. At Teotihuacan the pyramids rival those of ancient Egypt in size, and the site can reasonably be regarded as the capital of a Mexican empire whose history is now lost. Further south, in the Mayan zone, the political structure was one of rival chiefdoms, each with its own ceremonial center.

Note that the growing of maize has now spread to the Mississippi. Note also the first appearances by two Southeast Asian kingdoms, Champa (an intrusive Austronesian state in central Vietnam) and Funan (a precursor of Cambodia).

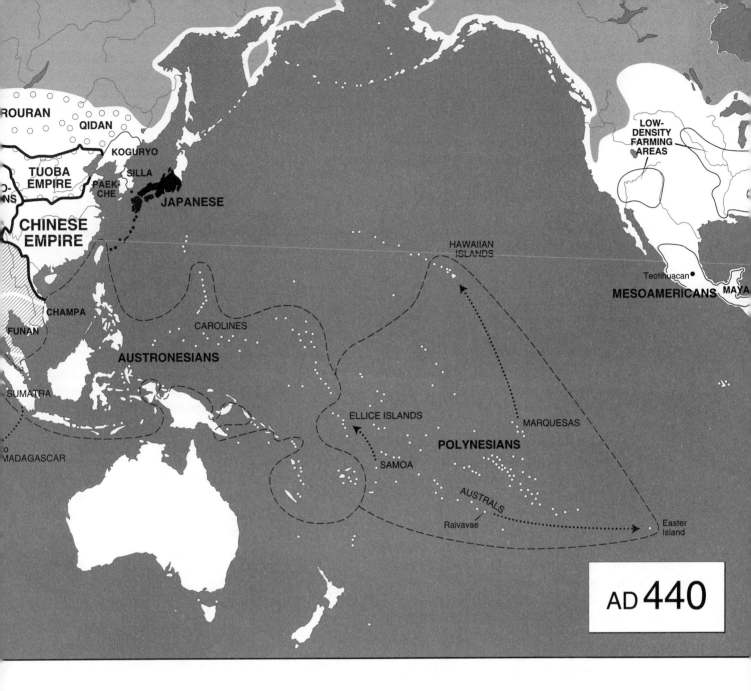

ROURAN

QIDAN

KOGURYO

TUOBA
EMPIRE

SILLA

PAEK-
CHE

JAPANESE

CHINESE
EMPIRE

CHAMPA

FUNAN

SUMATRA

MADAGASCAR

AUSTRONESIANS

CAROLINES

ELLICE ISLANDS

SAMOA

HAWAIIAN
ISLANDS

MARQUESAS

POLYNESIANS

AUSTRALS

Raivavae

Easter
Island

LOW-
DENSITY
FARMING
AREAS

Teotihuacan

MESOAMERICANS   MAYA

AD 440

*1. By this time new Mongol confederations, the Rouran and Qi-
dan, had replaced the Xiongnu and Xianbei in Outer Mongolia and
Manchuria.

*2. No one nowadays believes that Polynesia was colonized from
South America, and Thor Heyerdahl—who thought up the idea, and
who in 1947 sailed his balsawood raft *Kontiki* from Callao, Peru, to
Raroia in the Tuamotus to prove it—didn't prove anything of the sort:
he merely showed that a voyage of this type was possible. In fact, the
linguistic and anthropological data make it quite plain that none of the
Pacific islands has ever had a significant South American population.

The occasional raftload of unfortunates is a different matter.
Easter Island has a wall of what looks very like Inca masonry. More
significantly, the sweet potato, an Andean plant, and the Andean
name for it, was known to the Marquesans before they began their
round of discoveries. *Kontiki* certainly had one or two predecessors.

If the story so far seems to have been mostly about China, that is not unreasonable: 80 percent of the people in the region covered by the map were either Chinese or living under Chinese rule. This is not just conjecture. The Han authorities held a census in AD 1, which returned figures indicating a total population for the empire of around 50 million—this is at a time when what we know of later demographic developments makes it unlikely that the other areas of the map contained more than 10 to 12 million.[1]

Of the people who were not Chinese, nearly half would have lived in Southeast Asia and the Malay archipelago, places where rice-growing was well established if not, as yet, very intensively practiced. A fair guess for this region's population in the fifth century AD would be 3 million in the mainland and the same number in the islands. China's northern neighbors had gotten off to a slower start, because developing strains of rice suitable for higher latitudes was a slow business, but Korea's population must have been approaching 1 million by this time, and Japan's 2 million. In fact, at this date these two countries were probably notching up higher growth rates than anywhere else in the Pacific. By contrast, low totals and slow rates of increase characterized the pastoral peoples of Tibet and Mongolia, who are unlikely to have numbered more than 1 million between them. To these figures we can add something over 2 million for the visible parts of America (most of them in Mesoamerica) and 1 million in Oceania.

The figure for Oceania is, of course, purely hypothetical, and any attempt to break it down must be equally so. The bulk of the population would surely have been in the Neolithic area (perhaps 500,000 in New Guinea and 150,000 in the outer Melanesian islands), most of the remainder (perhaps 300,000) in the Old Stone Age world of Australia. That leaves a notional 50,000 for Micronesia and Polynesia.

The degree to which these different peoples were aware of each other—and of the rest of the world—varied greatly. Most would have lived out their lives with little mind to what lay over the horizon. However, there were by this time two international trade routes connecting the East Asian sphere with the countries to its west. One was the "silk road" which had gradually extended until, by the first century AD, it spanned the entire width of Asia. The other was the "spice route," developed at much the same time, which skirted the southern rim of Asia, linking up Arabia, India, Southeast Asia, and the Indonesian archipelago.

The Chinese, rather surprisingly, played no part in the development of these trade routes. They provided the silk road with its staple, but the caravans that made the long journey across the wastes of Central Asia to the markets of India, Iran, and Syria were organized by the inhabitants of the intervening oases. Similarly, the spice route, as visible on this map, was an entirely Indian enterprise. One consequence of this was that the nations bordering this route were incorporated in the Indian—not the Chinese—cultural sphere. The religious and social vocabulary of the kingdom of Champa, for example, was not that of its near neighbor the Chinese empire, but that of the far distant Indian subcontinent.

Both of the major Indian religious systems traveled the spice route, the Hindu pantheon having more success in Southeast Asia and Buddhism doing better in the Indonesian archipelago. The Buddhist gospel also made its way along the silk road to North China, where it made many converts among the Tuoba elite. To obtain instruction, enlightenment, and more accurate versions of the Buddhist scriptures, Chinese monks began journeying to India: accounts of their travels provide us with some useful information on the lands they passed through.[2]

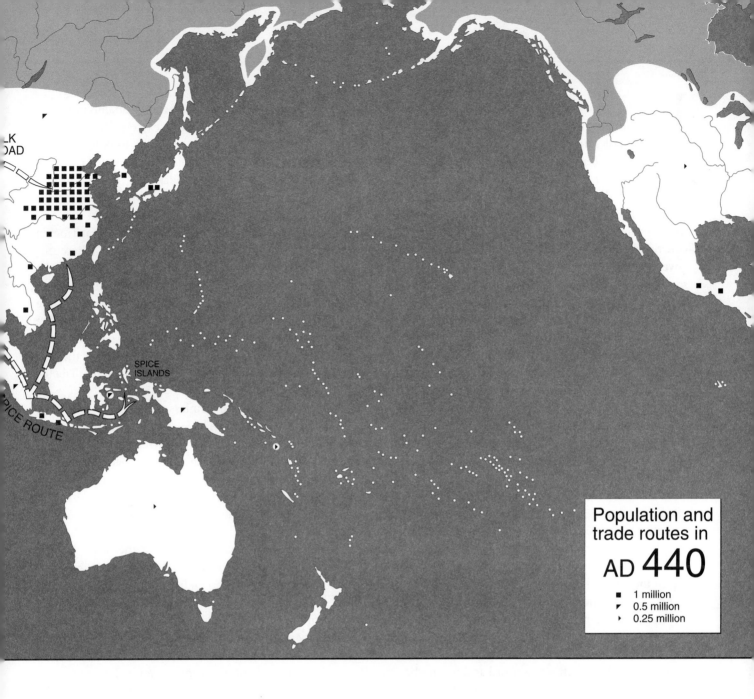

SPICE
ISLANDS

SPICE ROUTE

ILK
ROAD

Population and trade routes in

AD 440

■ 1 million
▶ 0.5 million
▸ 0.25 million

*1. Excluded from these totals, as from the subsequent discussion, are the 3 million or 4 million people living in the visible portion of India. Note that the populations of the shaded areas in the north of the map are too small to score with the symbols used: they perhaps amounted to 60,000 in the area west of the Bering Strait and 40,000 east of it. The uninhabited area is down to New Zealand and the small islands nearby (Norfolk, the Kermadecs, and Chatham), plus the Galapagos group.

*2. Journey times were unpredictable, but the general rule was that travel by sea was quicker. The Buddhist monk Faxian, the first person we know of to make use of both routes, took three years to get from China to India via the silk road (399–402) but only one year to get back via the spice route.

In 589 the armies of North China conquered the south and reunited the country. The founding dynasty, the Sui, didn't last long; but its successor, the Tang, ruled China for three centuries (618–906), an era generally regarded as one of the most glorious in the history of the "Middle Kingdom." It is easy to justify this view. Initially, at least, the Tang empire achieved all its goals—secure frontiers, a peaceful countryside, and a suitably splendid court and capital. Moreover, under the Tang, China was governed in exactly the way the educated class thought it should be: by civil servants, at least some of whom owed their position to a newly introduced system of written examinations. It seemed that the Confucian ideal was well on the way to being realized.

The reality was somewhat different. The main military resource of the empire was the assortment of nomad tribes that had settled in Inner Mongolia. Keeping these unassimilated pastoralists happy with their lot—and, just as important, giving their leaders rewards and responsibilities commensurate with their potential for trouble-making—was absolutely essential to the safety of the state. Up to the middle years of the eighth century, the Tang emperors managed the necessary balancing act well enough; but in 755 mistrust between court and army precipitated a revolt by the most powerful general of the day, and the resulting civil war very nearly brought the empire down. In the end the court managed to save itself by calling in the Uighur Turks, but things were never the same again. The frontiers contracted; worse still, the whole northern tier of provinces became effectively independent—the warlords who ran them ceased to take any notice of the emperor's edicts and paid no taxes to his treasury. By playing off one warlord against another and inserting extra commands where it could, the imperial administration managed to maintain a nominal authority throughout the country, but the later Tang empire was only a shadow of its former self.

The Turks, who make their first appearance on this map, are given a filled-in version of the Mongols' circles. This somewhat overstates the difference between the two, for they had identical lifestyles and spoke closely related Altaic languages: the Turks were simply the Mongols' western neighbors on the Central Asian grasslands. In the sixth century they defeated the Rouran Mongols and replaced them as masters of Outer Mongolia; another upheaval in the next century made the Uighurs the dominant group within this Turkish hegemony.

The Uighurs turned out to be rather unambitious politically, doing little or nothing to exploit Chinese weakness. The Tibetans, on the other hand, took up the task with gusto. It was Tibetan armies that occupied the Central Asian oases previously under Tang protection and conquered the province of Gansu; they also terrorized China's western borderlands and first held to ransom, then sacked the Tang capital. The most important Tibetan thrust, however, was made in the southwest, where migrant tribes overran what is now Yunnan, founding the kingdom of Nanzhao. And from there even more adventurous groups moved southwest to settle, under the name of Pyu, along the central stretch of the Ayeyarwady. The Pyu movement gave Burma its nuclear population of Burmans and allows us to distinguish between the two components of what had previously been a single Tibeto-Burman stock.

Both Sui and Tang armies campaigned in Korea, though with little profit. The Sui failed to win any ground (a failure that brought down the dynasty); the Tang succeeded in destroying the kingdom of Koguryo but then withdrew. Nonetheless, the Tang intervention had important effects: in the course of it, Paekche was destroyed along with Koguryo, and the peninsula ended up divided between the Tungus (Manchurian) kingdom of Pohai and the sole remaining native monarchy, the south Korean kingdom of Silla. Also affected was Japan, whose attempted intervention had ended in such humiliating defeat that it decided to reorganize itself on more modern—i.e., Chinese—lines. On the surface the Japanese polity was recast after the Tang model, with an emperor, an imperial capital, and a civil service. Underneath, nothing much changed except insofar as Japan was getting more populous, more prosperous, and more sophisticated. Power remained with the clan chiefs, whom the new system simply confirmed in office: the emperor was merely a repackaged version of the Yamato king, with ritual importance but no real political clout. The capital, though, was real enough, and it provided a focus for such aristocratic factions as sought wider power than that provided by their baronies.

During this period we begin to get some political data for the Indonesian archipelago. One source is the memoirs of Yi Jing, a Buddhist monk who traveled by sea between China and India in 671–695. Two of the places he describes, Malayu and Srivijaya, can be identified as Jambi and Palembang, Sumatran principalities with a long life

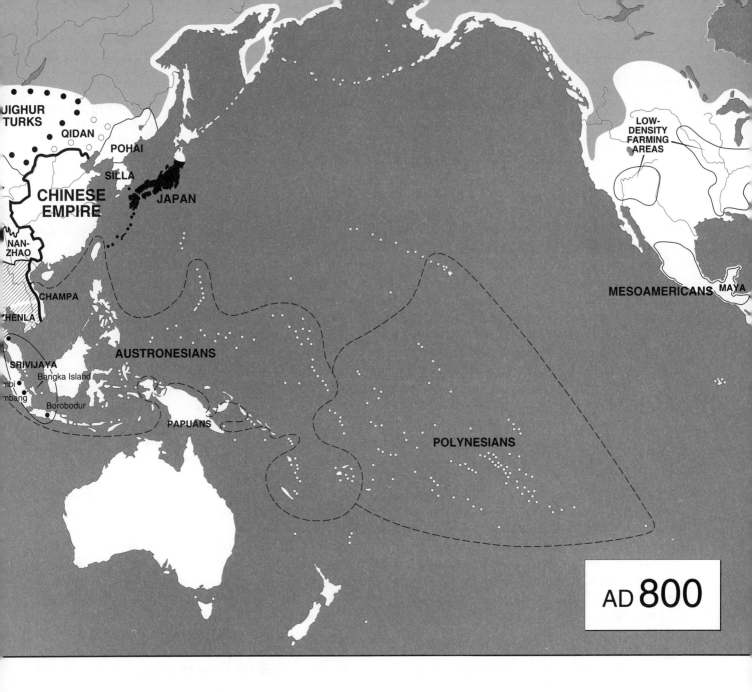

AUSTRONESIANS

PAPUANS

POLYNESIANS

UIGHUR
TURKS

QIDAN

POHAI

SILLA

JAPAN

CHINESE
EMPIRE

NAN-
ZHAO

CHAMPA

HENLA

SRIVIJAYA
Bangka Island
 mbi
mbang
Borobodur

LOW-
DENSITY
FARMING
AREAS

MESOAMERICANS MAYA

AD 800

ahead of them. Both were ardently Buddhist at the time, though this didn't stop Palembang from conquering Jambi, an event noted by Yi Jing and confirmed by a contemporary Srivijayan inscription. Other inscriptions indicate that Srivijaya was expanding all around: it had conquered Bangka Island and was about to invade Java. We don't know the outcome of this particular expedition, because there are no more inscriptions for the better part of a century; in the long run, however, Srivijaya's campaigning must have gone well, because the next set of inscriptions, dating from the 770s, indicate that members of Srivijaya's royal house, the Sailendra, were wielding power in places as far apart as Ligor on the isthmus of Malaya

and Mataram in central Java. They were also presumably responsible for the Malay raiding reported by the Khmers, Chams, and Viets at this time.[1]

As will be clear from this account, the evidence for a unitary Srivijayan empire is at best ambiguous: it could equally well be used to support the idea of a loose federation of Sailendra principalities. About the prestige of the Sailendras, however, there can be no doubt, and it is for this reason that they are generally credited with the construction of medieval Indonesia's most famous (but entirely anonymous) monument, Borobodur. This structure—really a cased-in hill—is not a building in the usual sense: it is a model of the universe as conceived by Buddhists. The pilgrims who followed the corridors built along its sides could see the story of the Buddha's life unfolding in the scuptured reliefs that line the walls. They could see how the Buddha achieved enlightenment and, thus enlightened themselves, proceed to the open platform at the top where three circular arrays of 72 Buddhas around a central stupa allowed them a glimpse of the world beyond the one we know. What with all the tourists, it doesn't seem to work so well nowadays.

As FAR AS OUR AREA is concerned, the oldest form of writing is Chinese, and by a long way at that. The essentials of the script were established in Shang times (1500–1000 BC), and both the system and the format (in columns read from right to left) have remained unchanged ever since. But though it is both ancient and, as regards present-day practice, unique, it was probably not entirely original. Scripts based on similar principles had appeared in the Middle East at an even earlier date (around 3200 BC), and it is likely that the Chinese had at least hearsay knowledge of these. In fact, the only script we can be entirely certain was a local invention is the Mesoamerican set of glyphs (standardized, though very elaborate, pictographic signs). This script first appears in the form of calendrical inscriptions (the earliest from 36 BC) and was subsequently developed to the point where it could be used to commemorate events the ruling elite considered important. Curiously, the grandest of the Mesoamerican states, Teotihuacan, ignored the invention; indeed, of all the Mesoamerican peoples only the Maya made regular use of it.

The Mesoamerican glyphs are a cumbersome form of writing. At the opposite end of the scale is the alphabet, which, at its best, is convenient, flexible, unambiguous, and easy to learn. Like writing itself, alphabets evolved in the Middle East: in 500 BC the one in general use there was the 22-letter, consonants-only Aramaic alphabet, written from right to left. This was soon copied in India and Central Asia. The Central Asian variant was used to write Sogdian, an Iranian language that was the *lingua franca* of the silk road. This was the first alphabet to enter our area, around AD 500. Not long after, a modification of it was being used to write Turkish. The Tibetan alphabet appeared somewhat later, in the mid-seventh century: it is based on the Gupta script, a North Indian derivative of Aramaic.

The role that the silk road played in the introduction of the alphabet to Central Asia was mirrored by the spice route as regards the south. However, the earliest inscriptions of Southeast Asia are not commercial but scriptural, and they are in Sanskrit, not any of the local languages. The alphabet is the South Indian variant of Aramaic known as Pallava (after the dynasty that ruled much of southern India during this period): by the eighth century forms of it were being used to write Cham, Khmer, and Malay.

These advances brought the alphabet up against the vast and immovable Chinese cultural bloc. Being monosyllabic, Chinese is the language least likely to benefit from alphabetization, so it is understandable that the Chinese have never wavered in their attachment to the one character–one word system that they know and love. However, the opposite is true of Korean and Japanese, which are polysyllabic and cry out for alphabetic expression. Sadly for them, China got in first. Phonetic scripts were developed for both Korean and Japanese, but the educated classes spurned them. The mark of the gentleman was the purity of his Chinese calligraphy.[2]

As regards the technology of writing, there is no doubt that the Chinese were the world leaders, and the Koreans and Japanese had nothing to complain about in this respect. Originally the Chinese had used strips of bamboo as their writing material. In the course of experiments intended to cover these parallel strips with a continuous film, they invented paper. Subsequently they discovered how to take thin paper rubbings of texts inscribed on stone, a somewhat laborious procedure justified by the need to make multiple copies of examination tests. From there it was but a short step to easy-to-carve wood with the text in relief, i.e., wood-block printing. Examples of Buddhist scriptures printed by this method were circulating throughout the Chinese cultural zone by the eighth century AD.

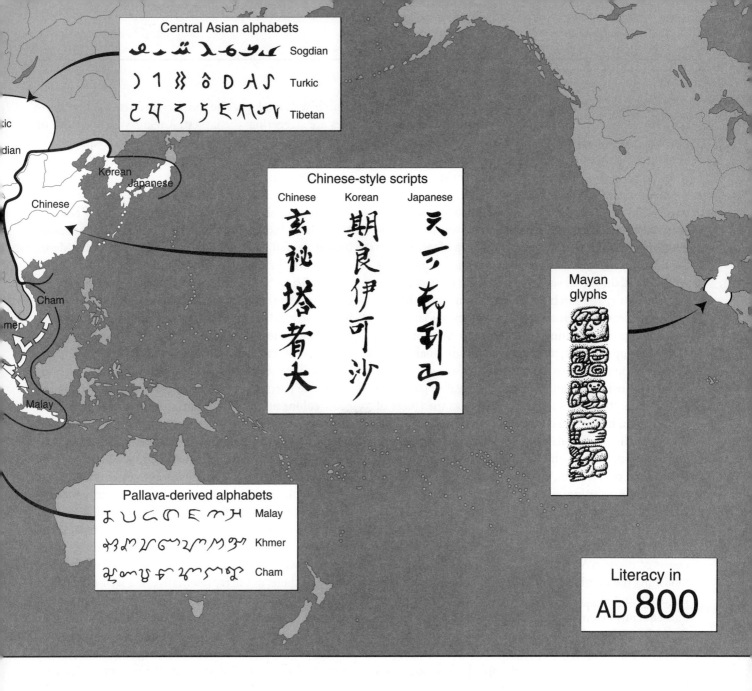

*1. Around 550 Zhenla replaces Funan as the designation of the Cambodian region. The change indicates the start of a new ruling house; it also corresponds to a decline in the royal authority.

*2. The Koreans created their alphabet, using Tibetan as a model, in the fifteenth century. At the date of this map the only way of writing Korean was to use Chinese characters phonetically. This was done sparingly, for the odd word or phrase in what was basically a Chinese text. So it could be argued, very reasonably, that to class Korean as a Chinese-style script, as the map does, is understating the case. It wasn't just Chinese style, it was unmodified Chinese applied to a different language.

The Japanese script, on the other hand, though it looks similar to Chinese, was, from the start, an instrument for writing Japanese. There were several variants, which were combined with Chinese characters to produce the wildly complicated, often ambiguous hotchpotch that has proved so perfect a match for the Japanese psyche.

After a period of disunity following the demise of the Tang, China's imperial dignity was restored by the first emperors of the Song dynasty. Like the Tang, the Song lasted a long time—from 960 to 1276, or just over three centuries—and because their government followed the traditional Chinese pattern they have, on the whole, been well regarded. Even at its best, however, the Song empire was smaller than the Tang (Gansu was held by Tibetan princes of the Xia dynasty, and a strip of territory in the north by the Qidan Mongols); and when things went wrong for it, they went very wrong indeed. Early on in the twelfth century the Jurchen, a Tungus clan whose homeland was in eastern Manchuria, replaced the Qidan as the dominant power in Inner Mongolia; to the Song this seemed an opportunity to recover the traditional "Great Wall" frontier, but their attempt to do so was a catastrophic bungle. The entire Yellow River valley passed to the Jurchen: the Song survived, but only as the rulers of the southern half of the country.

Two of the present-day states of Southeast Asia made their first appearance during this period. Dai Viet, the forerunner of Vietnam, declared itself independent of China in 938, shortly after the collapse of the Tang. Thereafter it successfully defended itself against China's attempts at reconquest while advancing its southern frontier at the expense of the Chams. Bagan, the predecessor of modern Myanmar (Burma), defeated Bago, establishing the dominance of the central Ayeyarwady over the delta, and of the Burmans over the Mon (circa 1050). Subsequently Mon craftsmen, masters of the international Buddhist style, conferred on Bagan the fantastic array of stupas, temples, and pagodas that have maintained the fame of this now-deserted capital. Eclipsing even Bagan, however, is its Cambodian rival Angkor. In the first half of the ninth century, Jayavarman II began the process of transforming the modest Cambodian kingdom of Zhenla into the all-conquering Khmer empire: this attained its maximum extent some 200 years later, in the reign of Suryavarman II (1113–1150), by which time it had added most of present-day Thailand and Laos (both then inhabited by people of Mon stock) to the Cambodian heartland (present-day Cambodia plus South Vietnam). As their names attest, the Khmer monarchs were devotees of the Hindu pantheon (Jaya is the Hindu god of victory, Surya the sun god; *varman* means "protégé of"). Their chief constructions at Angkor were temples that did for the Hindu worldview what Borobodur had done for

Buddhist cosmology. The number and size of these temples are staggering: the largest, Angkor Wat, the work of Suryavarman II, covers the better part of a square mile and is, on its own, enough to justify Angkor's claim to be one of the wonders of the world.[1]

Polynesia's last major colonization got under way with the arrival of the Maori on the shores of New Zealand's North Island sometime in the eleventh century. Archaeological as well as linguistic data suggest that the Maori came from the Society Islands, with a particularly close match being found recently in a site excavated on Huahine. The new environment was difficult for them, being too cold for most of their plants, and initially at least they leaned heavily on the local livestock. One consequence of this was the extinction of the moa, New Zealand's version of the ostrich. Such extinctions were an inevitable part of Polynesian, and subsequently of European, colonization. Most island species lacked experience of predation and were hopelessly trusting; others simply couldn't compete with the animals introduced by humans—the Polynesians' pig, for example. Flightless birds were particularly vulnerable—it's not chance that makes the dodo the archetype of the doomed island species—and no less than 20 different flightless birds disappeared on Hawaii within a few centuries of the Polynesians' landing. But that is not particularly relevant to the moa, which hadn't flown to New Zealand and then lost its wings but had been there, as the representative of a well-established flightless order, from Pangaean days. The moa's problem was having had it too easy over the subsequent 150 million years: no enemies, no sense of danger, no moa.

In North America an Athapascan group, the Apache, moved south and began to harass the farming folk of the American southwest. The farmers—termed the Anasazi in later tradition—responded by regrouping into more easily defended pueblos. In Mesoamerica the Toltec hegemony associated with the sites of Tula (in Mexico) and Chichen Itza (in the Mayan zone) was already ebbing.

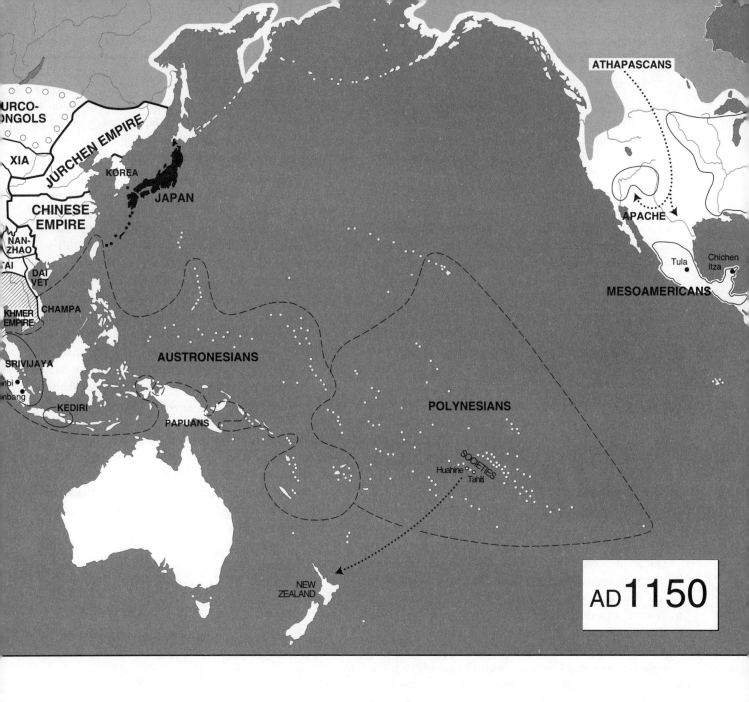

ATHAPASCANS

APACHE

MESOAMERICANS

Tula   Chichen
         Itza

AD1150

**TURCO-
MONGOLS**

XIA

JURCHEN EMPIRE

KOREA

JAPAN

**CHINESE
EMPIRE**

**NAN-
ZHAO**

TAI

**DAI
VIET**

**KHMER
EMPIRE**

CHAMPA

SRIVIJAYA

nbi
nbang

KEDIRI

AUSTRONESIANS

PAPUANS

POLYNESIANS

SOCIETIES
Huahine
         Tahiti

**NEW
ZEALAND**

Burman—control, this Tai movement can plausibly be interpreted as an attempt to reestablish lost freedoms. As for the Indonesian archipelago, we know so little about what was going on there that it is hardly worth commenting. The power of Srivijaya was certainly greatly reduced following a raid by the Cholas of South India during which the capital, Palembang, was put to the sack (1025); subsequently Jambi seems to have taken over many of Palembang's functions. Java was now independent, with most if not all of it under the control of the kingdom of Kediri.

In the northern half of Asia, note the collapse of the Uighur hegemony in Outer Mongolia, which has left the region divided among a medley of Turco-Mongol tribes; and the transformation of the kingdom of Silla into the kingdom of Korea (more a matter of a new dynasty than a new kingdom). Note also the completion of the Japanese domination in Honshu and its extension to the southern tip of Hokkaido.

*1. An important though largely silent event of this period is the infiltration of Tai tribes into the previously Mon areas of northern and eastern Burma. Since the Tai homeland, the southern third of China, was now under Chinese—or, in the case of Nanzhao, Tibeto-

In 1205 the Mongol chieftain Temujin, who had spent the better part of 20 years fighting to impose his rule on the squabbling tribes north of the Gobi, finally succeeded in bringing the last of them to heel. The next year he called all of them to a *kuriltai* (gathering of the clans) at which he raised the nine-tail standard that symbolized lordship over the peoples of the steppe. He also used the occasion to take the title by which history remembers him, Genghis Khan, meaning "world ruler." If it wasn't true at the time, Genghis had every intention of making it so. In 1209 he led the Mongol army on a foray south of the Gobi that reduced the Xia kingdom to vassaldom; in the years that followed his forces demolished the Jurchen kingdom of North China, mastered Central Asia, and—moving west from there—inflicted egregious defeats on the Persians, Georgians, and Russians. The empire he left at his death in 1227, already bigger than any previously achieved by the steppe peoples, was further expanded by his sons, until by 1260 the Mongol writ ran from the Carpathians to Korea. In fact the empire had become too big for one man to run, and when Genghis's grandson Kublai was proclaimed Great Khan, it was on the understanding that he would limit himself to its eastern half—essentially Mongolia, Manchuria, and the northern half of China. Other family members became khans in Russia, Persia, and Central Asia.

The main task facing Kublai was to overthrow the southern Song and complete the Mongol dominion over China. This achieved, as it was by 1276, little else needed to be done, but that didn't stop Kublai from doing it: expeditionary forces were dispatched against Japan, Burma, Dai Viet, even Java. Few of them met with lasting success, though Dai Viet and Champa eventually agreed to pay a token tribute to avoid further harassment, and the invasion of Burma, which put an end to the kingdom of Bagan, briefly added two small provinces to the empire. As to the operations against Japan, they brought nothing but humiliation. A relatively small army that landed on Kyushu in 1274 was forced to withdraw after losing many of its transports in a storm. Seven years later the same fate overtook a much larger force, said to number 140,000 men, that Kublai had assembled to avenge this rebuff. The Japanese gave thanks to the *kamikaze,* the "divine wind" that had saved them from their enemies, but it is difficult to believe that they had been in any serious danger: in amphibious operations of this type the Mongols were completely out of their element.[1]

The Mongol conquest of Bagan allowed the Mon to reestablish their independence in the south: control of the Ayeyarwady valley was subsequently split four ways, with Tai princes ruling the northern reaches, the Mongols the central section, a surviving Burman lineage a principality at Taungoo, and the Mon kingdom of Mottama the delta. Elsewhere the Mon-Khmer peoples were doing less well: Tai tribes had overrun the northern half of present-day Thailand, and though the Mon kingdom of Lavo still held the southern half of the country, both it and the Khmer empire were by now in decline. In the Indonesian archipelago Srivijaya had disappeared from the region's scanty records, though its two most important constituents, Jambi and Palembang, are still present as principalities. Joining them is Aru, near the northern tip of Sumatra. In Java Majapahit replaces Singhasari, the last capital of Kediri. None of these minor states deserves more than the simple symbol allocated to it on the map.

Note that Kublai established tribute-collecting posts within the forest zone of Siberia, and, in the far northeast, at the mouth of the Amur and on the island of Sakhalin. Note also that, around the date of this map, the Polynesians checked out the Kermadecs and Norfolk Island, only to discover that neither had the resources necessary for permanent settlement.

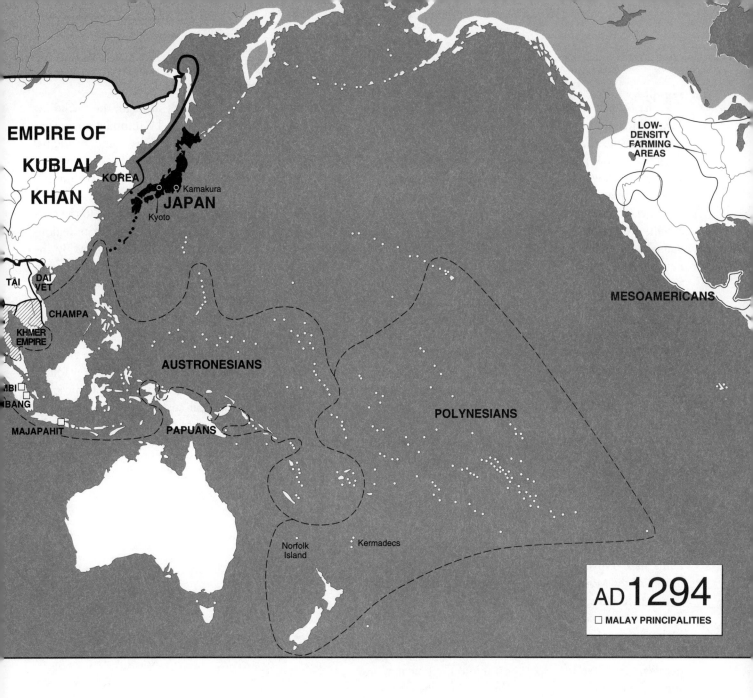

EMPIRE OF
KUBLAI
KHAN

KOREA

Kamakura
JAPAN
Kyoto

TAI
DAI
VET

CHAMPA

KHMER
EMPIRE

MBI

BANG

MAJAPAHIT

AUSTRONESIANS

PAPUANS

POLYNESIANS

MESOAMERICANS

LOW-
DENSITY
FARMING
AREAS

Norfolk
Island

Kermadecs

AD 1294
☐ MALAY PRINCIPALITIES

*1. The Japanese response to the Mongol threat was coordinated by the office of the shogun, or supreme military ruler, situated at Kamakura. This office had been created by Minamoto-no-Yoritomo in 1192 following his victory over a rival clan (and its puppet emperor) in the Gimpei war of 1180–1185. A lesser politician might have moved his entourage to the imperial capital, Kyoto, but this would have blurred the distinction between the rituals of the court and the exercise of power. By staying where he was, Yoritomo made it clear where Japanese barons seeking favors should look.

The Japanese overlordship of southern Hokkaido was extended to the whole island in 1222.

The Mongol court at Beijing remained in control of China until the middle years of the fourteenth century, when the country broke up into a jigsaw of squabbling baronies. What they were fighting about, apart from sheer survival, was the "mandate of heaven," the right to rule all China; and provincial governors, army generals, rebel peasants, and local opportunists all pitched in with a will. Eventually, in 1368, a winner emerged: Zhu Yuanzhang, warlord of Nanjing. As Zhu's troops closed on Beijing—the only time in Chinese history when the south has conquered the north—Toghun Temur, the last Mongol emperor, fled into the Gobi. Zhu, born the son of a destitute tenant farmer, mounted the throne as first emperor of the Ming dynasty.

Zhu gave China boundaries it could be proud of. In the north he established control over Inner Mongolia, in the south he imposed Chinese authority on Dai Viet. His son, Yong Le (1402–1425), went further, campaigning in person on the far side of the Gobi. Yong Le also dispatched a series of tribute-collecting fleets to Southeast Asia and beyond. Neither activity brought the empire any material profit, but both speak for the vigor that the new dynasty brought to its affairs.[1]

The Ming fleets found Southeast Asia in a state of flux. The Tai peoples, continuing their advance, were now in possession of most of Laos and all of Thailand. The Burmans had recovered their independence on the withdrawal of the Mongols but had not regained their former dominance within the country. And Islam, making its first appearance on our map, was winning converts among the Malay rulers of Sumatra and peninsular Malaya. These are changes that need to be looked at in some detail. A necessary first step is to split the Tai into the four major substocks distinguished today: the Zhuang (the stay-at-homes in southern China), the Shan (in northern and eastern Burma), the Lao (in Laos), and the Thai (in Thailand). The relative positions of these substocks are indicated on the main map. As to the political picture they and their neighbors presented, this is shown on the inset map. The Shan area was tribal, with a dozen different chieftains: Laos, in theory at least, had only one. The Thai had generated two states, Chiang Mai in the north of the country, and Siam (alternatively the kingdom of Ayuthia, after its capital) in the south. Other important contributions to the inset are provided by the Burmans (dividing their allegiance between Rakhine, Ava, and Taungoo), and the Mon-Khmer peoples (the Mon kingdom of southern Burma, with its capital currently at Bago; the dwindling Khmer empire, for which the label Cambodia now seems more appropriate; and, barely visible, some aboriginal tribes in the hinterlands of present-day Malaya). The final element consists of the Malay states, both Muslim and non-Muslim, in the peninsula and archipelago.[2]

The entry of Islam into this area dates back to the thirteenth century, when traders from the Indian regions controlled by Muslims began visiting Sumatra. By the date of this map the three northernmost of the Sumatran entrepots—Atjeh, Samudra, and Aru—had Muslim kings, and at the beginning of the fifteenth century the ruler of Malacca converted too. A similar process was conveying Islam along the silk road, where the Turkish ruler of Hami, the oasis town closest to the Chinese frontier, was a Muslim by the date of this map. Text and key follow the present-day fashion of referring to these Islamic kings as sultans. In actuality, local custom prevailed, with the Malay princes generally referring to themselves as rajahs and the ruler of Hami using the title khan.

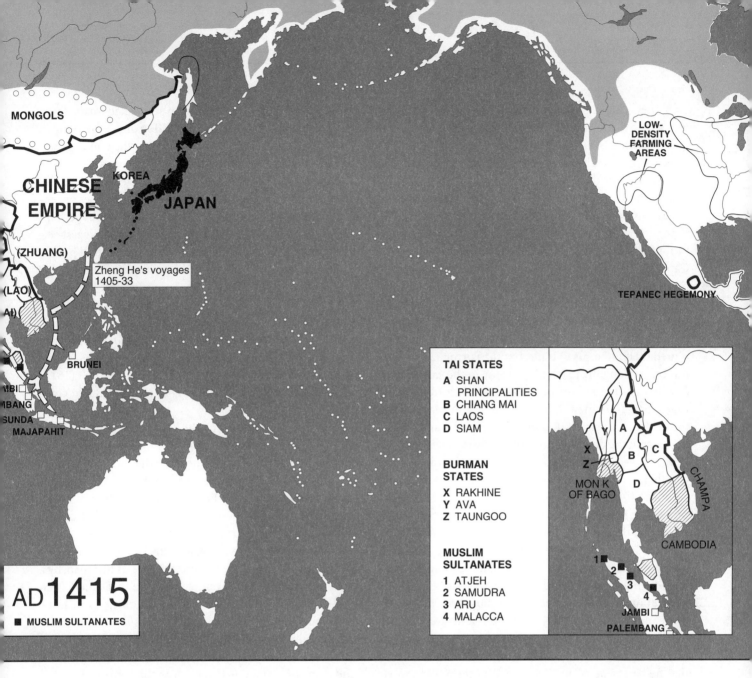

MONGOLS

CHINESE
EMPIRE

(ZHUANG)

(LAO)

AI)

BRUNEI

MBI

MBANG

SUNDA
MAJAPAHIT

KOREA

JAPAN

Zheng He's voyages
1405-33

LOW-
DENSITY
FARMING
AREAS

TEPANEC HEGEMONY

AD1415

■ MUSLIM SULTANATES

TAI STATES

A SHAN
   PRINCIPALITIES
B CHIANG MAI
C LAOS
D SIAM

**BURMAN
STATES**

X RAKHINE
Y AVA
Z TAUNGOO

**MUSLIM
SULTANATES**

1 ATJEH
2 SAMUDRA
3 ARU
4 MALACCA

MON K
OF BAGO

CHAMPA

CAMBODIA

JAMBI

PALEMBANG

*1. The Ming fleets sailed at roughly four-year intervals. Each was a veritable armada, with dozens of ships of the largest size (up to 1500 tons) and thousands of fighting men (as many as 20,000, according to the Chinese sources). All of them were organized and commanded by the same court official, the eunuch Zheng He, and it is his name rather than Yong Le's that is associated with the endeavor. Voyages usually began with visits to Majapahit, Palembang, Malacca, and Samudra. From Samudra the fleet proceeded across the Bay of Bengal to Ceylon and South India; on occasion some vessels would go on from there to Arabia and East Africa.

Clearly, there was never any intention of bringing such far-flung places into the Chinese tributary system: Zheng He simply bestowed lavish gifts on the local rulers and received whatever presents were offered in return. Nearer home, though, there was a little more to

Chinese claims that the local potentates had made a meaningful acknowledgment of Chinese suzerainty. The best example is Malacca, where the sultan, newly installed on his throne and in some danger of losing it to the Siamese, was quite prepared to travel to China for an investiture.

*2. Currently the Thais call their early kingdoms after their capitals: kingdom of Sukhothai, kingdom of Ayuthia. They refer to their country as Thailand, a habit which began in the eighteenth century and was made official in 1939. However, up to 1939 all Thai monarchs called themselves kings of Siam, regardless of wheher the capital was at Sukhothai (the original Siam), Ayuthia (a principality that supplanted Sukhothai in 1378) or Bangkok (after 1782). Siam is preferred here for the period up to 1939, on the gounds of common usage, and—no small matter on a map of this scale—because it takes up less space.

A new chapter in the history of the Pacific—and for that matter a new era for the world as a whole—opened with the European voyages of discovery of the late fifteenth and early sixteenth centuries. The one that caught the world's imagination, of course, was Columbus's transatlantic crossing of 1492, which at first seemed to have given Spain a new and very fast track to the orient. Vying for attention, however, was the Portuguese exploration of the Atlantic coast of Africa, which reached the Cape of Good Hope in 1488, enabling Vasco da Gama to make the first direct passage from Europe to India in 1499. From there the Portuguese picked up the spice route, arriving at Malacca—and making their first appearance on our map—in 1509. The sultan of Malacca rebuffed their attempts to trade, but the Portuguese weren't put off for long. In 1511 their viceroy in the east, Afonso de Albuquerque, arrived before the port with 18 ships and more than 1000 men. Militarily, the key to Malacca was the bridge at its center. Albuquerque seized it and, by doing so, split the defense into two equally ineffective halves. Within a week the sultan had fled and the Portuguese flag was flying over this, the most important of all the Malay emporia. If the voyages of discovery are to be seen as a race to the markets of the east—and it's not a bad way of looking at them—then the Portuguese had won.

What had held up the Spaniards was the American mainland, some parts of which Columbus had bumped into during his third and fourth voyages (1498–1502). Columbus still thought he was on target for China because, just as, to him the Caribbean islands were part of the Indonesian archipelago, so Panama was part of the Malay peninsula. But Europe's geographers soon realized that he had to be wrong: by 1507 Waldseemuller's world map was showing Columbus's discoveries as a new world, separated from the orient by a new ocean. In 1513 this conjecture was brilliantly confirmed by Vasco Núñez de Balboa, who led a party across the isthmus of Panama to its Pacific shore. Because he was facing south at the time, he named the new ocean the *Mar del Sur*, or "Southern Sea."

Columbus's voyages and Balboa's isthmus crossing lie off the right-hand border of our map. The first Spaniard to appear on it is Ponce de Leon, conqueror of Puerto Rico and discoverer of Florida, who in 1513 touched on the coast of Yucatán. This brought Spain's expanding empire within a few days' sail of America's most considerable political unit, the Aztec empire. The Aztecs, comparative newcomers on the Mesoamerican scene, had formed part of the alliance that overthrew the Tepanec hegemony in the 1430s. Soon afterward, they became the region's leading power. Vigorous campaining by such warrior rulers as Moctezuma I (1440–1468) and Ahuitzotl (1486–1502) gave the Aztecs dominion over nearly all the tribes of central Mexico. Their capital, Tenochtitlan, with perhaps 80,000 inhabitants, became far and away the biggest settlement of the Amerindian world, a vast, untidy pueblo sprawling across its island site like a Neolithic Venice.

The Portuguese put the years immediately following the capture of Malacca to good use. Within six months of taking the city, Albuquerque had dispatched an expedition to the Spice Islands, and the next year an embassy was sent to Canton. Local Muslim counterattacks spearheaded by the sultans of Demak (1511) and Atjeh (1513) were repulsed. All seemed set fair for a profitable commerce.

Portuguese success in the Indonesian archipelago should not be taken as indicating Muslim failure. Far from it: every decade saw more of the local rulers converting to Islam. This is, in fact, the period when power passed from the Hindu-Buddhist societies typical of the interior to the Islamic communities established on the coasts. An event that can be taken as symbolic of the whole process is the overthrow of the East Javan kingdom of Majapahit, sometime around the date of this map, by a coalition of northern Javan seaports led by Demak. Even the defeats the Muslim rulers suffered turned out to be less damaging than they seemed: the sultan of Malacca successfully reestablished his court on the island of Bintan (near present-day Singapore), while his son set up as an independent sultan at Perak (near the Siamese border). The rulers of the most important Spice Islands, Ternate and Tidore, had converted to Islam before the Portuguese got to them, and never wavered in their faith. Elsewhere, Atjeh absorbed Samudra.

In China, Ming prestige took a knock when the sixth emperor, Ying Zong, was captured by the Mongols (1449). The Ming pulled in their horns, shortening their northern frontier and leaving the Jurchen of Manchuria and the Koreans to their own devices. In the south Dai Viet had already been abandoned (1428). The Viets celebrated by conquering most of Champa (1471).

Some minor happenings: On the silk road, the ruler of Turpan occupied Hami (1513), the Siamese sacked Angkor (1430), and the Maori colonized Chatham Island

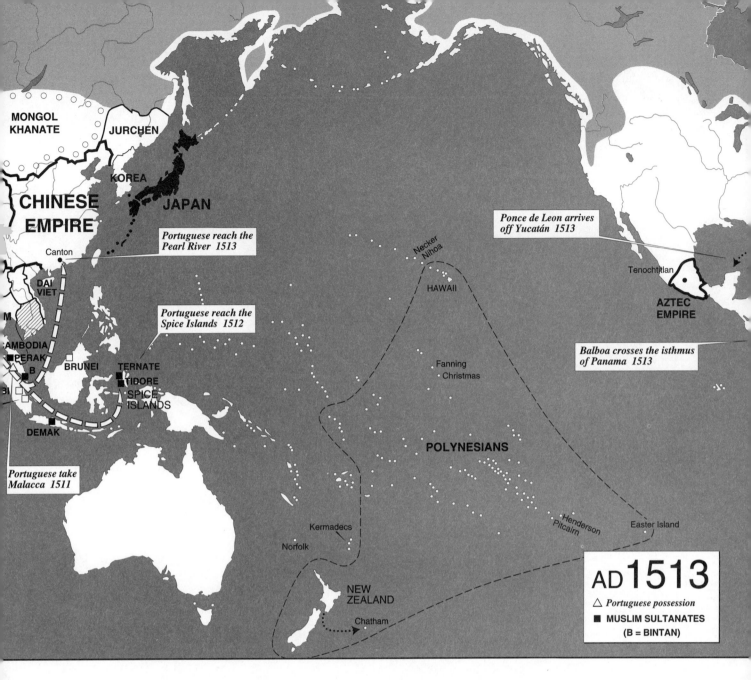

Portuguese reach the
Pearl River 1513

Portuguese reach the
Spice Islands 1512

Portuguese take
Malacca 1511

Ponce de Leon arrives
off Yucatán 1513

Balboa crosses the isthmus
of Panama 1513

MONGOL KHANATE

JURCHEN

KOREA

JAPAN

CHINESE EMPIRE

Canton

DAI VIET

M

AMBODIA
PERAK

BRUNEI

TERNATE
TIDORE
SPICE ISLANDS

DEMAK

B

Necker
Nihoa

HAWAII

Fanning
Christmas

POLYNESIANS

Tenochtitlan

AZTEC EMPIRE

Kermadecs

Norfolk

Henderson
Pitcairn

Easter Island

NEW ZEALAND

Chatham

AD **1513**
△ *Portuguese possession*
■ **MUSLIM SULTANATES**
(B = BINTAN)

(circa 1500). The Maori achievement was the final event in the long saga of Polynesian exploration, discovery, and settlement, which is summarized here by the dashed perimeter. Note that some peripheral islands, which had at one time been colonized—Necker and Nihoa in Hawaii, and Norfolk and the Kermadecs to the north of New Zealand—have now been abandoned. The same was true of many islands within the bounding line: Pitcairn and Henderson, for example, and Fanning and Christmas in the Line Islands. This has the effect of isolating the farther-flung communities, and by the date of this map the peoples at the apices of the Polynesian triangle—the

Hawaiians, Easter Islanders, and Maoris—had lost contact with the core area of the culture.[1]

*1. There are Polynesian populations on a number of tiny islands—too tiny to be shown here—within Melanesia. These "Polynesian outliers" represent a westward colonization that succeeded only on islands the Melanesians didn't know about or didn't want.

PART 2 THE OCEAN DEFINED

Portugal's remarkable thrust across the Indian Ocean had brought its seamen to the goal they had sought for so long, the fabled Spice Islands. The way, however, was long and hard, and some captains were more impressed by the dangers than the rewards. Among them was Ferdinand Magellan, who decided it was worth having a second look at Columbus's idea for a westward route to the orient. What was needed was an expedition to the South Atlantic to see if there was a way through, or around, the American barrier.

It is no surprise to find that the king of Portugal, to whom Magellan was duty-bound to offer his plan first, showed nothing but ill temper when approached. The king had committed his country's resources to the Cape route and didn't want to hear any talk of an alternative. Rebuffed, Magellan turned to Spain. Emperor Charles V was receptive: his grandparents had backed Columbus, and this seemed a logical follow-up. He gave Magellan five ships and the 250 men needed to crew them.

Magellan set sail from Seville in late September 1519. By the time the southern winter set in, he had explored the Atlantic coast of South America as far as 49°S, nearly 15° further than anyone else had gone. There was no sign of a passage, though, and the expedition had to spend five months holed up in a desolate Patagonian bay before the search could be resumed. Eventually, in October 1520, a further 4° to the south, Magellan found his strait. Of the original five vessels, one had gone aground in Patagonia, and the crew of another had mutinied and run for home; but Magellan led the three surviving ships through the passage and out onto Balboa's "Southern Sea"—or, as Magellan called it in an attempt to raise the flagging spirits of his sailors, the Pacific.

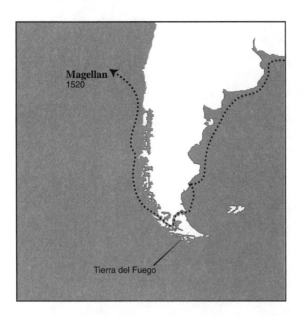

The Pacific lived up to its new name: the expedition enjoyed fair weather and made good time. But the three or four weeks that the voyage was expected to take failed to produce a landfall. A small, obviously uninhabited island was seen in late January 1521 (probably Puka Puka, a northerly outlier of the Tuamotu archipelago) and another (probably Caroline Atoll, at the southern end of the Line Islands) in early February. After that there was nothing except empty ocean day after day, week after week. Supplies ran low, then ran out: the crews chewed leather and began to die of scurvy. Finally, on March 6th, more than three months after the ships had left the strait, two large islands appeared on the horizon. They were Rota and Guam, the southernmost of the Marianas. A safe harbor was found at the southern end of Guam, and contacts were made with the island's inhabitants, the Chamorros. In fact, the Chamorros were soon swarming all over the flagship, stealing anything that wasn't nailed down, and Magellan had to drive them off. The next day the Spaniards went ashore and took the rice and fresh

fruit they needed by force. On March 9th they were ready to begin the last leg of their epic crossing, which was completed six days later when lookouts sighted the island of Samar in the eastern Philippines.

The remainder of Magellan's commission should have been relatively easy to execute: all he had to do was find his way to the Spice Islands and get home. There was no shortage of native pilots and, thanks to Enrique, a Malay slave Magellan had acquired during his earlier service at Malacca, no language problem. But Magellan decided to build up a power base in the Philippines before moving on, a plan that involved overawing the native chiefs and converting them to Christianity. At first all went well, with the important rajah of Cebu figuring among the converts. Then an ill-planned raid against the neighboring rajah of Mactan brought disaster. Magellan, reluctant to withdraw, was killed on the beach, and the expedition suffered further grievous losses as hitherto friendly rulers turned treacherous. Only when the Spaniards took to the sea again were they able to recover confidence and restock their vessels. Six months of judicious piracy put them back on course and finally, on November 6th, the two remaining vessels (the third had been abandoned for lack of men to crew her) arrived at the Spice Islands.

Fortunately, there were no Portuguese vessels in the Spice Islands when the Spaniards arrived, so they were able to refit their ships and take on cargo at their leisure. They were well aware, however, that they could expect no mercy if the Portuguese caught up with them; and to spread the risks of the homeward voyage it was decided that one ship, the *Victoria*, would take the westward route back to Spain and the other, the *Trinidad*, would return via the Pacific. The *Trinidad*, which didn't set out till April 1522, made it to the Marianas but subsequently failed to find favorable winds despite voyaging far to the north—according to the captain, as far as 43°N. Limping back to the Spice Islands, the ship fell into the hands of the Portuguese: such of the crew as still survived were imprisoned.

Del Cano, the captain of the *Victoria*, had more determination and better luck. Steering south, he cleared the Indies as quickly as he could and made the long voyage to the southern tip of Africa in the mid-30s, well below any latitude used by the Portuguese. After rounding the Cape and sailing the South Atlantic he put in at the Cape Verde Isles, where the Portuguese authorities accepted his story that he was returning from a Caribbean voyage and gave

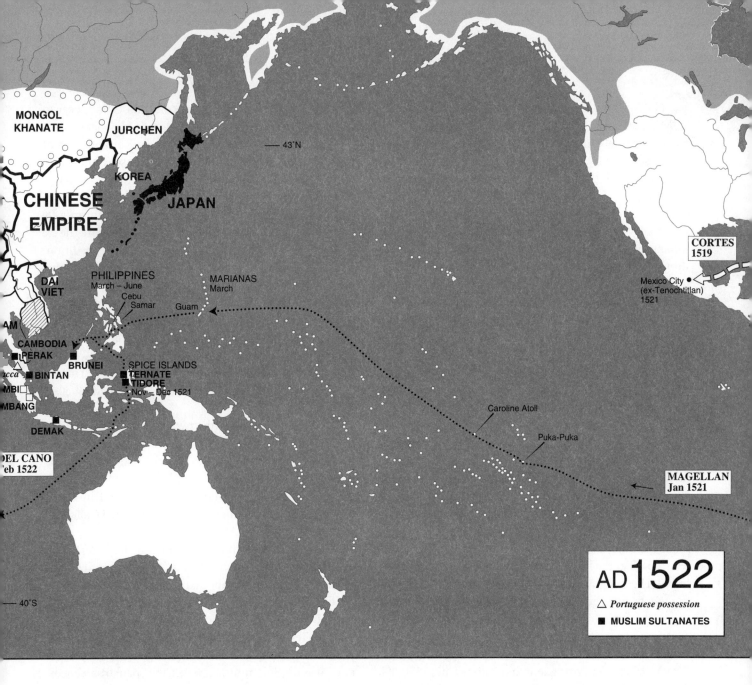

MONGOL
KHANATE

JURCHEN

KOREA

JAPAN

CHINESE
EMPIRE

— 43°N

DAI
VIET

PHILIPPINES
March – June
Cebu
Samar

MARIANAS
March

Guam

CAMBODIA
PERAK

BRUNEI

SPICE ISLANDS

acca BINTAN

TERNATE
TIDORE
Nov – Dec 1521

MBI

MBANG

DEMAK

Caroline Atoll

Puka-Puka

EL CANO
eb 1522

— 40°S

CORTES
1519

Mexico City
(ex-Tenochtitlan)
1521

MAGELLAN
Jan 1521

AD 1522

△ *Portuguese possession*

■ **MUSLIM SULTANATES**

him permission to take on supplies. Unfortunately, he had nothing to offer in payment except spices, and this gave the game away. Hastily abandoning the 13 men who were ashore, del Cano set sail for Spain with the remaining 18, barely enough to work a ship that was designed for a complement of 50. The final weeks were the hardest of the whole voyage, with exhausted men working the pumps day and night to keep the *Victoria* from foundering. At last, on September 4, 1522, Cape Saint Vincent came into sight; four days later, after a voyage that had lasted three years and one month, the *Victoria* docked at Seville.[1]

Aside from Magellan's voyage the map records another major Spanish exploit, Cortés's conquest of Tenochtitlan. Cortés, the archetypal *conquistador*, marched his tiny army into the Aztec capital in 1519 and almost succeeded in bluffing his way to control of the empire. Forced to pull back, he returned in 1521 and fought his way across the city house by house. Renamed Mexico City, it became the center of a rapidly expanding Spanish-American empire.

*1. For note see p. 111

Spain's follow-up to Magellan and del Cano's expedition set sail in 1525 with García de Loaysa as its commander and del Cano as its pilot. Luck was not with them. Of the seven ships that set out from Spain, three didn't make it through the Straits of Magellan, and the four that did were scattered by a typhoon shortly after emerging. One ended up in New Spain (meaning Mexico); one disappeared (its remains have recently been found on Amanu atoll in the Tuamotu archipelago); a third was shipwrecked on Mindanao in the Philippines. However, the flagship, the *Santa Maria del Victoria*, did manage to complete its mission. Both Loaysa and del Cano died in the course of the long voyage, but finally, via Guam and Mindanao, the *Victoria* made it to the Spice Island of Tidore.

The Spaniards received a warm welcome from the sultan of Tidore. He had been severely punished by the Portuguese for entertaining del Cano five years earlier and was burning for revenge on both them and their ally, the sultan of Ternate. The Spaniards fought in his corner as best they could, much encouraged by an unexpected reinforcement from New Spain (a single ship, the sole survivor of three dispatched by Cortés in 1528). Unfortunately, attempts to send spices back by the same route were a failure: in neither of the two tries that the Spanish made were they able to find the winds they needed. Meanwhile, back at the home farm, Charles V was changing his mind. His geographers told him that legally the Portuguese had the better case (see over), and it was becoming increasingly obvious that they had the better line of communication (they were losing one ship in ten en route to the Spice Islands, whereas he was losing two out of three). When the Portuguese king offered him 350,000 ducats for his claim and free passage home for such Spaniards as remained in the islands, Charles decided to call it a day (1529).

The Philippines were another matter. Spain had discovered them and was determined to have them. An expedition from Mexico in the 1540s failed to achieve anything except the naming of the archipelago (after the heir apparent, the future Philip II) and, once again, had no luck at all when it came to finding a way back. In 1564 Miguel de Legazpi made a new attempt, with four ships and clearer plans. A short bombardment persuaded the people of Cebu township to return to the allegiance they had briefly given Magellan more than 40 years earlier: this provided Legazpi with the necessary lodgement. The next step was to establish his line of communication. Legazpi ordered the expedition's pilot, Andrés de Urdaneta, to take one of the flotilla's three ships (one had disappeared on the way out), sail to the north Pacific, and see if there were winds there that would carry him back to the Americas. Urdanta found the wind he needed and made a successful crossing in the high 30s, though it took him four months to do it. That the route had been discussed before the expedition set out is clear from the fact that the expedition's stray, the *San Lucas*, after an independent cruise in Philippine waters, had already returned on a very similar course. It was, in fact, the *San Lucas* that made the first west-to-east crossing of the Pacific, and if this was a bit of a blow for Urdaneta, the man who had probably worked out the way to do it, the *San Lucas*'s captain, Alonso de Arellano, put more into his achievement than just setting out earlier: he sailed higher and faster and made the better time.[1]

New Spain was one of the two Spanish viceroyalties in the Americas, the second, the viceroyalty of Peru, being responsible for Spanish South America. News of Legazpi's success prompted the Peruvian administration to attempt something similar in southern latitudes, and in 1567 a modest flotilla (two ships, 100 men) departed Callao under the command of Alvaro de Mendana. There seems to have been no very definite plan, just the hope of finding an island that was rumored to exist somewhere to the east of New Guinea. Stories about it varied, but one version referred to it as Solomon's Isle and suggested that it had been the source of the gold that embellished the court of this Old Testament monarch. This explains why the island chain that the expedition discovered in early 1568 is now known as the Solomons. However, the Spaniards were disappointed in their hope of gold, and it soon became clear that the "Indians" in these parts were too poor, too fierce, and above all too few for a colony to be a practical proposition. After a six-month stay during which Mendana checked out all the major islands south of his first discovery, Ysabel, the frustrated Spaniards made their way home on a course that took them first north, skirting the Marshalls and Wake Island, then east, to a landfall in Baja California.

During this period the Portuguese began to draw real benefits from their Far Eastern enterprise. The fort they built on Ternate in 1522 and their alliance with its sultan enabled them to dominate the spice trade: a generation later the shipwreck on Tanegashima of a vessel seeking a

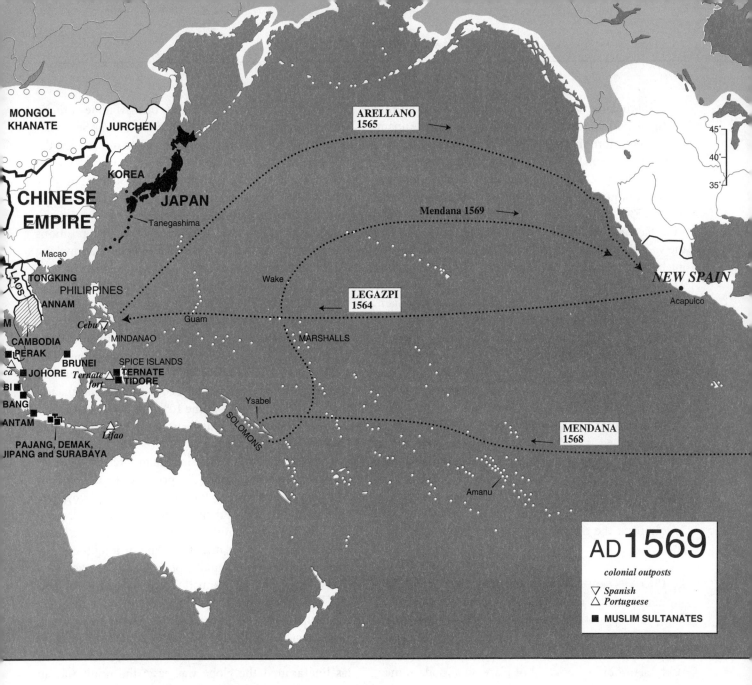

MONGOL KHANATE

JURCHEN

KOREA

CHINESE EMPIRE

JAPAN

Macao

Tanegashima

TONGKING
LAOS
PHILIPPINES
ANNAM

Cebu

MINDANAO

M

CAMBODIA
PERAK

ca
JOHORE
BI
BANG
ANTAM
PAJANG, DEMAK, JIPANG and SURABAYA

BRUNEI

SPICE ISLANDS
TERNATE
Ternate fort
TIDORE

Lifao

Guam

MARSHALLS

Wake

Ysabel

SOLOMONS

Amanu

ARELLANO 1565

Mendana 1569

LEGAZPI 1564

NEW SPAIN

Acapulco

MENDANA 1568

45°
40°
35°

AD **1569**

colonial outposts

▽ *Spanish*
△ *Portuguese*
■ MUSLIM SULTANATES

Chinese port opened up useful opportunities in Japan (1543). The Japanese had been excluded from China because of their piratical behavior: the Portuguese proved themselves acceptable intermediaries in the exchange of Chinese silk for Japanese silver. In the 1550s the three interested parties agreed on rules for this trade. Every year one or two "great ships" would leave Goa, the Portuguese base in India, for Macao, the Chinese customs port designated to receive them at the mouth of the Pearl River. There they would take on silk, plus some gold, spices, and porcelain, before proceeding to one of the small harbors dotting the coast of Kyushu. The Chinese goods were sold at double their cost in silver, the silver forming the bulk of the return cargo. European goods played only a trifling part in the exchange.

As well as serving Mammon, which they did with enthusiasm, the Portuguese made a genuine effort to serve God. They had no success in the Muslim parts of the Malay archipelago, but they established a successful mission at Lifao, on East Timor, where the Indo-Pacific aborigines were still pagan (1565). Proselytizing got off to an equally promising start in Japan: the Jesuit Francis Xavier, who was in the country from 1549 to 1551, was persuaded that great things could be expected from this quarter.

In Southeast Asia, note the division of Dai Viet into northern and southern halves (Tongking and Annam, 1533) and, more importantly, the appearance of a new kingdom of Burma, the creation of princes of the Taungoo line. The first stage in the revival of Burman fortunes was the conquest of the Mon kingdom of Bago by Taungoo in 1534–1535; the rest of the country was subdued by King Bayinnaung (1550–1581), who conquered Ava and the various Shan principalities of the north before moving beyond the natural borders of the country and taking Manipur (on the northwest) and Chiang Mai (on the east). Subsequently Bayinnaung led armies against Siam, whose capital he captured twice in the 1560s, and Laos, where he had some temporary success in the 1570s. His honorific "victor of the ten directions" was surely well earned.[2]

Brunei joined the list of Muslim sultanates circa 1520 (in time for the previous map): Jambi and Palembang followed suit in the course of the sixteenth century, though it is not known exactly when. In Java the sultanate of Demak split four ways in 1550: the eastern half of the island had acquired a sultanate of its own, Bantam, in 1526. The sultan of Bintan (ex-Malacca) was chased from this island by the Portuguese in 1526: he set up shop again in Johore, at the tip of the Malay peninsula, a few years later.

IN 1569 GERARDUS MERCATOR published a world map summarizing the results of three-quarters a century of European exploration. If we ignore the fanciful fill-ins for the areas not yet visited, the picture he presents is surprisingly accurate. The outlines of Europe, Africa, and mainland Asia wouldn't look out of place on a modern map, and North and South America, though a bit lumpy on the Pacific side, are perfectly recognizable. The Pacific archipelagos are not so good: Indonesia is roughly right, but Japan is a jumble. As for Australia, it doesn't appear at all, though New Guinea does, its northern coast having been sighted and named during Spanish attempts to get back to New Spain from the Spice Islands. The Spaniards had also picked up some of the Carolines and Marshalls during their voyaging.[3]

From a sailor's rather than a geographer's point of view, what this boils down to is a working knowledge of Pacific latitudes between 40°N and 12°S. There are important omissions. No one as yet had made contact with any of the Polynesian communities. The Spaniards sailed north and south of the Hawaiian Islands but saw none of them, while the few atolls that had been sighted in the South Pacific were either uninhabited or unvisited or both. On the other hand, the Galapagos Islands—also uninhabited—were known, thanks to their chance discovery by Fray Tomás de Berlanga, third Bishop of Panama, blown off course during a mission to Peru (1535).

Getting all these new finds into their correct positions on the map was even more of a challenge than making them. Latitude could be determined with relative ease and accuracy, but longitude was a real problem: it could only be guessed at by "dead reckoning," estimating the distance traveled in the course of each day's journey. As a result, most mapmakers were still working with a picture of the world derived from antiquity, which overstated the width of Eurasia by 20°. Mercator knocked 10° off this, but that still left the continent's eastern edge—China, Japan, and the Malay archipelago—some 10° too far to the east. Balance was achieved by underestimating the width of the Pacific by the same amount.

The overestimate of Eurasia had an interesting consequence in the Spice Islands. The primacy of Spain in westward expedition and of Portugal in eastward voyaging encouraged the two of them to agree to a formal division of the world into Spanish and Portuguese spheres, based on an Atlantic Ocean meridian (line of longitude) 370 leagues to the west of San Antonio in the Cape Verde Islands. In present-day terms this work out as 46°W. This line, known as the Tordesillas meridian after the 1494 treaty that established it, served its purpose well enough until Magellan and del Cano demonstrated the need for a similar divider in the Pacific. Prolonging the Tordesillas line around the globe was easy: the result was an antimeridian at 134°E. But where exactly did this antimeridian run? The Portuguese said just to the east of the Spice Islands, which therefore belonged to them (and they were right); the Spaniards, relying on the traditional overestimate of Asia's size, said that it ran through Malacca and that consequently the Spice Islands, like the Philippines, belonged to Spain. Priority in discovery was probably more important than cartography in persuading the Spanish to settle: certainly the Portuguese made little attempt to use their victory in the Spice Islands to press their equally valid claim to the Philippines. To the Spanish, though, it seemed that they might, so on their maps the moved the Philippines a few hundred miles to the east, putting them safely on Spain's side of the line.

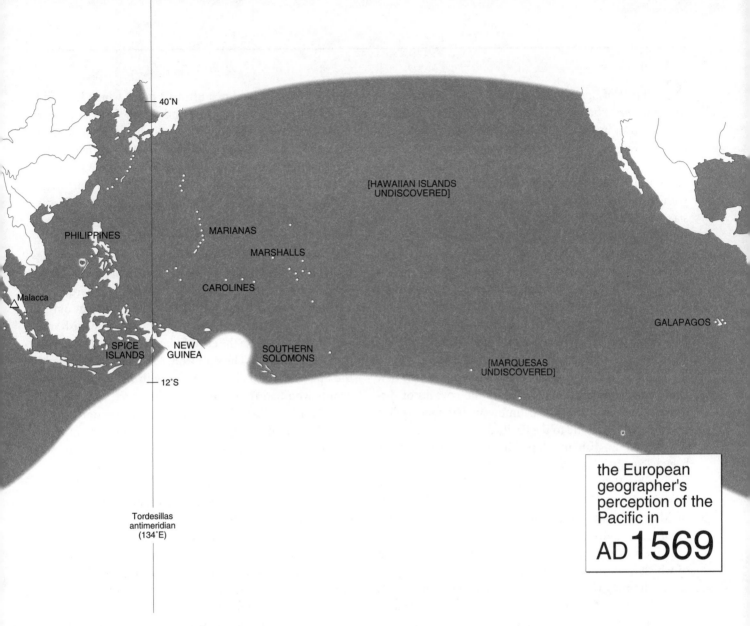

40°N

[HAWAIIAN ISLANDS
UNDISCOVERED]

PHILIPPINES

MARIANAS

MARSHALLS

CAROLINES

Malacca

SPICE
ISLANDS

NEW
GUINEA

SOUTHERN
SOLOMONS

GALAPAGOS

[MARQUESAS
UNDISCOVERED]

12°S

Tordesillas
antimeridian
(134°E)

the European
geographer's
perception of the
Pacific in

AD**1569**

*1. The outline of the Californian coast was already known to the Spaniards. Baja California had been visited by Cortés as early as 1533, and its peninsular nature was subsequently demonstrated by his lieutenant Ulloa in 1539–1540. Two years later, Cabrillo and Ferrer set sail on a voyage that eventually (in 1543) reached the present-day border with Oregon at 42°N.

*2. The Siamese got in Bayinnaung's bad books by refusing to give him a white elephant he wanted. White elephants, according to Buddhist theology, were born in lands where the ruler was particularly virtuous, and in turning down the request the Siamese king implied that Bayinnaung had some way to go in this area. True or not, the remark cost him his throne. The kings of Burma subsequently became "Lords of the White Elephant, the Red Elephant, the Mottled Elephant and All Other Elephants."

*3. Mercator ("the measurer," born Gerhard Kremer in the Netherlands in 1512) is the dominant figure in cartography of the late sixteenth century. He published a vast number of maps (many of which he engraved himself), invented the projection that bears his name (a modified version of which provides the base map for this book), and also the term *atlas* (personified in a title-page vignette of the giant Atlas holding up the globe). But Mercator didn't always have access to the most up-to-date information on the Far East; and from the hand-drawn world map of 1554 produced by Lopo Homem (and now in the *Bibliothèque Nationale*) it is clear that the Portuguese knew rather more about the Asian coast opposite Japan than he did. Mercator doesn't show either the Shandong or the Korean peninsula: Homem has both. Where the two of them do agree is in bringing Asia to an end at this point: the current assumption was that America extended right across the North Pacific and that the strait dividing the Asian and American continents—assuming it existed at all—was to be looked for somewhere due north of Japan.

Philip II of Spain ruled an empire the like of which the world had never seen before: besides his extensive holdings in Europe (Spain, most of Italy, and—initially—all of the Netherlands), he was master of Mexico, Central and South America, and, in the Pacific, the Philippines. In 1580 he acquired the Portuguese crown, together with its colonial possessions in Africa, India, and Indonesia. Truly this was an empire on which the sun never set. But Philip also had a knack of making enemies. His unnecessarily high-handed ways provoked a rebellion in the Netherlands, which, much to his surprise, proved impossible to extinguish. And the rebellious Netherlanders, founders of the astonishingly successful Dutch Republic, had an ally in Elizabeth of England, who shared their Protestant faith, disliked and feared Philip's form of militant Catholicism, and, perhaps more to the point, had no intention of allowing the Iberians a monopoly of the new lands and opportunities revealed by the voyages of discovery. The result was a maritime war that soon spilled over from the Atlantic to the Pacific.

The first English interloper in what had previously been a "Spanish lake" was Francis Drake, who had spent the early 1570s honing his piratical skills in the Caribbean. In 1577–1578 he led three ships to the Straits of Magellan and one of them, his flagship the *Golden Hind,* through the straits and on to the sack of Valparaiso (all nine houses of it). The payoff came the next year, most of which he devoted to cutting up the completely unprotected shipping responsible for ferrying the silver of Peru up to Panama. After stuffing the *Golden Hind*'s holds with plunder, Drake took it up to a latitude of at least 43°N (one account says 48°N) before turning back for a refurbishing stop just outside the fog-obscured entrance to San Francisco Bay. From there Drake sailed across the Pacific to Mindanao, then, via Tidore and Java, to the Indian Ocean, the Atlantic, and a tumultuous welcome home.

Contemporaries were vastly impressed by Drake's feat, not least because the voyage returned a profit of 11,900 percent (£600,000 on an investment of £5000). Queen Elizabeth was happy to knight her bold mariner and even more pleased with her share of the take (50 percent of the total, doubling the crown's revenue for the year). The voyage also has its place in the annals of seafaring: apart from being the second circumnavigation and the first performed under one captain, it yielded useful new data on two fuzzy areas of contemporary geography. On emerging from the Straits of Magellan, Drake had encountered a storm, which blew him south to a point where he could see that "the Atlantic Ocean and South Sea meete in a most large and free scope." This was obviously something that would bear further examination. And his trip to the coast of Oregon, which many believe was made in the hope of finding the Pacific end of the fabled "Northwest Passage" showed that, if this channel existed at all, it was further north than he had been able to sail.

Six years after Drake's return another Englishman, Thomas Cavendish, set out on a very similar foray. He didn't do anything like as well as Drake off the coast of South America, but he made up some of the difference in Californian waters. To understand the how and why of this means taking a look at the Philippines, where Spanish rule was now centered on the city of Manila, founded on Luzon by Legazpi in 1571. The shift from Cebu to Luzon brought the Spaniards into closer contact with the Chinese merchants who had traditionally handled such traffic as existed in the northern Philippines. The connection proved the salvation of Legazpi's enterprise, for his hope of finding gold or spices in sufficient quantities to fund his administration was turning out to be wildly overoptimistic. What the Spaniards did have was access to Mexican silver, and this was worth a great deal more in silver-starved China than it was in the silver-rich Americas. Within a few years a lucrative trade had sprung up, with annual sailings from Acapulco to Manila (with silver) and from Manila to Acapulco (with Chinese silks and porcelain). Like everything else in the Spanish empire, this trade was the subject of extraordinarily detailed royal decrees, which instructed the captains exactly how much cargo they could take on in how many shares, and when they should sail and on what course. Usually there was one galleon per year in each direction, and the prosperity of the Spanish community in the Philippines—maybe 1000 strong, almost all of them residents of Manila—rested entirely on the safe arrival of the Acapulco galleon (on a direct route, via Guam) and the safe dispatch of the Manila galleon (steering northeast into the high 30s, making its landfall at Cape Mendocino, and then following the Californian coast southward). The Acapulco galleon usually completed its voyage in three months; the Manila galleon took twice as long, and its crews were often barely able to work their ship by the time they reached their destination.

Thomas Cavendish heard about the Manila galleon from a pilot captured off the coast of New Spain and decided to lie in wait for it off the tip of the Californian

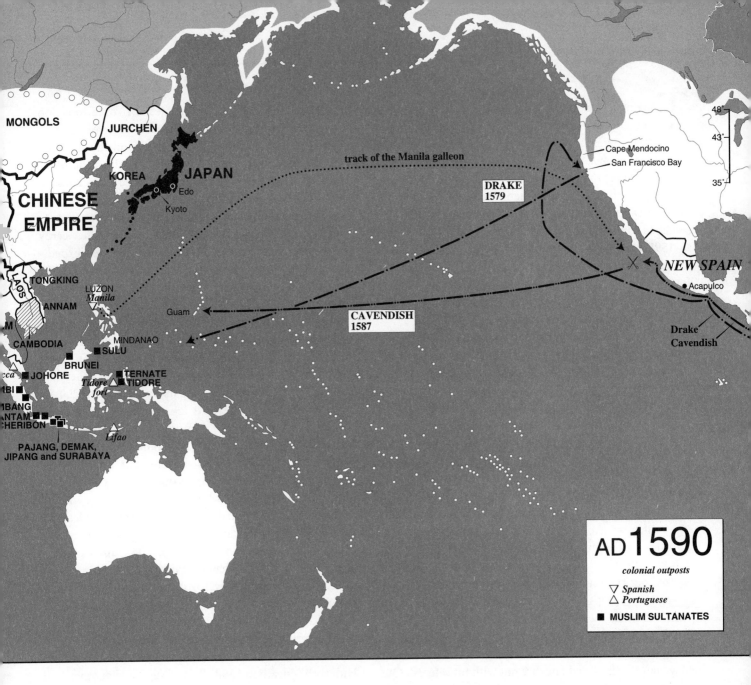

MONGOLS
JURCHEN
KOREA
JAPAN
CHINESE
EMPIRE
○ Edo
Kyoto ○
track of the Manila galleon
Cape Mendocino
San Francisco Bay
DRAKE
1579
48°
43°
35°
LAOS
TONGKING
ANNAM
LUZON
Manila
CAMBODIA
MINDANAO
SULU
BRUNEI
JOHORE
cca
*Tidore
fort* △ TERNATE
TIDORE
1BI
1BANG
ANTAM
HERIBON
Lifao
PAJANG, DEMAK,
JIPANG and SURABAYA
Guam
CAVENDISH
1587
NEW SPAIN
● Acapulco
Drake
Cavendish

AD**1590**

colonial outposts

▽ *Spanish*
△ *Portuguese*
■ MUSLIM SULTANATES

peninsula. After three weeks his patience was rewarded: the 600-ton *Santa Ana* came into view and was immediately set upon by Cavendish's much smaller vessels—the largest, the *Desire,* displaced 140 tons. It wasn't a fair fight: the Spaniards were so confident that the route was secure that they had stowed their cannon in the hold; within six hours they had been beaten into submission, and goods to the value of £125,000 had been transferred to English ownership. It was a well-satisfied Thomas Cavendish who crossed the Pacific and, via the Philippines, Java, and Saint Helena, completed his (and the world's third) circumnavigation.[1]

*1. These were significant years in Japan. The bigger barons had been swallowing up the smaller for some time, and in the 1570s Oda Nobunaga emerged as the biggest of them all, and a potential unifier of the country. One of the reasons for Nobunaga's rapid progress was a corps of 3000 men equipped with matchlocks copied from Portuguese examples; another was his lack of hesitancy in dealing with the militant Buddhist monks, who had been a destabilizing factor in the political life of the nominal capital, Kyoto, for more than a generation. By the time of his death—he was assassinated by a jealous general in 1582—Nobunaga was master of a third of Japan. His good work was continued by another of his generals, Toyotomi Hideyoshi, whose conquests of Shikoku (1585), Kyushu (1587), and the Kanto (the Edo region, 1590) brought the process to completion.

(footnote continued on p. 111)

The English offensive in the Pacific petered out in the 1590s: Drake never returned; and when Cavendish tried to, he failed to get through the straits. In 1594 Richard Hawkins, son of the more famous Sir John Hawkins, made the passage and took a few prizes off the coast of South America but then hung around too long and was captured by the Spanish. Subsequently attention switched to the Cape of Good Hope route. A trial voyage in 1598 reached Malacca, and prospects seemed bright enough to justify the creation of an East India Company for ventures in the Indian Ocean and Indonesia. But by this time the initiative in eastern waters had passed from the English to the Dutch.

The Dutch had the biggest fleet in Europe and the most advanced economy: these assets, plus their proverbial obstinacy, had enabled them to defeat the massive armaments brought against them by Philip II of Spain during the 1570s and 1580s. By the 1590s the Dutch homeland—the northern half of the Netherlands—was sufficiently secure for the new nation to go over to the offensive. As a first step Cornelis Houtman took four ships on the Cape route to Bantam in Java, where he managed to buy enough spices to turn a small profit. Two years later, in 1598, Jacob van Neck repeated this exploit, and four of his eight ships went on from Bantam to the Spice Islands. Cutting out the middleman had a huge effect on profitability: this time the return on the original investment worked out at a highly satisfactory 400 percent.

Van Neck's ships were not by any means the only Dutch vessels to make the Far East their destination in 1598: no less than 14 others set out in the course of the year. Of these, ten chose the westward passage via the Straits of Magellan. Their varied fates are not without interest. Out of five in the first flotilla one turned back for home shortly after clearing the straits, one was lost in a storm, one was captured by the Spanish, and one—the *Liefde* ("Charity"), under Jacob Quaeckernaeck—ran so far north that it ended up in Japan. Only one reached the Spice Islands, and it was eventually taken by the Portuguese. A second group of four ships had almost equal ill luck. One never made it to the straits; one reached the Spice Islands only to run aground when it got there. The remaining two reached the Philippines, where one was lost in an abortive attack on Manila. The commander of this foray, Olivier van Noort, managed to get himself home in the other, becoming the first Dutch circumnavigator (fourth overall). The heavy losses sustained by these expeditions confirmed Spanish experience: the western route took too heavy a toll of ships and men to be competitive.

The third of the trans-Pacific tracks on the map belongs to a survivor from an earlier era, Alvaro de Mendana, who discovered the Solomons three maps back, in 1568. They had proved unsuitable for colonization then, and there was no reason to think a second attempt would fare better, but Mendana managed to persuade the viceroy of Peru, the Marqués de Cañete, to finance a new expedition, and this—two galleons, two smaller ships, and 378 men and women—duly set sail in 1595. Five weeks out from Callao, Mendana happened on the Marquesas (named for his patron the viceroy), and these islands became the scene of the first encounter between European and Polynesian. Initial goodwill soon gave way to rows over pilfering, warning shots, and finally lethal volleys: by the time the episode had run its course, some 200 islanders were dead. The next leg of the voyage brought Mendana to where the Solomons were supposed to be but, as it turned out, weren't. Mendana declared that the island in view, which he named Santa Cruz, would do just as well, and went ashore. The second galleon sailed on regardless and found the Solomons, only to be lost with all its crew on San Cristobal. The Santa Cruz colony lasted a couple of months, during which Mendana and many others died; the expedition's pilot, Pedro de Quiros, eventually got a hundred famished survivors to Manila.

Japan, newly unified by Toyotomi Hideyoshi and eager to flex its muscles, launched an invasion of Korea in 1592. This was supposed to be merely a prelude to the conquest of China, but in fact Korea on its own proved too big a mouthful and the whole enterprise was abandoned on Hideyoshi's death in 1598. This precipitated another civil war, in the course of which the hegemony Hideyoshi had created passed to Tokugawa Ieyasu (1600). In Southeast Asia the Siamese staged a remarkable comeback, expelling the Burmese (1587), reducing Cambodia to tributary status (1594), and conquering Chiang Mai (1598). On Java the sultanate of Mataram absorbed Pajang and Demak, becoming the most powerful of the principalities on the island. New sultanates appeared on Borneo (Banjarmasin) and Sulawesi (Macassar).

In America, note the appearance of the isolated Spanish province of New Mexico. Back in the 1540s Francisco de Coronado had had a look at the area north of New Spain and concluded that in general the native population was too thin on the ground to support an administration.

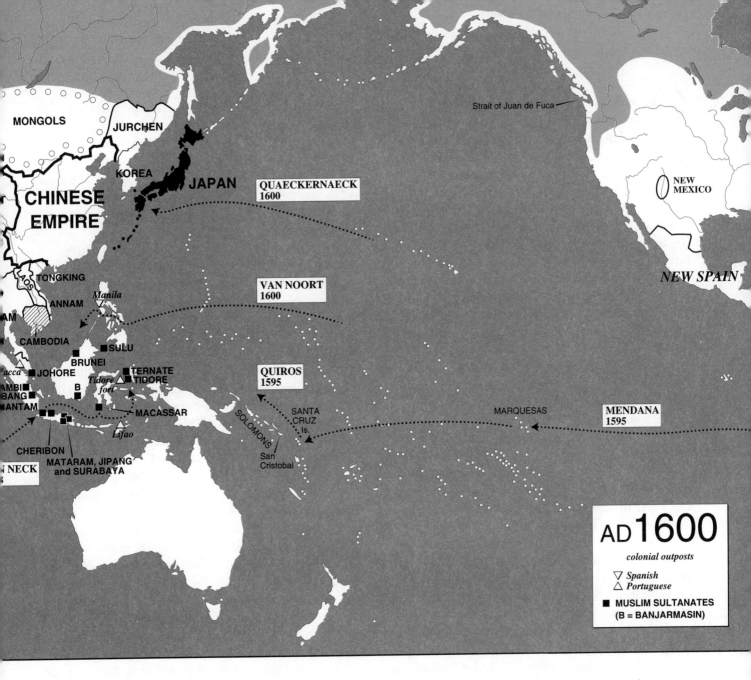

MONGOLS

JURCHEN

KOREA

JAPAN

QUAECKERNAECK 1600

CHINESE EMPIRE

TONGKING

Manila

ANNAM

CAMBODIA

■SULU

■BRUNEI

Strait of Juan de Fuca

NEW MEXICO

NEW SPAIN

VAN NOORT 1600

△*acca* ■JOHORE

■■TERNATE
■TIDORE

Tidore fort

QUIROS 1595

AMBI
BANG
ANTAM

B

■MACASSAR

SOLOMONS

SANTA
CRUZ
Is.

MARQUESAS

MENDANA 1595

Lifao

CHERIBON

San
Cristobal

NECK

**MATARAM, JIPANG
and SURABAYA**

AD**1600**

colonial outposts

▽ *Spanish*
△ *Portuguese*

■ MUSLIM SULTANATES
(B = BANJARMASIN)

He did, however, find a cluster of pueblos in the region of the upper Rio Grande, and it was this that provided the basis for the New Mexican province as finally set up in 1598.

A claim by Juan de Fuca to have sailed the Pacific coast of North America as far north as the strait that now bears his name has to be given a grudging mention, as the strait is there in apparent witness to his achievement. In fact, there is no documentary evidence at all to support his tale, which is only one of many dreamed up in support of the idea of a Northwest Passage.

Once the Dutch were satisfied that they had found the best way of tapping into the spice trade, they set about taking it over completely. There was no shortage of individual entrepreneurs—no less than 65 ships left for the east in 1601—but a coordinated effort by a company with monopoly rights seemed a better proposition. Agreement on the form this should take was soon achieved, and in 1602 the Vereenigde Ost-Indische Compagnie or "Chartered East-India Company," more readily referred to as VOC, was floated on the Amsterdam stock market. Within a month the offer had been fully subscribed, despite the fact that the sum required, £540,000, was eight times the amount raised by its English rival, the East India Company (EIC), floated in London the year before.

The Portuguese were poorly equipped to withstand the onslaught that now fell on their Far Eastern establishments. Within a few years they had yielded their position in the Spice Islands to the superior armaments of the Dutch, and though they managed to beat off attacks on Malacca and Macao, they could do little to prevent the steady buildup of VOC's forces in the region. Particularly ominous for the Portuguese were the periods when Jan Coen was the Company's governor-general in the east. Coen turned the trading post of Jakarta, granted to VOC by the sultan of Bantam on the express condition that it was to remain unwalled, into a well-fortified town, which in 1619 was proudly renamed Batavia (after the Roman name for the Netherlands). This became the nerve-center of Dutch operations in the east.

After 1610 the fleets dispatched by VOC's directors took a low (meaning high-latitude) route across the Indian Ocean, keeping between 35° and 42°S until they reached the longitude of Sumatra, then turning north for the Sunda Strait and Batavia. If all went well, this cut three months off what had been a six-month voyage. From Batavia the majority of new arrivals proceeded to the Spice Islands, but some were sent north to Fort Zeelandia on Taiwan (established in 1624 as a base for traffic with China), and a few went on from there to Japan (where a trading post had been set up at Hirado on the island of Kyushu in 1609).

Trailing along behind the Dutch were the English. Officially VOC was prepared to put up with a certain amount of cherry picking by EIC because the Dutch republic needed England's support in Europe; as a result, EIC was able to dip a profitable finger into the spice trade,

at least for a while. However, VOC's men on the spot had little time for their directors' hesitancy, and, when they thought they could get away with it, they put the boot into their "allies" in no uncertain fashion. This could have led to war, but in the late 1620s EIC decided to shift the focus of its operations from Indonesia to India, where the outlook seemed more promising. Guardedly the two sides drew apart.

Portugal's weakness meant that the main burden of confronting VOC fell on Spain, which, in the event, managed rather better than might have been expected. Manila was successfully defended against repeated Dutch assaults, the trans-Pacific galleon trade was sustained, and Spanish forces even managed a halfway successful counterattack in the Spice Islands, reoccupying the fort on Tidore abandoned earlier by the Portuguese. One other Spanish achievement of the period also deserves mention, the discovery of the Torres Strait between New Guinea and Australia's Cape York. This was an unexpected and entirely unplanned by-product of the expedition of Pedro de Quiros to Espíritu Santo, the last in the series of ill-starred attempts to found a colony in the South Pacific. Quiros, the pilot who had saved the remnants of Mendana's colonists in 1596, set sail from Peru in 1605. After a swing to the south, which took him through the previously unknown Tuamotu archipelago, he ran west for two months, ending up at Espíritu Santo, in present-day Vanuatu. This was clearly not the continent he declared it to be, and, as soon became apparent, it hadn't the population necessary to support a Spanish colony. The attempt at settlement was soon abandoned, and Quiros and his shipmates were lucky to survive the long return voyage, which took them first to 38°N and then, following the track of the Manila galleons, back to New Spain. So much for the bad news. The good news was that the expedition's second galleon, commanded by the highly competent Luis Vaez de Torres, had taken a westward course from Espíritu Santo and fetched up under the tail of New Guinea. Unable to round the tip, Torres was forced to take the route along the island's underside and, in doing so, discover the strait that now bears his name. As he said in the report he wrote on his arrival in Manila, "Such voyages are not made every day."

In Japan Tokugawa Ieyasu consolidated his control over the country so effectively that at his death in 1616 nobody challenged his son's right to succeed him as shogun (military ruler). This son, Tokugawa Hidetada,

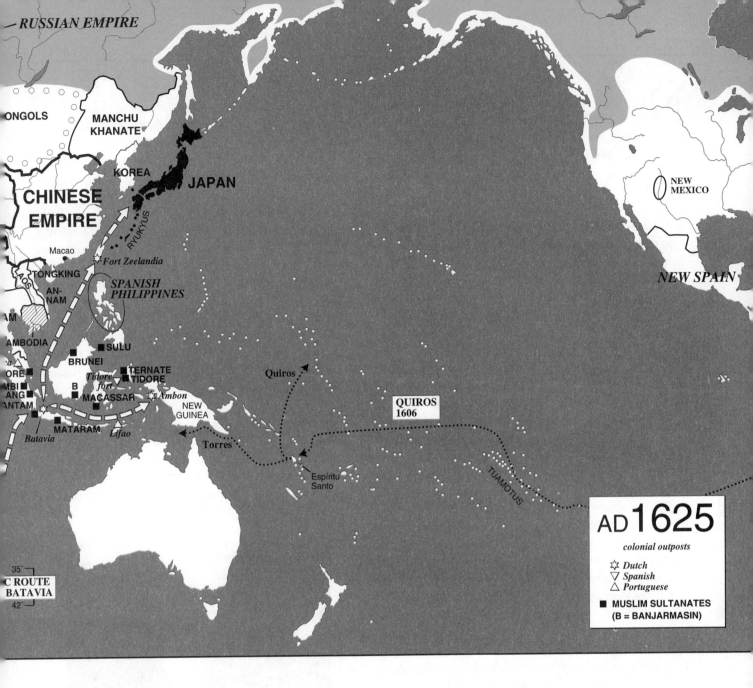

RUSSIAN EMPIRE

MONGOLS

MANCHU
KHANATE

KOREA

JAPAN

CHINESE
EMPIRE

Macao

☆ *Fort Zeelandia*

TONGKING

*SPANISH
PHILIPPINES*

AN-
NAM

NEW
MEXICO

NEW SPAIN

AMBODIA

ORE

SULU

BRUNEI

*Tidore
fort*

TERNATE
TIDORE

Quiros

B

Ambon

MACASSAR

ANTAM

NEW
GUINEA

QUIROS
1606

MATARAM

Batavia

Lifao

Torres

*Espíritu
Santo*

TUAMOTUS

35°
42°

C ROUTE
BATAVIA

AD **1625**

colonial outposts

☆ *Dutch*
▽ *Spanish*
△ *Portuguese*

■ MUSLIM SULTANATES
(B = BANJARMASIN)

shared the general Japanese mistrust of foreigners and soon began making life difficult for them. The English EIC, after ten years of losses, withdrew in 1623; the Spanish were ordered out the next year. Everywhere Christian missions were shut down, and converts were persecuted.[1]

In northern Asia, note the appearance of the Russians (of whom more later) and the union of the Jurchen tribes (by the Manchu clan, under the leadership of Nurhachi) in 1616. In Southeast Asia Burma recovered Dawei and Chiang Mai from Siam (1614–1618).

*1. The ethnically Japanese inhabitants of the Ryukyus were left to their own devices until 1609, when the islands nearest Kyushu—the two shown on the map are Yakushima and Tanegashima—were annexed by the Satsuma lords of southern Kyushu. The remainder continued under the rule of their own king, who resided on Okinawa; he paid token amounts of tribute to both China and Japan—as he had done since 1372 and 1572 respectively—but was not bothered by either even when he forgot.

Not a lot was added to European knowledge of the Pacific in the late sixteenth and early seventeenth centuries, and there is little to chose between this map and the one for 1569 as regards the amount left blank. Contemporary cartographers were less coy: typically they showed a vast "Terra Australis" ("Southern Land") sprawling across the bottom third of the map. The fact that this new land existed entirely in their imagination didn't stop them from giving it a firm shoreline: "common sense" told them that the world's land and sea areas had to be roughly equal, and there was nowhere else to put the balancing landmass.

This way of thinking was part of the intellectual baggage left behind by the Middle Ages. God was supposed to favor symmetry in such matters, just as He had opted for a heliocentric universe and circular orbits for the planets. This meant that, so long as there was no evidence to the contrary, Terra Australis would continue to have its place on the globe—admittedly usually qualified as "incognita" or "nondum cognita" ("undiscovered" or "not yet discovered")—and cartographers would depict its coasts and rivers in the same loving detail that they used for better-founded continents. But if the world was moving slowly, it did, as Galileo insisted, move. New facts were undermining old theological certainties and underpinning new hypotheses. Kepler's elliptical orbits now ringed Copernicus's central sun: voyagers' reports were beginning to put restrictions on the ballooning coasts of Terra Australis.

In the sixteenth century New Guinea provided the best evidence for a southern continent. Only its northern coast was known, and how far it extended to the south could still be a matter of speculation. This situation should have been resolved by Torres's voyage along the underside of the island in 1606; but the secretive Spaniards didn't publish his report, and such news of it as leaked out was offset by Dutch accounts of their ventures in the region. The Dutch didn't find anything interesting in either of the two probings they made: the first in 1606, when Willem Jansz took the *Duyfken* ("Little Dove") along the south coast of New Guinea and down the west side of the Cape York peninsula; and the second in 1623, when two ships repeated Jansz's voyage and clipped Arnhem Land (named for one of the vessels) on the way back. The problem was that both expeditions missed the Torres Strait and reported the coastlines they followed as continuous. Jansz, the European discoverer of Australia, remained entirely unaware of his achievement.

In the interval between these two voyages to Australia's northern shore, VOC captains made the first sightings of its western coast. Ships using the new high-latitude route to Batavia were never certain of their longitude and often missed the correct turning point: accidental landfalls on Australia's flank were correspondingly frequent. The first was made by Dirck Hartog in the *Eendracht* ("Concord") in 1616; another, in 1619, showed that this coast stretched down at least as far as 35°S. It was the best evidence yet for Terra Australis.

One voyage not illustrated on the main map is worth a small one (below). The driving force behind the venture was Isaac Le Maire, an ex-director of VOC who had no love for the company and had demonstrated this by carrying out a bear raid on its shares in 1605, the first recorded instance of this tactic. Ten years later he decided to challenge VOC's monopoly. The company's charter covered all voyages to the Pacific whether via the Cape of Good Hope or the Straits of Magellan. But would it apply if, as Drake's neglected but perfectly clear account suggested, there was an entry to the south of Magellan's? Le Maire thought not and dispatched a vessel, under the joint command of his son Jacob and the experienced sea captain Willem Schouten, to find out. In early 1616 Jacob

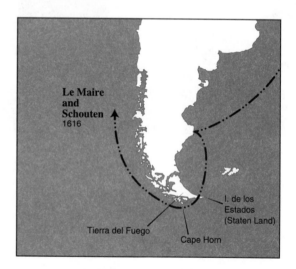

and Schouten found and rounded Cape Horn and set sail across the Pacific. Alas, when the two of them arrived in Batavia nine months later, Governor-General Coen refused to believe a word of their story, confiscated their ship, and packed them off home on one of the company's vessels. Though old Isaac eventually managed to get full restitution, plus costs, from the courts in Amsterdam, the

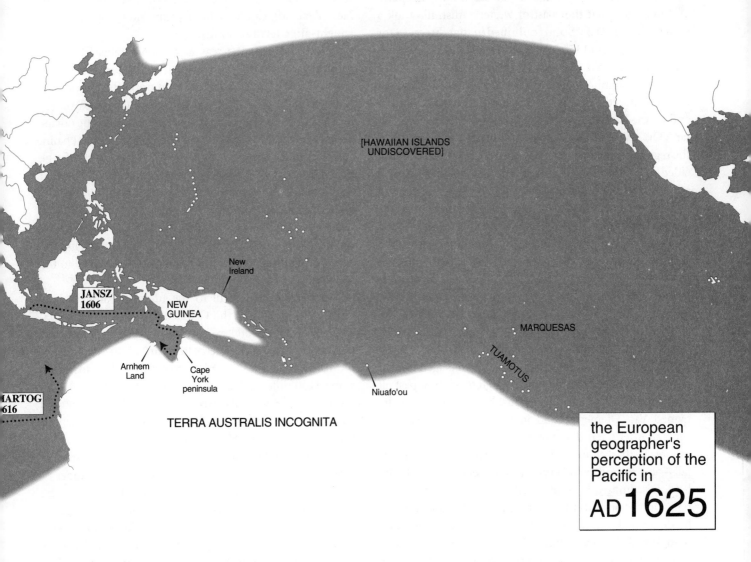

[HAWAIIAN ISLANDS
UNDISCOVERED]

New
Ireland

JANSZ
1606

NEW
GUINEA

Arnhem
Land

Cape
York
peninsula

MARQUESAS

TUAMOTUS

Niuafo'ou

HARTOG
616

TERRA AUSTRALIS INCOGNITA

the European
geographer's
perception of the
Pacific in

AD 1625

company continued to exercise its monopoly regardless.[1]

During the Pacific leg of their voyage Jacob Le Maire and Schouten raised a few coasts that hadn't been sighted before: some of the northern Tuamotus, Niuafo'ou (the northernmost of the Tongas), and the north coast of New Ireland (which they considered part of New Guinea). Other members of the Tuamoto group had been seen earlier by Quiros while on his way to Espíritu Santo. This meant that all the main island groups between 40° N and 15° S had now been touched on, except the Hawaiian archipelago. This remained completely unknown, missed both by the Acapulco galleon that sailed to the south of it and by the Manila galleon sailing to the north.

Note that the upper corners of the map have now been filled in: the top right-hand corner, Hudson Bay, by the discoveries of the Englishman Thomas Button and the Dane Jens Munck; the top left, the middle Yenisey, by the advance of Russia's Cossacks. The Cossacks had first crossed the Urals in 1581; by 1610 they had brought the Ob basin under control, and by 1619, when they established a fort at Yeniseysk, they were onto the area covered by our base map.

*1. Schouten named the cape for his hometown of Hoorn, but the English spelling suits the geography and has won general acceptance.

In 1627 Pieter Nuyts, master of the *Gulden Zeepard*, discovered that the coast of western Australia took a turn to the east at 35°S and continued in that direction for at least 900 miles (1450 kilometers). This made it exceedingly unlikely that the Australian landmass—New Holland in the terminology of Dutch cartography—was part of any Antarctic continent. Discouraged by this finding and by the barren aspect of the country as discovered so far, VOC's directors abstained from further exploration of the region for the next 15 years. In 1642, however, they decided to look on the positive side of Nuyts's findings and see if the waters south of New Holland offered a fast way of getting from the Indian Ocean to the Pacific. Governor-General Anthony van Dieman gave the commission to the experienced captain Abel Tasman, together with two ships, 110 men, and instructions to keep to high latitudes (52–54° S) until he had reached the longitude of the Solomons. From there he was to return to Batavia via New Guinea, taking time out to clarify the geography of the Gulf of Carpentaria if possible.

These were tall orders, but Tasman carried them out with surprising faithfulness. He never managed to get much below 44° S, but that was enough to get him past all of Australia except Tasmania. This, his first discovery, he named Van Diemen's Land in honor of the governor-general. After a ten-day stay and only the briefest of visits ashore, Tasman continued eastward, making his next land-fall—and second discovery—at New Zealand's South Island. Discomfited by a savage Maori attack on one of his boats, he didn't land either there or in North Island, nor did he discover the strait between the two. Nevertheless, Tasman thought "Staten Land," as he called it, a fine country.

Tasman now set out on the northward leg of his voyage. His track took him to Tongatapu, the southernmost of the Tongas, then to Fiji, both new additions to the map. He then returned to Batavia via New Ireland, New Britain (another new discovery, though not perceived as such), and New Guinea. The round trip (Batavia–Mauritius–Tasmania–New Zealand–Batavia) had taken him ten months. The next year he was at sea again, making the circuit of the Gulf of Carpentaria that van Diemen had asked for. Like nearly everyone else he missed the Torres Strait, but by following the coast westward he demonstrated its continuity with New Holland. This simplified the map in this area; his earlier voyage, by contrast, had raised more questions than it settled. Did New Holland and Van Diemen's Land form a single landmass? If so,

where was its eastern boundary? What was the nature of New Zealand? Could it be a promontory of the long-sought-after Terra Australis?[1]

Besides probing the seas around Australia, VOC also mounted a series of expeditions to waters east and northeast of Japan. In 1643 the most important of these saw Maarten Fries in the *Castricum* pass through the Kurils (to be specific, between Iturup and Urup) and chart the northeastern coast of Hokkaido and the east side of Sakhalin. This didn't do as much as it might have done to clarify the geography of the region: Fries came away with the view that Sakhalin and Hokkaido were joined and that the two together formed a peninsula hanging off the end of Asia. Urup he visualized as the tip of another peninsula jutting out from the northwestern part of America—much like the Alaskan peninsula but pulled 2200 miles (3500 km) to the southwest.

More obviously useful to the understanding of East Asian geography was the Cossacks' conquest of Siberia. The 1250-mile (2000 km) section between the Urals and the Yenisey had taken the better part of 40 years to explore, exploit, and organize; the remainder, spanning some 3100 miles (5000 km), was won in a mere 30. The motive power for this extraordinary achievement was supplied by the fur trade. Siberia, being both huge and hugely cold, had furs like nowhere else, and the first thing the Cossacks did when entering a new area was set the natives hunting. Each tribe had to deliver a fixed number of pelts a year or face savage retribution. However, as the quotas were always set at unrealistic levels—finite greed was not one of the Cossacks' failings—yields soon fell off whatever the reprisals. The result was that the Cossacks had to move on: in fact, they were constantly drawn forward by the lure, not of sustainable resources, but of the brief bonanzas afforded by virgin lands.

The final phase of the Russian advance began in 1631, when Peter Beketov used the Ilmin portage to cross from

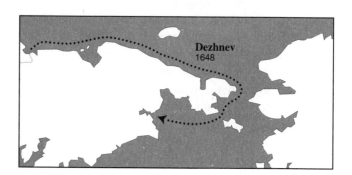

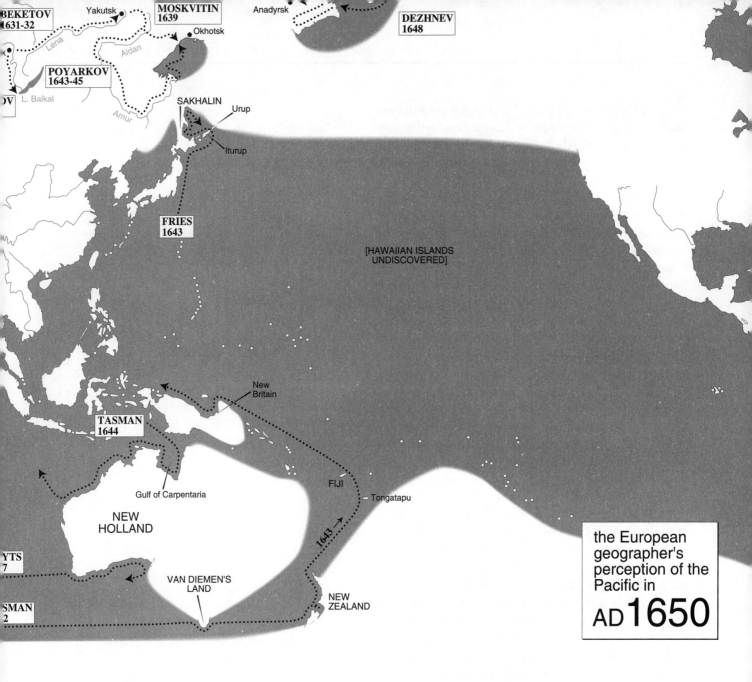

Yakutsk

MOSKVITIN
1639

Anadyrsk

Okhotsk

DEZHNEV
1648

Lena

Aldan

POYARKOV
1643-45

L. Baikal

Amur

SAKHALIN

Urup

Iturup

FRIES
1643

[HAWAIIAN ISLANDS
UNDISCOVERED]

New
Britain

TASMAN
1644

Gulf of Carpentaria

FIJI

Tongatapu

1643

NEW
HOLLAND

the European
geographer's
perception of the
Pacific in

AD 1650

YTS
7

VAN DIEMEN'S
LAND

NEW
ZEALAND

SMAN
2

the Angara, a tributary of the Yenisey, to the Lena. The next year Beketov built an *ostrog* (stockade) at Yakutsk, on the middle Lena, which became the departure point for further expeditions. One of these, led by Ivan Moskvitin, reached the Sea of Okhotsk as early as 1639; another, under Vasily Poyarkov, got to the sea via the Amur only a few years later. But perhaps the most remarkable of these Cossack explorers was Semyon Dezhnev, who made an epic voyage along the north coast of the continent in 1648, reaching and rounding its eastern extremity. Unfortunately, Dezhnev seems to have had no inkling of how far east his journey had taken him, and for all the effect he had on the map of Asia he might as well have stayed

home. Well into the next century atlases were still showing the continent coming to an end opposite Sakhalin.

*1. That Tasman thought so is indicated by his christening it Staten Land. The name had been used before, by Le Maire and Schouten, who had sighted their Staten Land as they made their way to Drake Passage; Tasman seems to have assumed that he was looking at the same landmass, despite the 5000-mile (8000 km) gap between the two sets of observations. It is difficult to imagine a more powerful example of the grip that Terra Australis had on the seventeenth-century mind.

Le Maire and Schouten's Staten Land, in reality a small island, is still known as Isla de los Estados (see the map on p. 46). Tasman's was renamed New Zealand as early as 1648 by Joan Blaeu, VOC's official cartographer, who was also responsible for the term New Holland.

By the early 1630s the Ming had begun to go the way of all Chinese dynasties: widespread corruption provoked a series of rebellions by the peasantry; feeble military leadership allowed the Manchu to encroach in the north. The end came in 1644, when the most successful of the rebel leaders occupied Beijing and mounted the throne left vacant by the suicide of the last Ming emperor. The usurper's reign was brief. Chinese troops stationed on the Wall combined with the Manchu forces attacking it, marched on Beijing, and extinguished his regime. The imperial inheritance passed to the Manchu, justifying their long-standing claim to the "mandate of heaven."

China is a big country, and in 1650 the Manchu were still not masters of all of it: a fugitive Ming prince was hanging on in the southwest, and some enclaves on the southeast coast were in the hands of a recalcitrant admiral. There was also trouble in the north, where Cossack bands had reached the Amur. As was their wont, the Russians were demanding furs from the hapless natives and inflicting murderous punishments on those who failed to meet their quotas. The Amur was the traditional, if little visited, frontier of the Manchu, and the natives' pleas for protection could hardly go unanswered.

The Dutch finally managed to take Malacca in 1641; they also obtained a monopoly of the traffic with Japan when the Portuguese were expelled in 1639. The Portuguese had got into the shogun's bad books by backing the now proscribed Christian mission; the Dutch reaped the advantage of this indiscretion, though they had to put up with nit-picking controls on their trading post (removed from Hirado to Nagasaki in 1641). Japanese policy was now running strongly against contacts with the outside world: natives were forbidden to travel abroad, and foreigners were forbidden to land, both on pain of death. The Tokugawa government had brought peace for the first time in 500 years: it was not going to let this achievement be challenged by alien interlopers or undermined by alien ideas.

The Spaniards managed to win control of the sultanate of Sulu in 1638, only to lose it again eight years later. They kept Zamboanga, at the tip of Mindanao, until 1662, but the only long-term result of their campaign was the appearance of Maguindanao, previously dependent on Sulu, as an independent sultanate.

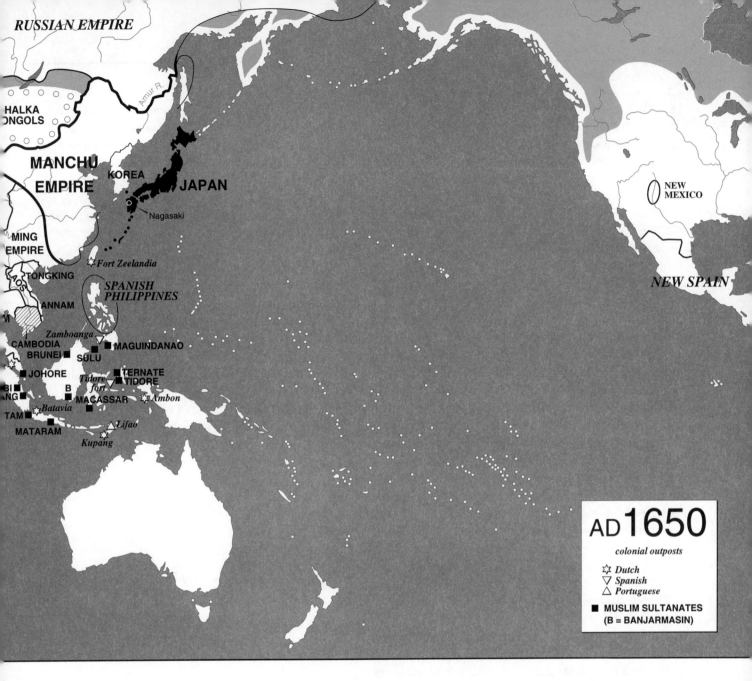

RUSSIAN EMPIRE

HALKA
ONGOLS

MANCHU
EMPIRE

Amur R.

KOREA

JAPAN

Nagasaki

MING
EMPIRE

☆ *Fort Zeelandia*

TONGKING

*SPANISH
PHILIPPINES*

ANNAM

Zamboanga

CAMBODIA
BRUNEI ■ SULU

■ MAGUINDANAO

■ JOHORE

*Tidore
fort* ■ TERNATE
▽ ■ TIDORE

B

■ MACASSAR

☆ *Ambon*

☆ *Batavia*

△ *Lifao*

TAM

☆ *Kupang*

MATARAM

NEW
MEXICO

NEW SPAIN

AD **1650**

colonial outposts

☆ *Dutch*
▽ *Spanish*
△ *Portuguese*

■ MUSLIM SULTANATES
(B = BANJARMASIN)

In the late 1680s the Manchu decided to meet the challenge posed by the Cossacks' infiltration of the Amur valley. The military confrontation was brief—the logistics strongly favored the Manchu—and the Russians were soon forced to sign away the entire region. In fact, the treaty of Nerchinsk (1689) gave the Manchu more territory than they ever intended to occupy: the lands north of the river were seen simply as a buffer zone, enabling them to keep the Russians at arm's length while they concentrated on more serious opponents elsewhere. The most pressing of these was the Mongol leader Galdan Khan, who had built up a formidable empire embracing Turkestan (his starting point in 1676), the Tarim basin (1678), and Outer Mongolia (1688).

Not that the Manchu had much to worry about as regards land battles. They had long since completed their conquest of China, chasing the last Ming emperor out of Yunnan and into Burma (1659), and then extracting him from there and sending him back to Beijing for execution (1662). Where they did have a problem was with naval campaigns: it took them more than 30 years to eliminate the pirate state established on Xiamen and other offshore islands by Zheng Chenggong. Zheng's major coup was the capture of Zeelandia from the Dutch, which brought with it control over Taiwan (1662). It wasn't until 1683 that the Manchu were able to muster a fleet strong enough to take Taiwan and bring it, for the first time, within the boundary of China.[1]

Despite the loss of Zeelandia, these were good years for the Dutch. Up until the 1660s, VOC's grip on the spice trade had been less than complete: considerable amounts were still picked up by Portuguese, Spanish, English, and native traders, with Macassar acting as a safe haven for the interlopers. This leakage came to an end in 1667–1668, when Cornelis Speelman, the "sword of the company," took direct control of the sultanates of Ternate, Tidore, and, after a long siege, Macassar. The new, more powerful image presented by VOC vis-à-vis the local potentates was subsequently enhanced by the reduction of the sultanates of Mataram and Bantam (i.e., all of Java except the eastern tip) to vassal status.

The Spanish had withdrawn their garrison from Tidore in 1663, four years before Speelman's conquest of the sultanate. In a compensating advance they set up the first European post in the Pacific islands, a Christian mission, with military backup, on Guam (1668). Previously the string of islands of which Guam is at once the southernmost, the biggest, and the best-known, had been called the Ladrones, or "thieves' islands," a name given to them by a disgusted Magellan. To mark the impending conversion of the inhabitants, they were renamed the Marianas.

Minor points to note in the Indonesian archipelago are the reappearance of Perak (in the 1660s, after a long spell under the suzerainty of Atjeh) and the founding of trading posts for the west Sumatran pepper trade by VOC (at Padang, in 1663) and EIC (at Bencoolen, in 1685). Kutai in eastern Borneo, previously a dependency of Macassar, became independent on Macassar's fall.

In North America, Europeans were beginning to probe the interior of the continent, with the French, thanks to the opportunities presented by the Great Lakes, setting the pace. In 1660 Groseilliers explored the area between Lake Superior and Hudson Bay; in 1674 Louis Joliet and Father Jacques Marquette journeyed southwest from Lake Michigan, discovered the Mississippi, and descended that great river for much of its length. The name Louisiana, conferred on the Mississippi valley by La Salle in 1682, advertised French ambitions in this area.

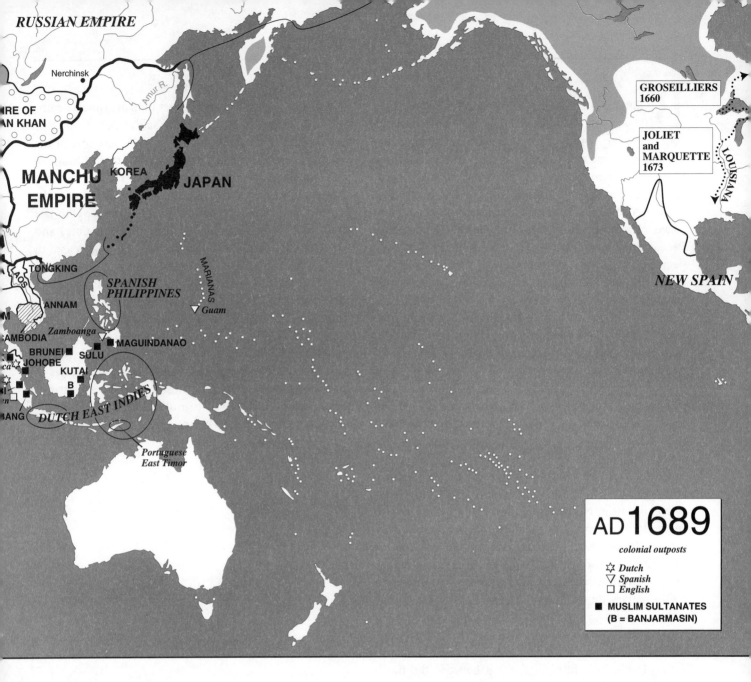

RUSSIAN EMPIRE

Nerchinsk

RE OF
AN KHAN

MANCHU
EMPIRE

Amur R.

KOREA

JAPAN

TONGKING

SPANISH
PHILIPPINES

MARIANAS

▽ *Guam*

Zamboanga

ANNAM

■ MAGUINDANAO

AMBODIA

BRUNEI

SULU

JOHORE

KUTAI

B

DUTCH EAST INDIES

*Portuguese
East Timor*

GROSEILLIERS
1660

JOLIET
and
MARQUETTE
1673

LOUISIANA

NEW SPAIN

AD **1689**

colonial outposts

☆ *Dutch*
▽ *Spanish*
□ *English*

■ MUSLIM SULTANATES
(B = BANJARMASIN)

*1. In European accounts Xiamen appears as Amoy, Taiwan as Formosa, and Zheng as Coxinga (from his title, Guo-xing-ye, "Lord of the Imperial Surname"). The Manchu acquisition of Taiwan opened up the island to Chinese settlers, who gradually displaced the Austronesian aboriginals. These still survive today, but form only a small part—less than 2 percent—of the total population.

By the date of this map Europeans had chalked up 200 years of Pacific navigation and had acquired a good knowledge of the ocean's boundaries and behavior. The benefits were surprisingly few. The commercial route to the orient remained the eastward one, via the Cape of Good Hope and the Indian Ocean. The Portuguese had never used any other, and the Dutch, once they had established their monopoly, followed suit: they rarely crossed the Pacific and found little profit when they did. The only people to work a regular trans-Pacific route were the Spaniards, whose Manila and Acapulco galleons performed an annual shuttle between New Spain and the Philippines. One or two ships each way each year was the extent of the traffic; a thousand or so Spaniards, almost all resident in Manila, were the sole colonial fruit. Not a lot to show for two centuries of epic voyaging.

Contemporaries obviously shared this sense of disappointment. There was very little activity in the Pacific in the late seventeenth and early eighteenth centuries, and there were only two maritime discoveries of any significance. In 1699 the English adventurer William Dampier sailed through the strait now named after him, demonstrating that New Britain (which he named) was a separate entity from New Guinea. Eleven years later Spanish missionaries, responding to tales told by Caroline Islanders shipwrecked in the Philippines, mounted a search of the area east of Mindanao; they were rewarded by the discovery of the Palaus, but, after a hostile demonstration by the natives, decided not to land.

More useful to cartographers was the continuing advance of Russia's Cossacks, in particular Vladimir Atlasov's discovery and conquest of the peninsula of Kamchatka (1697–1699). This filled in the gap between the north shore of the Sea of Okhotsk and the extreme east of Siberia. It also provided, in the person of Dembei—a Japanese sailor who had been shipwrecked on the peninsula a few years earlier—a clue to the geographical relationships of the entire region. Atlasov signally failed to sort out Dembei's story; he thought that Dembei was a Hindu and that the homeland he was describing was the Indian subcontinent. This goes some way toward explaining why Cossack ideas on geography didn't always get much of a hearing in Moscow. Dembei's true origin was realized as soon as he arrived at the Russian capital, and subsequent exploration of the Kurils (beginning in 1711) eventually brought confirmation that the land to the south was indeed Japan.[1]

The other changes since the last map are quickly summarized. The Manchu defeated Galdan Khan and annexed most of Outer Mongolia in 1696. The seat of the war subsequently moved to Tibet, where the Manchu were equally successful, taking Lhasa in 1720 and with it control of the entire country. Annam advanced its southern frontier at the expense of both Champa (the last remnant of which was absorbed around this time) and Cambodia (which was forced to yield the Saigon area in 1691). The sultanate of Johore shifted its base to Riau, on the island of Bintan, in 1699; Siak in Sumatra, a vassal of Johore-Riau, became independent in 1721. In the Philippines the Spanish reoccupied Zamboanga in 1718. In North America the British established outposts in Hudson Bay, while the French began to give their claim to the Mississippi valley some substance by building a series of forts along the river and the nearer reaches of its tributaries. This French activity provoked the Spanish into advancing across the Rio Grande and occupying southern Texas (1716–1721).

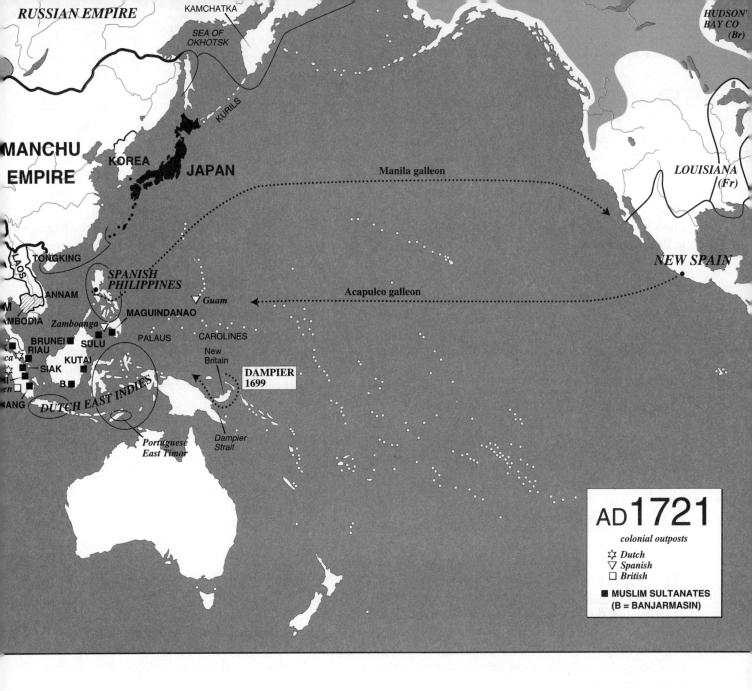

RUSSIAN EMPIRE

KAMCHATKA

SEA OF
OKHOTSK

*HUDSON'
BAY CO
(Br)*

MANCHU
EMPIRE

KOREA

JAPAN

KURILS

Manila galleon

*LOUISIANA
(Fr)*

TONGKING

*SPANISH
PHILIPPINES*

NEW SPAIN

ANNAM

∇ *Guam*

Acapulco galleon

MBODIA

Zamboanga

MAGUINDANAO

PALAUS

CAROLINES

BRUNEI
RIAU

SULU

New
Britain

DAMPIER
1699

KUTAI

SIAK

B

DUTCH EAST INDIES

ANG

*Portuguese
East Timor*

*Dampier
Strait*

AD **1721**

colonial outposts

☆ *Dutch*
∇ *Spanish*
☐ *British*

■ **MUSLIM SULTANATES**
    (B = BANJARMASIN)

*1. Dembei's ship had sailed from Osaka, his hometown, as part of the annual convoy taking supplies to Edo (now Tokyo), the seat of the shogun. The convoy was scattered by a typhoon, and Dembei and his companions ended up on Kamchatka's east coast. Only Dembei survived an early quarrel with the locals.

The Russian authorities told Dembei that he would be returned to Japan in due course, but the promise was never honored. A sad little figure, he passed his remaining years attached to one of Peter the Great's new scientific institutes.

Between 1689 and 1725 Russia was ruled by the most remarkable of its tsars, Peter the Great. His achievements were many and various, but underlying them all was a single determination—to make Russia a modern state. This often meant employing foreigners, and when Peter decided that the time had come to sort out the geography of the eastern end of his empire, he gave the commission to Vitus Bering, a Dane who had made his career in the Russian navy.

It took Bering 3½ years to get to Kamchatka, build a boat, and set sail. His instructions were simple: to follow the coast north and see if this led him to America. The trouble was that the region's perpetual fogs made it difficult to see anything at all. He stayed with the coast to 67° 30' N (a fraction above the top of our map), by which time

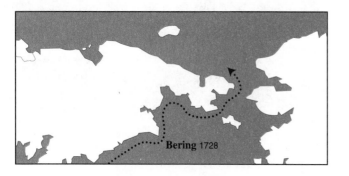

he was through the strait now named for him and the Siberian shore was clearly trending westward. At no stage had there been any sign of America, and he turned back confident that this was not the way to get there. And so he reported on his return to Saint Petersburg in 1730.

If America wasn't to be found by following the Siberian coast, it would have to be approached in a more adventurous manner, by sailing directly across the north Pacific. In 1733 Bering was told to do this, but he was given so many other duties as well that this time it was eight years before he and his lieutenant, Aleksey Chirikov, had built their boats and put out to sea. After making a joint detour to the south in search of a mythical "Gamaland," the two lost contact with each other. Chirikov in the *Saint Paul* was the first to sight America, reaching Prince of Wales Island after 40 days at sea. From there he coasted home via Alaska and the Aleutians, never setting foot ashore. Bering's voyage in the *Saint Peter* began in much the same way: he made his landfall, Mount Saint Elias, a day after Chirikov, then sailed westward with brief stops for water at various islands off the Alaskan coast.

At this point everything started to go wrong. A month behind Chirikov when he reached the Aleutians, Bering lost another month when storms blew the *Saint Peter* back toward America. With the planks and rigging rotting away in the foul climate, and the men starting to come down with scurvy from lack of fresh food, the situation looked increasingly desperate. Perhaps because of this the crew convinced themselves that they had reached the Kurils when they were still in the Aleutians and insisted on turning north, a course that brought them to the uninhabited Komandorskis. There they wintered among animals that had never seen men before, like the helpless, hopeless giant dugong. These provided easy meat, but the fresh food came too late for the very ill, including Bering. Next spring the survivors (46 out of 76) built a new *Saint Peter* from the timbers of the old and successfully completed the relatively short journey to Petropavlovsk.[1]

As part of the same program of exploration Martin Spanberg (a Dane) and William Walton (an Englishman) were sent south from Kamchatka to establish contact with the Japanese. In 1738 they sailed down the Kuril chain as far as Iturup; the next year they reached Honshu. Though they were received politely by the local Japanese, the voyages were not repeated: their function had been to clarify the geography and, given the results of their brush with the Manchu, the Russians were probably wise not to press their luck.

The only other voyage of importance during this period was the attempt by Jacob Roggeveen to find Terra Australis. This had the backing of VOC's rival, the Dutch West India Company (WIC), which wasn't supposed to operate in the Pacific at all. Apparently WIC had taken legal advice and had gotten an opinion that, provided Roggeveen entered and left via Cape Horn, he wouldn't be breaching the VOC's monopoly. This was a more sophisticated version of Isaac Le Maire's thesis, with the advantage that, accept it or not, VOC would be hard put to do anything about it. Roggeveen set sail with three ships in 1721 and rounded the Horn early the next year. His first discovery was Easter Island (named for the day it was sighted); he was impressed by the famous statues but wasn't puzzled about how they had been transported or erected because he thought they were made on the spot, out of mud.[2] From Easter Island he steered a course similar to that of Schouten and Le Maire a century earlier: he saw a few more of the Tuamotus than they did, glimpsed the northernmost Societies (the first sightings of any

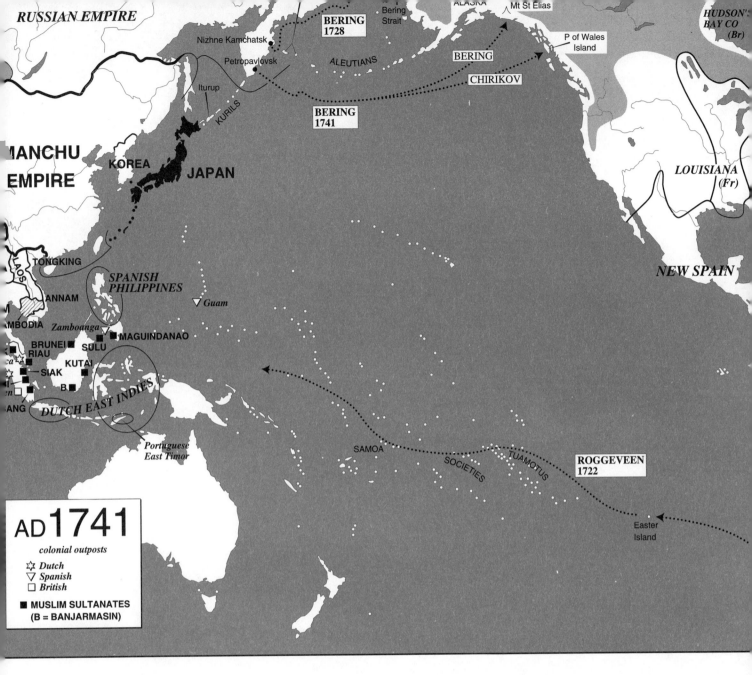

members of this island group), and saw, but did not visit, the main islands of Samoa. What he didn't do was turn around, and, despite his plea that sheer necessity had forced him to keep on westward, he ended up having his ships seized by the VOC authorities in Batavia. It hadn't been a great enterprise, but, considering that Roggeveen was a lawyer by profession, and that he took up this, his first command, at the age of 62, it provided a creditable coda to the era of Dutch exploration.

*1. Bering is remembered in the strait he discovered, the island where he died, and the group this belongs to—the Komandorskis, after his title, commodore. The Gamaland he sought was a false sighting by one Juan de Gama, who had sailed through these waters on a voyage from Macao to Acapulco in 1598.

*2. There were about 1000 of these huge statues on the island, which, if one accepts a population figure of 2000 for the early eighteenth century, amounts to one for every two islanders. Roggeveen was quite wrong about the material of which they are made; they are monoliths carved from volcanic tufa. The quarry and a series of statues in various stages of completion still exist on Rano Raraku, an extinct volcano on the eastern side of the island. Finished statues—the vast majority—are found near the shoreline, usually in rows of half a dozen or more.

(footnote continued on p. 111)

PART 3   FROM COOK TO PERRY

During the seventeenth century the Dutch had done better than the English as regards the area covered by the map: globally, however, there wasn't all that much to choose between them. England had acquired an equivalent overseas empire (in America and India), and when the two clashed, as they did with some frequency, the result was usually a standoff. This situation changed in the opening decades of the eighteenth century, when the balance began to tilt toward the British (call them British after the union of England and Scotland in 1707). Mostly this was a matter of scale: the United Kingdom was a much bigger country than the Netherlands (10 million in the mid-eigh-

teenth century, as against 2 million), and its economy was growing faster. Consequently it was better able to shoulder the burdens of the long war that the two fought, as allies, against the France of Louis XIV. But the changing nature of navies was also important. The Dutch war fleet had always consisted of armed merchantmen; the contemporary move to professional navies, with purpose-built battleships, was one that the Dutch couldn't really afford.

The first Pacific episode to feature Britain's new-style Royal Navy took place in the early 1740s, when the War of the Austrian Succession was being waged in Europe and the British were, as usual, fighting France and Spain. The protagonist was Captain George Anson, who brought the 60-gun battleship *Centurion* around the Horn in 1741. Anson initially headed north in the hope of capturing the Manila galleon. Failing to get to Acapulco in time to make the interception, he moved off to the Philippines to lie in wait for the Acapulco galleon, but the Spaniards assumed that he had done just that and kept the ship in port. Undaunted, Anson took the *Centurion* to Macao for a refit, returned to the Philippines in 1743, and captured the *Nuestra Señora de Covadonga* as it approached the San Bernardino Strait. In its hold was treasure to the value of half a million pounds sterling, two-thirds of it in silver.

This was fun but not really an advance on the achievements of the Elizabethan circumnavigators, Drake and Cavendish. The more important part of George Anson's career came after his return home, when he became the Royal Navy's most effective administrator yet. The next time Spain sided with France, the British response was much grander: a fleet of ten ships sailed from Madras (in British India) and forced the surrender of Manila (1762). The same conflict—the Seven Years' War of 1756–1763—saw even more conclusive victories won against the French in America and India. The results can be seen on the map, where most of Louisiana has been swallowed up in British North America (Spain got the part west of the Mississippi) and the British empire in India has been given a firm base by the annexation of Bengal (1765).

The end of the Seven Years' War released resources for more peaceable activities. In 1764 John Byron was given two ships, the *Dolphin* and the *Tamar,* for a voyage of exploration in the region of California and the supposed Northwest Passage. Unfortunately, rounding the Horn reduced the ships to such a state of unseaworthiness that Byron, somewhat pusillanimously, decided to make straight for home, and his only claims to fame are the speed with which he made his circumnavigation (22 months, easily the fastest yet) and the discovery of some minor islands in the Tuamotos, Tokelaus, and Gilberts. His successor in command of the *Dolphin,* Samuel Wallis, did much better. Wallis's instructions were to sail across the Pacific in the latitude of Cape Horn, and though he didn't manage to do that, he did achieve a much more southerly track than any previous navigator. He was rewarded by the discovery of Tahiti, the Eden of the South Seas. For once the warmth of the welcome survived the cycle of thieving and reprisal that formed an inevitable part of the clash of cul-

tures, and Sam Wallis was not the only one with a moist eye when the time came to wave good-bye to his comely Dido, Princess Purea. The other ship in his little squadron, Philip Cartaret's *Swallow,* had parted company soon after entering the Pacific, taken a different course, and made different discoveries. The first was tiny Pitcairn Island; the most important concerned the nature of New Ireland, which Cartaret showed was separate from New Britain by sailing through the channel between the two.

The Chinese conquered the last independent Mongols in 1755; this meant that China's frontier with Russia now extended for more than 2200 miles (3500 kilometers). However, trade between the two empires was restricted (at China's insistence) to a single post at Kyakhta, south of Lake Baikal. Here the *promyshlenniks* (Russian hunters and trappers) brought their furs and exchanged them for tea, silks, and porcelain. The trade received a significant boost from the opening up of the Aleutians, home to the sea otter, whose pelt was particularly highly prized by the Chinese. By 1763 Cossacks searching for sea otters—and for Aleuts to hunt for them—had ventured as far as Kodiak Island, off the Alaskan peninsula.

The Burmese monarchy made a remarkable recovery during this period, first reestablishing control over the Mons of the south (1757; they had been in revolt since the 1740s), then going on to take Tanintharyi from Siam (1760), and, in the year of this map, the Siamese capital Ayuthia. In the East Indies Selangor seceded from Riau in 1766.

WHILE WALLIS WAS STILL on his way home, the Admiralty began preparing for a third expedition to the South Pacific. The inspiration this time was a request from the Royal Society, which wanted the impending transit of Venus—of which more in a moment—observed from an appropriate point in the antipodes. The Navy, with researches of its own to pursue, agreed. A sturdy craft, previously engaged in carrying coal from Newcastle to London, was purchased, refurbished, and renamed *Endeavour;* command of it was entrusted to Lieutenant James Cook, an officer who had proved himself a master of chart making during the recent war in North America. As the *Endeavour* completed her fitting out, Wallis arrived home with news of Tahiti, whose position turned out to be ideal for observing the transit. Cook's instructions were consequently drawn up with Tahiti as his initial objective, to be followed by a foray to the south in search of

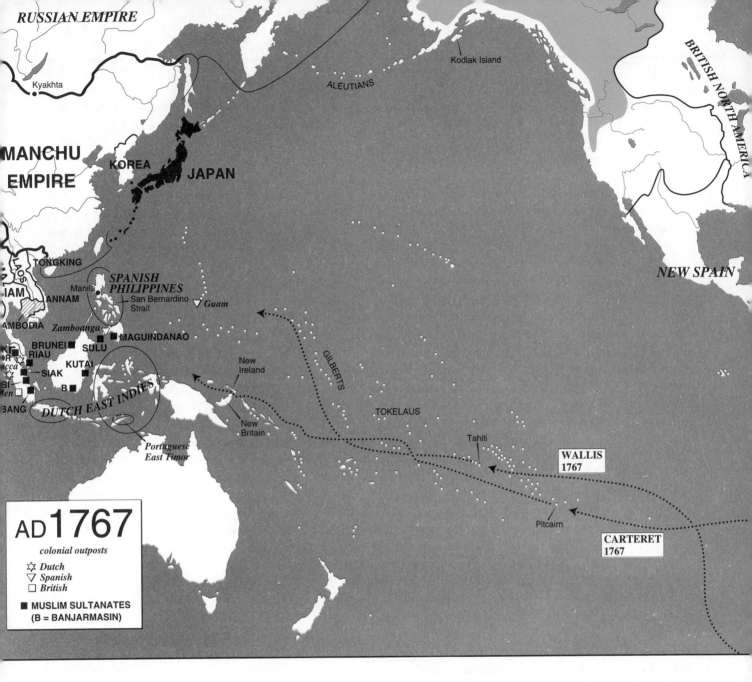

the supposed southern continent, and, failing any sign of that, an exploration of Tasman's New Zealand.

One of the interesting things about all this is that Wallis was confident that he had valid coordinates for Tahiti, longitude as well as latitude. This represented a big step forward in the science of navigation, because previously estimates of longitude had been little more than guesswork. Back in 1714 the Admiralty had been so concerned over the losses this caused that it had offered a prize of £20,000—millions in today's money—to anyone who could find a way of fixing a ship's longitude to within half a degree, the equivalent of 30 miles (55 kilometers) at the equator. Now two different methods were yielding excellent results, the measurement of "lunar distances" and the use of the marine chronometer. The trouble with the first, which depended on exact observation of the angles between the moon and various other heavenly bodies, was that the observations were difficult to make at sea and the subsequent calculations beyond the capacity of most seamen. The marine chronometer, which was simply a clock accurate enough to enable local noon to be compared with noon at the notional starting point of the voyage—Greenwich so far as the British Admiralty was concerned—seemed a more practical proposition. And a chronometer made by a Yorkshire clockmaker, John Harrison, had actually met the conditions laid down by the Board of Longitude. Rather meanly, however, the board limited Harrison's payment to £10,000 on the ground that it wasn't clear that copies of his clock could be made to work as well as the original. So Cook set sail with tables of the moon's movements supplied by the astronomer royal, but no chronometer.

This was not something that was likely to upset James Cook, who prided himself on his observational skills. By the time he reached Cape Horn, he had mastered the art of "lunar distances" and was turning in very acceptable determinations of longitude; on arriving at Tahiti he set up his observation post confident that he would be equally successful as regards the transit of Venus. This event—the passage of the planet Venus across the face of the sun—offered astronomers a chance to calculate the distance of the sun from the earth with unprecedented accuracy. Widely spaced observation posts were necessary (hence Tahiti), and so was luck with the weather; everyone hoped for the best, because the next transit wasn't due till 1874. As it turned out, the observations proved unexpectedly difficult because the planet's penumbra made the cutoff points imprecise. Nonetheless, the final figure for the sun's distance was within 1 percent of the true value, a considerable improvement on previous estimates.[1]

Departing Tahiti, Cook made a brief exploration of the other members of the island group—which he called the Societies because they were all relatively close together—and then headed south. He went as far as 40° S, then, finding no sign of a southern continent and deciding from the ocean swell that there was nothing of the sort to be found in this latitude, he turned for New Zealand. Once there, he set himself the task of producing an accurate map of the country, which he achieved by discovering the channel between North Island and South Island and circumnavigating both. A Tahitian who had elected to accompany Cook had no difficulty conversing with the Maoris, but despite this the relationship between the Endeavour's crew and the islanders was always tense: the Marois were a warrior people and required very little in the way of provocation before they reached for their clubs.

Cook had now discharged his instructions and could head for home whatever way he thought fit. He chose a course that took him toward the southern end of New Holland's unknown east coast. He found it at Cape Howe, named it New South Wales, and followed it northward past Botany Bay (named after the successful plant-collecting forays of the Endeavour's chief scientist, Joseph Banks) to Cape York. A nasty episode in which the Endeavour was holed on one of the coral outcrops in the narrowing gap between the Great Barrier Reef and the coast of present-day Queensland forced a seven-week stay and gave Banks the opportunity to add a kangaroo to his list of specimens. There were also occasional contacts with the country's inhabitants, who clearly lived in a totally different world from the Polynesians. In August the voyage was resumed, Cape York rounded, and Torres's passage confirmed. Thence to Batavia, where the Endeavour refitted, and finally home via the Cape.[2]

Meanwhile Russian activity in the Aleutians (which they officially annexed in 1772) upset the Spaniards, who felt they had a prescriptive right to every part of the Americas. They couldn't, of course, do anything about the far north, but they could protect their more proximate interests. In 1769 complementary land and sea expeditions were launched up the Californian coast, and the new province of Alta California was established. San Francisco Bay, hidden for so long behind its wreath of cloud and finally discovered overland, marked its northernmost point. The administration operated from Monterey, and at first the province consisted of little more than this outpost, a fort at San Diego, and some Franciscan missions on the coast between the two.

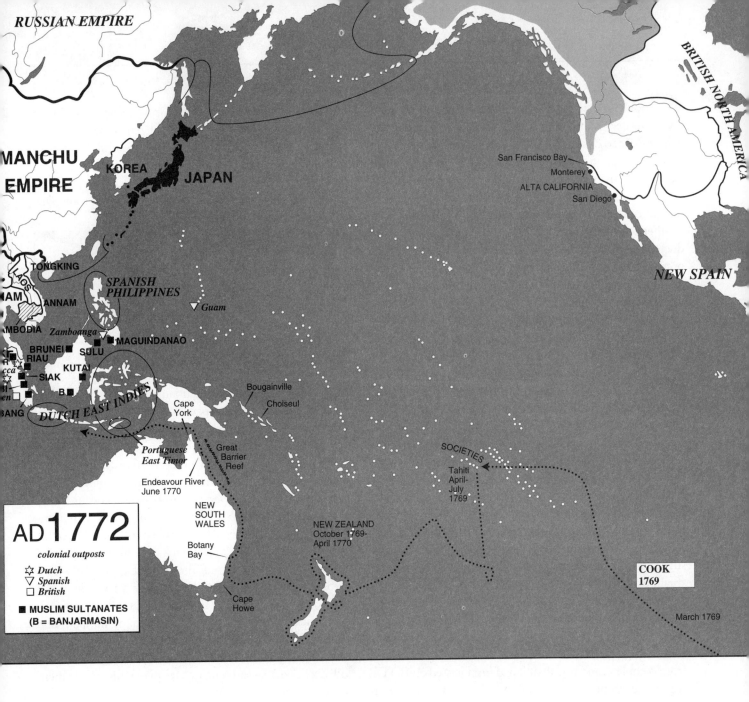

MANCHU

EMPIRE

KOREA   JAPAN

BRITISH NORTH AMERICA

San Francisco Bay
Monterey
ALTA CALIFORNIA
San Diego

NEW SPAIN

TONGKING

*SPANISH
PHILIPPINES*

∇ *Guam*

AM

ANNAM

Zamboanga   ∇ **MAGUINDANAO**

AMBODIA

BRUNEI
RIAU   **SULU**
cca
el — **SIAK**   **KUTAI**
en   **B.**

BANG   *DUTCH EAST INDIES*

Bougainville
Choiseul

Cape
York

*Portuguese
East Timor*

Great
Barrier
Reef

Endeavour River
June 1770

NEW
SOUTH
WALES

Botany
Bay

NEW ZEALAND
October 1769-
April 1770

SOCIETIES

Tahiti
April-
July
1769

**COOK
1769**

March 1769

Cape
Howe

AD 1772

colonial outposts
☆ *Dutch*
∇ *Spanish*
☐ *British*

■ **MUSLIM SULTANATES
(B = BANJARMASIN)**

*1. When Cook got to Tahiti, he found that two European ships had called there the year before. He thought they were probably Spanish, but in fact they were French, Louis-Antoine de Bougainville's *La Boudeuse* and *l'Étoile.* Bougainville had hoped to restore France's maritime prestige, wilting after the defeats of the Seven Years' War, by making significant discoveries in the South Pacific; he had the bad luck to be too late in Tahiti, and to be forced to turn away from the east cost of Australia by an outlier of the Great Barrier Reef. Where he did score was with his write-up of Tahiti (as *Nouvelle-Cythère,*

Cythera being the Greek island where Venus was supposed to have been born), which was a runaway best-seller. He also provided a couple of new names in the Solomons: Choiseul (after his patron, the minister of war) and Bougainville (named in his honor in the nineteenth century).

*2. Part of Cook's success lay in his care for his crew's health. At a time when mortality rates of 50 percent per annum were commonplace, he lost only two of his crew of 70 in the 26 months it took him to get to Batavia. In Batavia, which was notoriously unhealthy, malaria and dysentery played havoc with this record, and by the time he arrived back in England his total loss was an undistinguished 32. An unexpected survivor was the goat which provided the officers' milk and which had already been around the world once before with Wallis. It was rewarded with a silver collar, for which Dr. Johnson composed a suitable inscription ("*ambita bis terra . . . altrici Capra . . .*" etc.).

Cook's first voyage to the Pacific had shown such mastery that within a few months of his return the Admiralty had decided to send him back again. This time he was given two ships—the near-disaster on the Barrier Reef had convinced both Cook and his superiors of the perilous nature of single-ship expeditions—and was told to find out whether there was anything to the idea of a southern continent or not. The search was mainly conducted in areas off the bottom of the map, so apart from noting that between them the *Resolution* and *Adventure* finally put paid to Terra Australis, we can limit our focus to the winter months of 1774. During this period Antarctic exploration was impossible, so Cook filled in by fixing the positions of the known but inaccurately plotted islands between Easter Island and Australia. He also discovered several new ones, most notably New Caledonia. The longitudes were obtained by a combination of "lunar distances" and chronometry, and proved a triumph for a copy of John Harrison's watch, for which the Board of Longitude had reluctantly made full payment in 1773. The era of exact navigation had finally dawned. In recognition of this, Cook was elected a Fellow of the Royal Society when he arrived back in England in 1775. Equally feted was Omai, a young Tahitian who had shipped back in the *Adventure*. "How do, King Tosh," he said when presented to King George, who gave him an allowance and suggested, sensibly enough, that he be vaccinated before smallpox carried him off.

A year later Cook was off to the Pacific again. This time he was to take *Resolution* and its new companion *Discovery* to the North Pacific to test out the old tales of a Northwest Passage. Russian knowledge of Alaskan waters was far from complete, and not all of it had been passed on to European geographers: it was still possible that there was a gap between Alaska and Canada; if not, the Bering Strait would be used to reach Arctic waters. From there the expedition could attempt the passage around the north of Canada and, if such a passage proved possible, return home via the North Atlantic. Alternatively, Cook could attempt a Northeast Passage around the top of Russia.

The Admiralty must have known that these instructions were more than a mite fanciful and probably expected no more of Cook than a tidying-up operation on the geography of the North Pacific region. This he certainly delivered. After dropping Omai off at Tahiti he headed north, discovering Christmas Island, the largest of the Line Islands, and, much more important, the Hawaiian archipel-

ago. Neither detained him long, for he needed to be in the north by spring, and he planned a refit before that. He found a good spot for this at Nootka Sound, Vancouver Island,[1] then moved on to begin his American survey at 55°N, near enough to where the present-day state of Alaska has its southern border. By June *Resolution* and *Dis-*

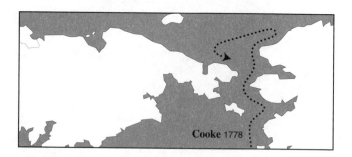

Cooke 1778

covery were through the Aleutians; in August 1778 they reached the edge of the pack ice on the far side of the Bering Strait. There was clearly no viable Northwest Passage.

With half his task done, Cook turned south for Hawaii, where he intended to winter and which obviously needed mapping. He was received rapturously, as a god, and after a two-month stay on Big Island, he sailed away with nothing but fond memories. Alas, a broken foremast forced his return less than a week later. This time his reception was sullen. The cycle of Lono, the harvest god with whom Cook had been identified, had ended; a rival deity, the warrior god Ku, was now in the ascendant. With the visitors officially unwelcome, thieving became rampant and tempers flared: finally a confrontation over a stolen ship's boat escalated into a running battle in which Cook was killed. His end is a sad echo of Magellan's, his achievement an equally enduring monument.

The voyage was not yet over. Charles Clerke, Cook's second in command, took the ships back to the Bering Strait that summer for a second look at the ice pack's edge. Clerke then succumbed to tuberculosis, and the expedition acquired its third commander, John Gore. After a stopover at Macao, where all hands were amazed at the prices the Chinese were prepared to pay for the sea otter skins collected in the north, Gore brought the expedition home, arriving in England in October 1780. French privateers were operating in the Atlantic, but any worries this may have caused Gore were unnecessary: such was Cook's standing that his ships had been exempted from the general war.

This war had begun in 1775 with the rebellion of the

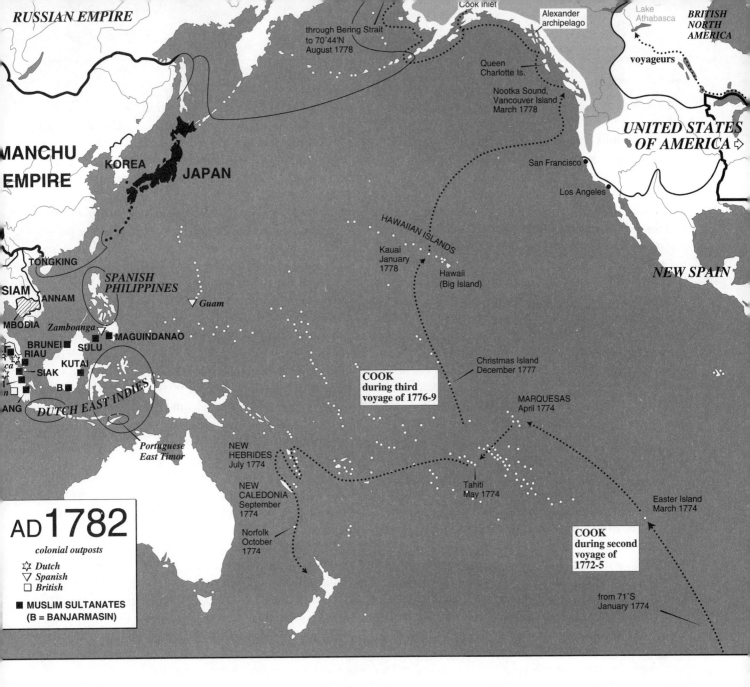

RUSSIAN EMPIRE

through Bering Strait
to 70°44'N
August 1778

Cook Inlet

Alexander
archipelago

Lake
Athabasca

BRITISH
NORTH
AMERICA

voyageurs

Queen
Charlotte Is.

Nootka Sound,
Vancouver Island
March 1778

UNITED STATES
OF AMERICA ⇨

MANCHU
EMPIRE

KOREA   JAPAN

San Francisco

Los Angeles

HAWAIIAN ISLANDS

Kauai
January
1778

Hawaii
(Big Island)

NEW SPAIN

TONGKING

SPANISH
PHILIPPINES

▽ Guam

SIAM   ANNAM

MBODIA   Zamboanga
BRUNEI   ▽ MAGUINDANAO
RIAU   SULU
KUTAI
SIAK
B
ANG   DUTCH EAST INDIES

Christmas Island
December 1777

COOK
during third
voyage of 1776-9

MARQUESAS
April 1774

Portuguese
East Timor

NEW
HEBRIDES
July 1774

Tahiti
May 1774

Easter Island
March 1774

NEW
CALEDONIA
September
1774

COOK
during second
voyage of
1772-5

AD 1782

colonial outposts

☆ Dutch
▽ Spanish
□ British

■ MUSLIM SULTANATES
(B = BANJARMASIN)

Norfolk
October
1774

from 71°S
January 1774

thirteen colonies of British North America. The colonies became the United States with their official Declaration of Independence in 1776; the next year the new nation won its first major victory by forcing the surrender of an invading British army at Saratoga. The French, who had been aiding the Americans surreptitiously, now entered the war openly; Spain followed suit in 1779. The climax came in the campaign of 1781, when the British failed to sustain their command of the sea and consequently lost a second army, boxed in and forced to surrender on the York peninsula. Preliminaries of peace were signed at Versailles in 1782, and the definitive treaty in 1783. With its

western border along the Mississippi, the United States had as yet no claim to be a Pacific power, but in its own eyes it was already a world leader by virtue of its democratic constitution. Other sources of pride would not be long in coming.

*1. The Spaniards had preceded Cook in this area, mounting expeditions to what is now the Canadian coast in 1774 and 1775. In the first, Juan Perez reached the Queen Charlotte Islands; in the second, Bruno Heceta got only as far as Vancouver Island himself, but his subordinate, Bodega y Quadra, took a tiny schooner on to the Alexander archipelago. Neither the Spaniards nor Cook realized that Vancouver Island was separate from the mainland, and all of them

(footnote continued on p. 111)

The loss of the American colonies put the British penal system into crisis. The courts had been sending convicted felons across the Atlantic at a rate approaching a thousand a year; now there was nowhere for them to go, and the "hulks"—the decommissioned warships used as temporary prisons—were filled to overflowing. In 1786 the home and colonial secretary, Lord Sydney, decided that the way to solve this problem was to establish a penal colony in New South Wales. Captain Arthur Phillip was put in charge of the operation, and in January 1788, after an uneventful eight-month voyage, the 11 ships of the First Fleet dropped anchor in Botany Bay.

It was immediately apparent to Captain Phillip that, whatever Cook and Banks might have thought, Botany Bay was not a suitable site for a colony: its harbor was unprotected, its soil was thin, and there was insufficient freshwater. Luckily, the next inlet up the coast—Cook's Port Jackson—turned out to be much more promising; and it was here, at Sydney Cove, that the First Fleet discharged its human cargo: 736 convicts (188 female) and 294 guards and officers. One boatload was sent off to Norfolk Island, where Cook had noticed pines and flax plants that he thought might make useful spars and sails for the Royal Navy; the remainder set about unloading the stores that would, with a bit of luck, see the colony through till 1790, when the Second Fleet was due.

A few days after their arrival at Botany Bay, the British had been surprised to find themselves playing host to two French vessels, the *Astrolabe* and the *Boussole* ("Compass"), under the command of Jean-François de La Pérouse. La Pérouse had persuaded his superiors that national honor demanded a Cook-style scientific expedition to the Pacific and that he was the man to command it. Departing France in 1785, he visited Easter Island, Hawaii, Alaska, and Alta California in the course of the next year; wintered at Macao and Manila; and then (the part of his track shown on the map begins here) set off for the Sea of Japan. After a survey of its northern shores he declared that Sakhalin was, as some European geographers had suggested, a peninsula of Asia, but went some way toward redeeming this error by exiting between Sakhalin and Hokkaido, putting an end to the idea that the two might be one and the same. From his next stopover, Petropavlovsk, he steered south, to make his unexpected rendezvous with the First Fleet in January 1788. Three months later he set out for the last time, his announced intention being to chart the west coast of New Caledonia

and then head home via Torres Strait. Neither he nor either of his vessels was ever seen again. In 1791 the French government sent Bruni d'Entrecasteaux with two ships to look for him, but their fruitless search of New Caledonia and adjacent islands served only to deepen the mystery. Much later, in 1827, a few scraps of French uniform and equipment were found on Vanikolo, an island in the Santa Cruz group, which solved the problem of where the expedition had come to grief, but how La Pérouse had managed to lose both ships and whether there were any survivors ashore when d'Entrecasteaux sailed by in 1793 are questions to which there are still no answers.

Both Spain and Russia established posts in the Pacific northwest during this period, the Spanish at Cook's old anchorage in Nootka Sound, the Russians on Kodiak Island and some points on the mainland. None of this was regarded as proving anything by the British, who looked on the region as open to all comers. And the British were coming there more frequently than anyone else: Cook's men had discovered that Canton was the best market in the world for furs, and British merchants soon made this discovery the basis for a trans-Pacific trade that yielded high profits for shippers engaged in it. The Russian fur traders relied on the Chinese market too, but their route to it, via Kyakhta, was far more circuitous and correspondingly less profitable. As a result, an increasing proportion of the region's peltry ended up with British traders. The Spanish, as could have been predicted, failed to make anything of the trading opportunities: they also failed to impose their sovereignty on the region. In fact, in 1790, after a British threat of naval action, they were forced to concede that, north of San Francisco, their posts had no more status than anyone else's.

One British endeavor in this region that didn't pay off was Alexander Mackenzie's exploration of the far northwest of Canada. He allowed his mentor Peter Pond to persuade him that Great Slave Lake was a thousand miles further west than it is, and that its outflow was probably into the Pacific. In June 1789 he set out to test this theory, his pockets full of rubles for the Russians he expected to meet. Six weeks later he had reached the mouth of the great river that now bears his name, only to find that he was on the Arctic Ocean, not the Pacific. By September he was back at Fort Chipewyan, discouraged but not defeated.

Southeast Asia registered some significant changes during this period. The Burmese conquered the coastal kingdom of Rakhine (1785); Siam got a new dynasty and a

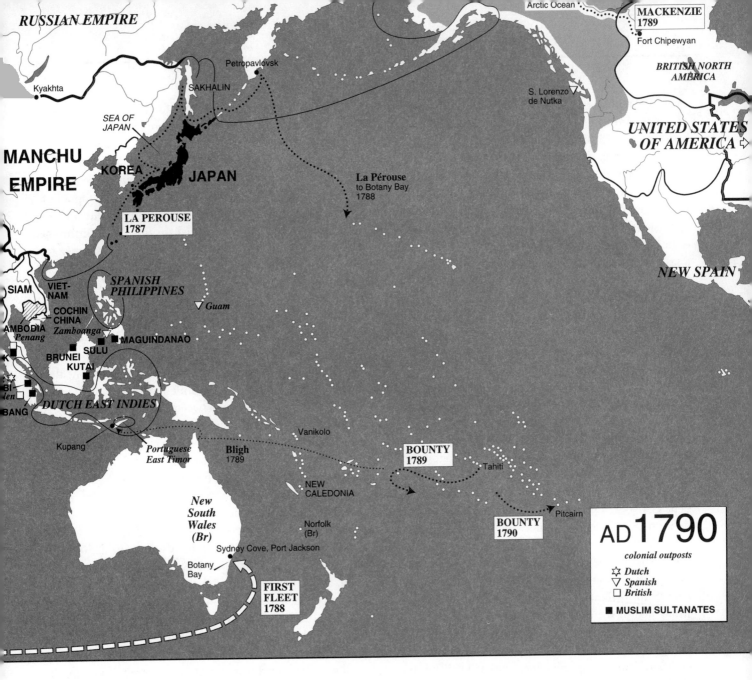

RUSSIAN EMPIRE
Kyakhta
Petropavlovsk
SAKHALIN
SEA OF JAPAN
MANCHU EMPIRE
KOREA
JAPAN
LA PEROUSE 1787
La Pérouse to Botany Bay 1788
Arctic Ocean
MACKENZIE 1789
Fort Chipewyan
BRITISH NORTH AMERICA
S. Lorenzo de Nutka
UNITED STATES OF AMERICA ⇨
NEW SPAIN
SIAM
VIET-NAM
COCHIN CHINA
Zamboanga
AMBODIA
Penang
BRUNEI
KUTAI
SULU
MAGUINDANAO
SPANISH PHILIPPINES
Guam
K
BI len
BANG
DUTCH EAST INDIES
Kupang
Portuguese East Timor
Bligh 1789
Vanikolo
NEW CALEDONIA
BOUNTY 1789
Tahiti
BOUNTY 1790
Pitcairn
New South Wales (Br)
Botany Bay
Sydney Cove, Port Jackson
Norfolk (Br)
FIRST FLEET 1788

AD 1790
colonial outposts
☆ Dutch
▽ Spanish
□ British
■ MUSLIM SULTANATES

new capital, Bangkok (1782). Vietnam was reunited by the Tay Son brothers, who then proceeded to lose the southernmost region (known to Europeans as Cochin China) to the Nguyen, the dynasty that had previously ruled Annam. The British obtained the island of Penang from the sultan of Kedah (1786); the sultan, who was a vassal of Siam, hoped that the British would help him achieve independence, but he was to be disappointed in this. In Riau intervention by the Dutch, and counterinterventions by the regional Muslim powers, left the town in ruins and the sultan a fugitive: subsequently Selangor and Siak, and, in South Borneo, Banjarmasin, accepted a de-

gree of Dutch control. In the northern sector of the map, note the de facto division of the Kurils between the Russians and Japanese, with the Russians getting all except the last three (1785).[1]

*1. Better remembered than many of these events is the episode of the *Bounty,* a Royal Naval vessel that had been given the job of carrying breadfruit cuttings from Tahiti to the West Indies. The *Bounty* had its problems on the way out: the voyage was hard; the quarters were cramped; and the captain, William Bligh, though far from the sadistic flogger Hollywood has made of him, was ill-tempered and foulmouthed. Life on Tahiti made a telling contrast: many of the men slept ashore, and few slept alone. Four weeks into the return (footnote continued on p. 111)

In 1790 reports of a clash between the British and Spanish at Nootka Sound brought the two countries to the brink of war. Spain, lacking the means to enforce its claims, had to back down, and in 1791 the British Admiralty dispatched Captain George Vancouver to accept the formal restitution of British installations at Nootka (in truth nonexistent) and observe the withdrawal of the Spanish garrison established there two years before. This done, Vancouver, who had trained under Cook, set about a task nearer his heart, the detailed mapping of the coast northward from the Strait of Juan de Fuca to Cook Inlet. The Strait of Juan de Fuca had been found and named—overgenerously, considering the apocryphal nature of the Greek pilot's tale—by John Meares, the British trader who had stoked up the Nootka incident, but Meares had been looking for furs and hadn't followed up his discovery. Vancouver charted the strait and its offshoot, Puget Sound, then circumnavigated the island that now bears his name. Subsequent years saw the fearsomely complicated maze of islands and inlets north of Vancouver Island probed and plotted. Sadly, Vancouver just missed meeting Alexander Mackenzie, who on his second attempt reached the Pacific via the Peace River, the upper reaches of the Fraser, and the Bella Coola (1793). This was the first crossing of the continent north of the Rio Grande.

The British had established their predominance on this coast; whether they could maintain it was another matter. The Russians were moving forward again, establishing Fort Saint Mikhail on Baranof Island in 1794 and strengthening their organization by setting up the monopolistic (and entirely Russian) Russian-American Company in 1799. They suffered a setback in 1802, when the local Indians, the Tlingit, captured Fort Saint Mikhail, but the arrival of the *Neva*, a warship that had sailed out from Saint Petersburg, gave them the firepower to recover the fort, which was then rebuilt under the name of Novo-Arkhangelsk. The most active traders, though, were neither British nor Russian but American. By the opening years of the nineteenth century, American ships were carrying ten times as many pelts to Canton as the British. The Americans were also making contributions to the area's geography, Captain Robert Gray of the Boston-based *Columbia* being the first to investigate the great river subsequently named after his ship (1792); this was the same Gray who had earlier completed the first American circumnavigation, taking furs from the northwest to Canton and tea from Canton to Boston.

The British had some excuse for their fading performance in the North Pacific: they were once again engaged in a life-and-death struggle with France. The war started out as a conflict of ideologies (a semidemocratic but deeply conservative Britain standing against the revolutionary values trumpeted by the new French republic), but it soon assumed a more familiar guise (British interests against French, personified on this occasion by the emperor Napoleon). The most obvious consequence for our map came in the opening years of the nineteenth century, when Napoleon, toying with the idea of reviving French interests in North America, bullied Spain into returning the half of Louisiana it had received in 1783. He then changed his mind—sensibly enough, in view of Britain's overwhelming naval superiority—and instead took up an American offer to buy the province. The deal was settled in 1803, with the United States paying $15 million for all the territory between the Mississippi and the Rockies. President Jefferson, the moving force in the Louisiana Purchase, then put down a marker on the lands beyond the Mississippi basin, dispatching captains Lewis and Clark overland to the Pacific coast. Their 31-man expedition left Saint Louis in 1804 and reached the mouth of the Columbia the next year.

In Southeast Asia the Nguyen succeeded the Tay Son as masters of the reunited state of Vietnam (1802), the Siamese took a substantial slice out of Cambodia (1794), and the British took over Malacca, a move that allowed the sultan of Riau to return home (1795) and the sultans of Selangor and Siak to recover their independence. The Dutch let the British have Malacca (and also Padang) because the French occupation of the Netherlands had put them willy-nilly in the French camp and they wanted, if possible, to avoid an all-out British assault on their colonial empire. This meant abandoning the attempt to stop up the Strait of Malacca, which the British, like the Portuguese before them, saw as an essential channel of communication between the Indian Ocean and the South China Sea. The British East India Company's trade with China had been building up steadily since 1699, when the first East Indiaman dispatched in this direction, the *Macclesfield*, had docked at Canton. Now the Dutch were forced to stand aside while the Batavia-based network they had imposed on the orient was replaced by an Anglo-Indian one.

Not that trading with the Chinese was easy. Canton was the only port open to foreigners, and even there dealings were subject to many restrictions. The British view was

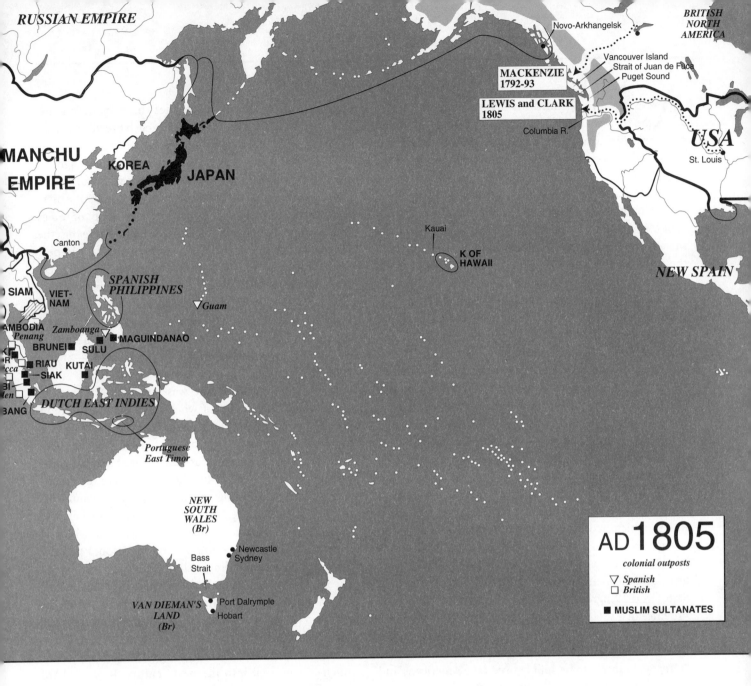

that many of the difficulties could be sorted out if the Chinese would agree to the establishment of formal diplomatic relations. The Chinese, who did well out of the traffic—getting much-valued silver in return for their exports of tea and porcelain—were prepared to be polite, and they agreed to receive a special envoy in the person of Lord Macartney. Preceded by a Chinese official bearing a banner inscribed "Tribute-Bearer from the Red Barbarians," Macartney was permitted to present his credentials to the emperor and submit a proposal for a permanent embassy. But that was as far as politeness went. When the ambassador received the emperor's reply, he discovered

that it dismissed the idea of a permanent embassy out of hand: "The request is contrary to all usage of my dynasty. . . . Europe consists of many other nations besides your own: if each and all demanded to be represented at our court, how could we possibly consent? The thing is utterly impracticable." And for good measure the emperor added, "I set no value on objects strange or ingenious and have no use for your country's manufactures."[1]

*1. Britain's antipodean colonies acquired a little more substance during this period. Secondary settlements were established at Newcastle to the north of Sydney and at Hobart and Port Dalrymple in (footnote continued on p. 111)

As Napoleon extended his hegemony over Europe, the British established a comparable dominion over the oceans. For the Dutch this meant that by the time the long war came to an end (in 1814–1815), most of the East Indies, including Java, were in British hands. In the subsequent settlement the British returned nearly all of their gains and even gave the Dutch Bencoolen; but they kept Malacca, plus a "sphere of interest" that included the Malay Straits and the Malay peninsula. This safeguarded the main British concern, the route to China. In terms of the local sultanates it meant dividing Riau into British-run Johore (the province at the end of the Malay peninsula) and Singapore (the island at its tip) and Dutch-run Riau (covering the rest of the islands between Malaya and Sumatra, plus the adjacent part of Sumatra). The British subsequently made Singapore their main base in the region. Like the other two "Straits settlements," Penang and Malacca, it was run as part of British India, which also included the ex-Burmese coastal provinces of Rakhine and Tanintharyi. These had been lifted from Burma after border troubles had provoked a British punitive expedition to the lower Ayeyarwady (1826).[1]

During this period the various powers with interests in North America sorted out their claims to the west coast. Russia, which had initially demanded exclusive rights to coastal resources as far south as 51° N, settled for 54° 40'N in 1824, and an eastern border of Alaska at 141° W the following year. Spain, as part of a treaty with the United States in 1819, agreed to an upper limit for its Californian province of 42° N. Two years later, when Mexico declared its independence from Spain, this became the frontier between the Mexican and American republics. That left the "Oregon country" to be split between the Americans and the British. The obvious dividing line was the 49th parallel, which had already been accepted for the sector of the frontier between British North America and the United States, running from Lake Superior to the Rockies. However, the British, who had their eyes on Vancouver Island, refused an offer on this basis, and eventually the two parties agreed that, for the time being, they would hold the territory jointly (1818, reaffirmed 1828).

While politicians played for the long term, the sea captains of old England and New England sought for immediate returns. Whatever riches the Pacific Ocean had—mostly a matter of its marine life, but on some of the islands there were valuable stands of sandalwood—these cossacks of the sea gathered in without thought of

the morrow. Within a few decades the trees were gone, and waters that had teemed with life each breeding season were reduced to emptiness and silence.

The North Pacific sector was the first to show signs of exhaustion. The Russians, and the Aleuts who worked for them, reached ever further down the west coast of America, setting up their final post, Fort Ross, only 65 miles (100 km) north of San Francisco in 1812. Despite this, the sea otter catch in the 1820s was running at a bare 10 percent of the figure for 1800, while sealing was off by 60 percent. At this level the trade was barely worth pursuing, and in 1841 Fort Ross was abandoned. The Aleuts had fared little better than the animals the Russians forced them to hunt: only about 5000 were left out of a starting population estimated—probably overestimated—at five times this number.

In the South Pacific there was a parallel slaughter of seals, and of the species of whales that came inshore to breed. "Bay whaling" brought a flush of prosperity to Hobart and Sydney in the period 1805–1835, but the recklessness with which it was pursued ensured that the game was soon over. By the 1840s the whales were "economically extinct"—meaning too few to be worth hunting. Seals had reached the same point ten years earlier. The shore stations established by the bay whalers, which at their peak had considerable if largely seasonal populations, were correspondingly short-lived; the number of Europeans in New Zealand, which had briefly touched the 500 mark (mostly bay whalers and sealers living on the southern coasts of South Island) fell back to less than 100 (traders and missionaries, nearly all on North Island).[2]

Deep-sea whaling drew on a larger biomass and lasted much longer, well into the next century. It was a hard trade. The most valued prey at this time, the sperm whale, moved in relatively small schools, and though the oil it yielded fetched a good price, it could take three years or more for a whaler to fill all the barrels in its hold. As far as the Pacific is concerned, the industry had only begun in the last decade of the eighteenth century, the starting date being the British discovery of the Galapagos whaling area in 1793. The British were soon overtaken by the Yankees, particularly the Nantucket-based vessels that made whaling their specialty. Hawaii was their favorite stopover, and as Yankee skippers came to dominate the trade, so American influence became predominant in the Hawaiian kingdom. When missionaries from New England arrived in the 1820s, an interesting tug-of-war developed between

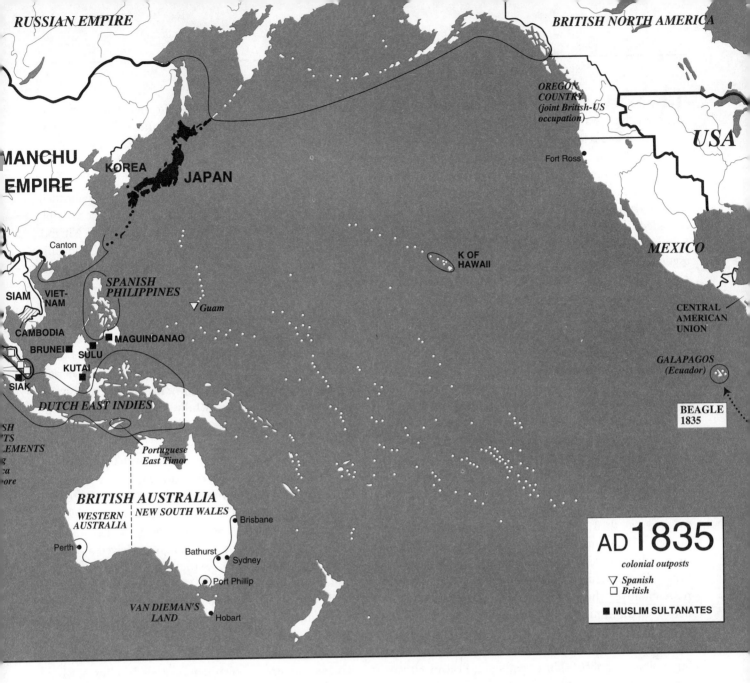

RUSSIAN EMPIRE

BRITISH NORTH AMERICA

MANCHU
EMPIRE

KOREA

JAPAN

OREGON
COUNTRY
(joint British-US
occupation)

USA

Fort Ross

MEXICO

Canton

K OF
HAWAII

SPANISH
PHILIPPINES

▽ Guam

CENTRAL
AMERICAN
UNION

SIAM

VIET-
NAM

CAMBODIA

BRUNEI

MAGUINDANAO

SULU

KUTAI

SIAK

GALAPAGOS
(Ecuador)

DUTCH EAST INDIES

BEAGLE
1835

SH
TS
LEMENTS
g
ca
ore

Portuguese
East Timor

BRITISH AUSTRALIA
NEW SOUTH WALES

WESTERN
AUSTRALIA

Brisbane

Perth

Bathurst

Sydney

Port Phillip

AD 1835

colonial outposts

▽ Spanish
☐ British

■ MUSLIM SULTANATES

VAN DIEMAN'S
LAND

Hobart

their spiritual program (less dancing, more clothes) and the R and R requirements of the whalers (more dancing, less clothes).[3]

actually hunted to extinction, Steller's sea cow, the giant dugong of the Komandorskis. It perished because it was an island, not an oceangoing, species, and its numbers were precariously low to start with—probably no more than a couple of thousand. Bringing this figure down to zero took less than 30 years.

*3. Other points to note on this map are: (1) The colonization of Western Australia, bringing all Australia into the British orbit, and the number of colonial governments there to three—New South Wales (established 1788), Van Dieman's Land (1825), and Western Australia (1831). (2) The recognition of an enlarged Portuguese "sphere of interest" around East Timor by the Dutch in 1818. (3) The formalization, without much in the way of implementation, of the Dutch claim to the western half of New Guinea. (4) The break between Mexico and the Central American Union (1823). (5) The annexation of the Galapagos by Ecuador (1832). Settlement began immediately: Darwin arrived in the *Beagle* three years later.

*1. The sultanates that became dependencies of the British and Dutch are dropped from the map: they include Perak, Selangor, and Johore in the British sphere; and Riau, Jambi, and Palembang in the Dutch sphere.

*2. Despite the orgy of killing, only one of the marine mammals was

By the 1830s British trade with China was booming, but there was mounting ill temper on both sides. The British had a long-standing grievance—the Chinese would not receive any official at all, not even locally, at Canton. The Chinese faced the more immediate problem of a sudden reversal in the balance of trade. Traditionally western demand for Chinese silks, porcelain, and tea had exceeded Chinese demand for western products, the gap being covered by deliveries of silver. These silver transfers, a godsend to the cash-poor Chinese economy, had been one of China's main reasons for tolerating the traffic in the first place. Now, because of a steady growth in the import of Indian opium, the trading surplus had disappeared, and the silver that had been flowing into China for more than two centuries was flowing out again. This was not a situation that could be tolerated. The opium trade was damaging not just the economy but the health and well-being of the Chinese people. Moreover, it was totally illegal. If the local officials were too corrupt to put a stop to it—and they were—then a special commissioner would have to be sent to do the job.

Lin Zexu, the commissioner the emperor appointed, arrived in Canton in 1838. By confining all western merchants to their compounds, he forced the opium traders to disgorge their stock, which he then ceremonially burned, to the consternation of those who had been expecting him to return it on receipt of a suitably large bribe. He also refused to negotiate with Britain's official representative, who wanted to define the conditions under which trade might be resumed. Do it my way, said Lin, or not at all. When trade started up again nonetheless—the complicated estuary of Canton's Pearl River is almost impossible to police—Lin assembled a fleet of 80 warjunks to bring the unruly foreigners to heel. No doubts appear in the poem he composed after reviewing his forces: "A vast display of imperial might has shaken all the foreign tribes, but if they now confess their guilt we shall not be too hard on them."

Lin's magnanimity was never put to the test: any of his junks foolish enough to approach the British ships were quickly blown out of the water. And that was before the Royal Navy arrived in force. When it did it was the Chinese who found themselves blockaded. Commissioner Lin, who had been sending back colorful but entirely imaginary accounts of Chinese naval victories (his "six smashing blows against the barbarian navy" is still widely quoted in Chinese histories) was dismissed by the court,

and a new official was sent out to negotiate terms. He tried to placate the British with the offer of Hong Kong Island and an indemnity of $10 million (£2.1 million), but the emperor refused to ratify these terms. So did Queen Victoria. The Opium War began again.

This time the British pressed harder. They fought their way up to Canton and made the city fork over the $10 million. More to the point, they sacked Amoy and Ningbo, and then moved up the Yangzi to Shanghai, Zhenjiang, and Nanjing. This was a threat to China's economical heartland. The Emperor, whose predecessor had seen no need to have much truck with foreigners, found himself agreeing to open five ports to British trade (Canton, Amoy, Fuzhou, Ningbo, and Shanghai), each with a British Consul in residence. He also agreed to hand over Hong Kong outright, plus a new indemnity of $35 million (£7.35 millions). It was a serious climb down for the "son of heaven," but, as he observed sorrowfully, "We have to make our choice between danger and safety, not between right and wrong."

Equally important rearrangements were in progress on the opposite edge of the Pacific rim. Ever since Lewis and Clark had planted the American flag at the mouth of the Columbia, the United States had been hovering on the brink of becoming a Pacific power. Now the time had come to fulfill what was increasingly perceived as the nation's "manifest destiny." Settlers following the Oregon Trail, opened up in the early 1840s, were already altering the demography of the Far West in America's favor, and if they numbered no more than a few thousands in the middle of the decade, thousands more were on the way. And what even small numbers of American settlers could achieve had already been demonstrated in Texas, where they had taken the province out of Mexico (1836) and into the United States (1845). Needless to say, this had brought Mexico and the United States to a confrontation which only goodwill on both sides was going to prevent from developing into outright war.

President Polk of the United States didn't think he had been elected as a man of goodwill: his campaign platform had been overtly annexationist. He wanted all of the Oregon country, all of New Mexico, and the province of Upper California. Congress was less greedy. There was no doubt that, left to itself, the Pacific Squadron of the U.S. Navy could take over California, because it had already done so once, in 1842, when there had been a false rumor that hostilities with Mexico had already begun. But if

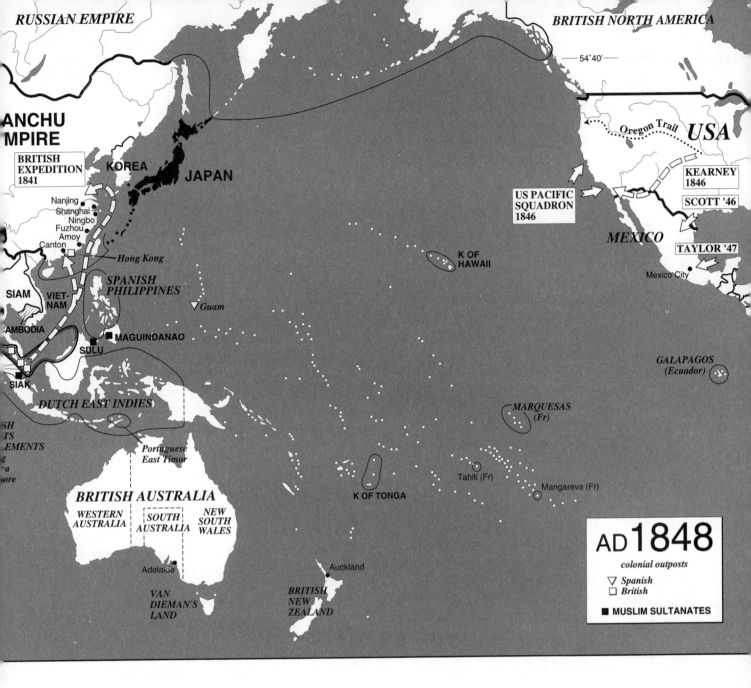

RUSSIAN EMPIRE

BRITISH NORTH AMERICA

— 54°40' —

MANCHU
EMPIRE

Oregon Trail

USA

**BRITISH
EXPEDITION
1841**

KOREA

JAPAN

Nanjing
Shanghai
Ningbo
Fuzhou
Amoy
Canton

— Hong Kong

SPANISH
PHILIPPINES

SIAM

VIET-
NAM

CAMBODIA

SULU

■ MAGUINDANAO

SIAK

DUTCH EAST INDIES

Guam

KEARNEY
1846

SCOTT '46

MEXICO

TAYLOR '47

Mexico City

**US PACIFIC
SQUADRON
1846**

K OF
HAWAII

GALAPAGOS
(Ecuador)

MARQUESAS
(Fr)

Portuguese
East Timor

BRITISH AUSTRALIA

WESTERN
AUSTRALIA

SOUTH
AUSTRALIA

NEW
SOUTH
WALES

Adelaide

VAN
DIEMAN'S
LAND

Tahiti (Fr)

Mangareva (Fr)

K OF TONGA

Auckland

BRITISH
NEW
ZEALAND

AD 1848

colonial outposts

▽ *Spanish*
☐ *British*

■ **MUSLIM SULTANATES**

---

there was one circumstance that could prevent the squadron from doing so again, it was war with Britain. So, despite Polk's slogan, "54-40 or fight," Congress offered Britain the old terms: a division along the 49th parallel, now with a prolongation along the Strait of Juan de Fuca. As this gave them all of Vancouver Island, the British were happy to accept (1846).

By this time the United States and Mexico were already at war. It was a one-sided contest. A small force of U.S. cavalry swept through New Mexico and then proceeded to upper California, where the U.S. Navy and the local settlers had laid the ground for another easy conquest.

Meanwhile, major U.S. Army units moved into action on the Gulf coast, eventually entering Mexico City itself. Through the Treaty of Guadalupe Hidalgo (1848), the Mexicans ceded the vast, if largely empty, territories that the United States wanted, in return for a payment of $15 million. At least they didn't have to pay an indemnity.

British Oceania underwent a notable expansion in 1840–1841, when New Zealand was annexed and three shiploads of colonists initiated the process of European settlement. The Maoris were cajoled into signing treaties whose full implications certainly escaped them; their resentment subsequently fueled "Maori wars," which, if they didn't significantly delay colonization, did require the deployment of British troops. Other events of the period include the organization of South Australia as a separate province (centered on Adelaide) in 1836, the breakup of the Central American Union into the five separate republics of today in 1838, and the reduction to dependent status of Brunei (by the British) and Kutai (by the Dutch) in 1846. In Polynesia British missionaries helped the Tongan chieftain Taufa'ahau eliminate his rivals; in 1845 he was crowned as King George Tupou I. In 1842 the French annexed the Marquesas and established an official protectorate over Tahiti, plus, a bit later, an unofficial one over Mangareva.

DEFEAT IN THE OPIUM WAR was far from being the only mishap to befall the Manchu in the middle years of the nineteenth century: they faced a series of risings by the desperately ill-used peasantry, one of which, the Taiping rebellion, very nearly brought the dynasty down. Taiping ("Great Peace") was the brainchild of Hong Xiuquanin, a would-be civil servant who had taken the entrance examination four times without success. Following his fourth failure Hong had a vision of a utopian state—Taiping—in which land was free, justice impartial, and exams a lot easier. Converts flocked to his banner, and in 1853 he entered Nanjing in triumph. However, Hong proved unable to provide the movement with the strategic direction it needed, and his increasingly odd pronouncements alienated the gentry, who might otherwise have been inclined to see in him the founder of a new, and native, dynasty. Gradually the government rebuilt its forces, and began to roll back the Taiping armies.

The suppression of the Taiping had barely begun when the Manchu found themselves involved in what is often termed the Second Opium War. This certainly followed from the preceding war, though opium wasn't involved, the proximate cause being differences of opinion about the treaty terms for Canton. But, in back of this, the British (and French) had become convinced that without a direct line to Beijing they would never be able to make any deal stick, and, as far as they were concerned, the aim of the war was to make the Manchu court accept permanent ambassadorial representation. For the Chinese this was unthinkable, and they engaged in a great deal of bobbing and weaving to avoid any such thing. An Anglo-French fleet extracted an agreement in 1858, only to have the Chinese renounce it as soon as it was safe to do so. Two years later the allies returned, this time with an army that could and did carry their plenipotentiaries to the gates of Beijing. After some final prevarications the court capitulated, and the representatives of the West were given appropriate accommodation.

China's northern frontier was also under pressure. The Russians discovered that the Manchu had never made any attempt to occupy the lands north of the Amur, and had no means of preventing a Russian advance to the line of the river. In 1858 they persuaded the Manchu to cede this buffer zone, and the Amur became the official boundary between the two empires. Equally important was the Russians' discovery that the Manchu had abandoned the posts that justified their claim to the coastal regions opposite Sakhalin. For the next two years this "Maritime Province" became an area of shared sovereignty. Then, in 1860, when the Anglo-French expeditionary force was camped outside Beijing, the Russian ambassador talked the Chinese into abandoning their half-title, and the province passed to Russia—this in return for a dubious promise of diplomatic support.

The Manchu had now been thoroughly humiliated. The bannermen, their once formidable military caste, had proved incompetent at every level. Important territories had been lost in the north; civil war was endemic in China proper. And all along the coast the cities were passing out of Chinese control. Leaving aside the sovereign enclaves of Hong Kong (substantially enlarged in 1860) and Macao (unilaterally proclaimed as such by the Portuguese in 1849), the arrangements entered into after the Second Opium War raised the number of "treaty ports" to 15. In all of these, westerners were entitled to live under their own laws; in the case of Shanghai the purchase of the Bund (waterfront) by the foreign community in 1854 had created what was effectively a "free city" under international protection. Then there was another colossal indemnity to pay off: $12 million (£2.5 million) split 2:1 between British and French. Yet the Manchu survived. As the treaty ports geared up to the West's commercial needs, exports boomed, and silver again began to flow China's way. The creation of a British-officered customs service provided the central government with revenues that had previously been pocketed by local dignitaries. Even the ending of the ban on opium proved a financial, if not a social, plus, as homegrown opium began to replace Indian imports. The dynasty endured, saved by forces it couldn't control or even understand.

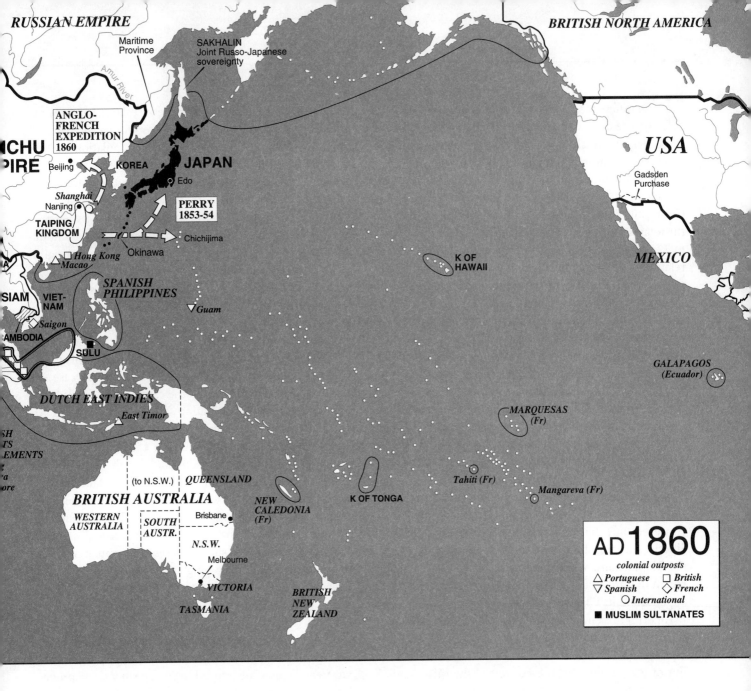

RUSSIAN EMPIRE

BRITISH NORTH AMERICA

Maritime
Province

SAKHALIN
Joint Russo-Japanese
sovereignty

ANGLO-
FRENCH
EXPEDITION
1860

CHU
PIRE

Beijing

KOREA

JAPAN

USA

Edo

Gadsden
Purchase

Shanghai
Nanjing

PERRY
1853-54

Chichijima

TAIPING
KINGDOM

Okinawa

Hong Kong
Macao

MEXICO

SIAM

VIET-
NAM

SPANISH
PHILIPPINES

▽ *Guam*

K OF
HAWAII

Saigon

CAMBODIA

SULU

GALAPAGOS
(Ecuador)

DUTCH EAST INDIES

MARQUESAS
(Fr)

SH
TS
EMENTS

East Timor

a
ore

QUEENSLAND

(to N.S.W.)

Tahiti (Fr)

Mangareva (Fr)

BRITISH AUSTRALIA

Brisbane

NEW
CALEDONIA
(Fr)

K OF TONGA

WESTERN
AUSTRALIA

SOUTH
AUSTR.

N.S.W.

AD **1860**

colonial outposts

Melbourne

△ *Portuguese*   □ *British*
▽ *Spanish*   ◇ *French*
○ *International*

VICTORIA

TASMANIA

BRITISH
NEW
ZEALAND

■ **MUSLIM SULTANATES**

While Britain was opening up China, America determined to do the same for Japan. President Fillmore entrusted the mission, and command of an imposing flotilla, to his senior sailor, Commodore Matthew Perry. The commodore made a leisurely eastward passage out to China (where the new treaty ports would provide the logistical base for the expedition), then set sail for Japan via Okinawa and Chichijima (places he thought might be useful forward stations in the event of trouble). In the summer of 1853 Perry dropped anchor off Edo. He was, he said, just delivering a letter from the president of the United States; next year he'd be back for the answer. "Will you be bringing as many ships?" asked the worried Japanese officials. "Probably more," said Perry. This was enough to concentrate the minds of the men around the shogun, all of whom were well aware of the capital's vulnerability to blockade. On his second visit Perry got the reception he wanted, and subsequently the first American consul to serve in Japan negotiated a treaty as good as anything the British had gotten in China. Getting the genie out of the bottle had proved surprisingly easy.[1]

*1. For note see p. 112

The differences between this map and the previous one dealing with population (in AD 440) are in one sense striking: total numbers have risen nearly ninefold, from 63 million to 550 million. But in another way, perhaps equally important, the impressive thing is how little has changed, for Asia still dominates the picture, and China still dominates Asia. Admittedly China's share of the total is down a few points (from 79 percent in AD 440 to 72 percent in AD 1875); but this drop, which is due to relatively faster growth in Japan and, to a lesser extent, Korea and the Indonesian archipelago, hardly matters when it comes to absolute numbers. With 415 million inhabitants, more than a quarter of the world's population, the Chinese empire far outranks any rival. Small wonder that losses that sound horrifying to Western ears—25 million in the course of the Manchu conquest, the same again in the Taiping wars—could be made up in a generation and were regarded as of little moment by the country's rulers. As Zhou Enlei remarked in more recent days, "In China a million is not a large number."

One new element in Asia is the appearance of the Russians. With 93 million people in 1875 and a rate of increase even faster than China's, the Russians posed a real threat to China's sparsely populated outer provinces. However, only 3.5 million of the tsar's subjects lived in Siberia, and only 1.5 million of these in the lands east of the Ob that come within the framework of our map. This meant that there was a significant gap between the bear's appetite and its effective grasp.

America presents a mirror image of Russia. The population of the United States was increasing ever more rapidly and had reached 44 million by the mid-1870s. But of the 7 million who lived west of the Mississippi, 5 million resided in states bordering the river and less than 1 million in the lands facing the Pacific (California, 0.825 million; Oregon, 0.120 million; Washington territory, 0.04 million). Canada was even more lopsided: of its 4 million citizens only 150,000 lived west of Sault Sainte Marie.

California's population growth was much aided by the gold strike of 1848 and the consequent gold rush of 1849. Some of the "forty-niners" who had less luck than they would have liked in California subsequently began looking elsewhere, and in 1851 one of them started a second gold rush, this time in southeast Australia. The new colony of Victoria saw its population soar from 80,000 in 1850 to 800,000 in 1875 and its capital, Melbourne, displace Sydney from the number one spot in Australia's urban hierar-

chy. In 1861 the focus moved to New Zealand, where finds on the west coast of South Island produced a rush of immigrants that pushed the European population of the country up to 300,000. Gold is far from being the whole story as regards this antipodean boom: the major economic development in both Australia and New Zealand was sheep farming. But gold certainly played its part; it jump-started the population and added a bit of glamour to the otherwise slow and stolid business of pioneering.[1]

While European numbers soared, the native peoples of Oceania declined. The statistics are shaky because nobody knows for sure what the starting populations were, but it is thought that there were about 300,000 native Australians when the First Fleet arrived in 1788, and about 100,000 Maoris in New Zealand. By the date of this map, numbers were down to about 150,000 in the case of the Aborigines and 55,000 in the case of the Maoris. The next-largest native population in Oceania belonged to the Hawaiians, who seem to have suffered even more severely: the usual figures quoted are 150,000 at discovery and 50,000 in 1875. The major cause of these losses was disease. The agents responsible for smallpox and measles need large human reservoirs: if the population is below a certain size—something on the order of half a million—these illnesses, and others like them, soon disappear. Lacking experience of such diseases, the population loses its resistance to them. So long as the community remains isolated no harm is done, but reestablish contact with the wider world and the reintroduced diseases will, at least through their first few cycles, extract a much enhanced mortality. There is something to be said for the missionaries' view that sexual promiscuity played a part, for the venereal diseases introduced by European visitors probably reduced the natives' fertility at a time when maximum fertility was called for. But the main factor was the intrinsic vulnerability of these isolated populations: the attitudes and behavior of contemporary Europeans were relatively unimportant.

This is not to condone the frequent brutality of the colonial era, nor to deny that, in the case of smaller communities, it could well cause a total cultural or demographic collapse. In one particularly cruel episode Peruvian slavers removed 900 of Easter Island's 1500 inhabitants and worked most of them to death digging guano. None of those left behind could read the *rongorongo* boards, Polynesia's only indigenous form of writing, and as a result their meaning became another Easter

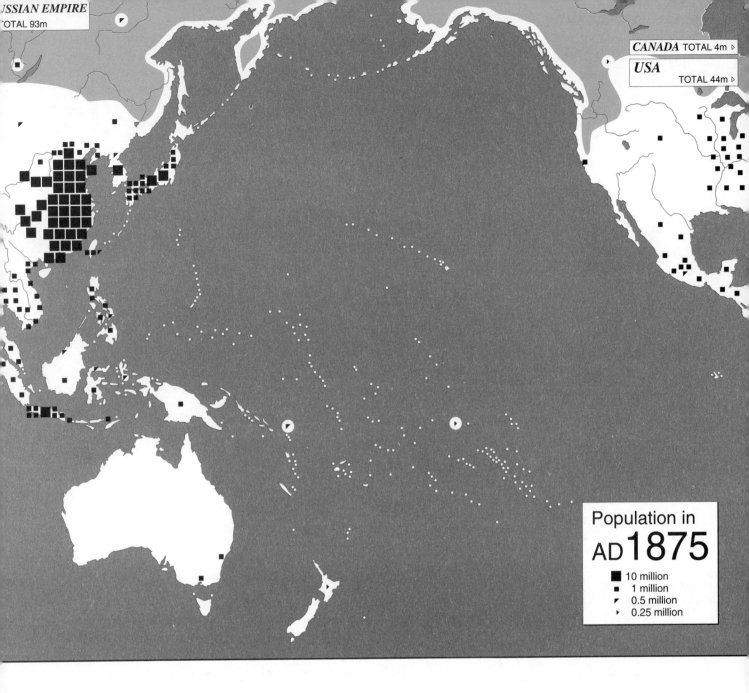

CANADA TOTAL 4m ▷

USA
TOTAL 44m ▷

Population in
AD 1875

■ 10 million
■ 1 million
▶ 0.5 million
▸ 0.25 million

Island mystery.[2] The Australian Aborigines also suffered harsh treatment. The colonial authorities might preach paternalism, but to the average colonist the native peoples were at best an irrelevance, at worst an impediment: the serious business at hand was the building of a new nation. This indifference allowed bushwhackers, the outlaws who formed civilization's skirmishing line, to murder and maltreat as the fancy took them. Even when the government stepped in, as it did on Tasmania, the results were little better. The last few hundred Tasmanians were rounded up in the 1830s, placed on reserves, and given rations; but they died just the same, the last in 1876. Of course the native peoples had their darker side too: a Maori invasion in 1831 disposed of the Chatham Islanders as speedily and completely as the advance of European settlement extinguished the Tasmanians.

*1. The transportation of convicts to Australia ceased in the 1860s, by which time the cumulative total had reached 150,000.
*2. The *rongorongo* script, which looks like a cross between Hittite hieroglyphic and Conan Doyle's dancing men, still hasn't been fully
(footnote continued on p. 112)

PART 4 MODERN TIMES

A history of the world in sound bites would make a straightforward tale of the opening up of Japan. From a policy of total seclusion, the Japanese switched to a program of all-out westernization. They did this overnight, and were rewarded with immediate success. What a contrast with China, which gave ground only when it had to, clung to the old ways as long as it could, and had to endure countless humiliations as a result.

The reality was more complicated. Xenophobia was just as strong in Japan as China, and many Japanese reacted with equal fury to the series of treaties opening up the country. There were attacks on foreigners and their

ships, and reprisals by western navies. As disorders mounted, confidence in the shogun gradually crumbled, and eventually, in 1867, he half resigned, half was pushed out. Subsequently, in what is termed the Meiji restoration, the emperor Meiji and the supposedly antiwestern faction that had brought the shogun down moved up from Kyoto to Edo. The city was renamed Tokyo ("Eastern Capital"): Edo castle, previously the residence of the Tokugawa shoguns, became the imperial palace. On the face of it, the forces of reaction appeared to have triumphed. But, as is often the case in Japan, things were not as they seemed. For instance, the idea that power was being restored to the emperor was simply humbug; the monarchy remained, as it always had been, purely ceremonial. For another, the new government was searching for a consensus and soon found it; top priority, it announced, would go to strengthening the armed forces. In a society that took great pride in its warrior caste, this was not a policy anyone could oppose. At last—15 years after Perry's first visit—the famous modernization program could begin.

The United States played a less prominent role in Japan's evolution than might have been expected. In the early 1860s there was the distraction of the Civil War: subsequently, the opening of the American west made such enormous demands on the nation's energy that there was little left over for foreign affairs. The building of the first transcontinental railroad (achieved by the junction of the Central and Union Pacific lines in 1869) symbolized the start of the new era; the completion of parallel routes to north and south in the early 1880s heralded its consummation. In the interim, Congress proved niggardly when it came to overseas projects. A start was made at setting up a coaling station on Midway Island in 1867, but the money ran out before anything much had been done, and both the work and the island were soon abandoned. The Hawaiian archipelago, however, was now generally perceived as lying within the American sphere. Though the whalers were long gone, sugar planters had taken their place and their market was America's west coast. The abolition of tariffs tied the two closer. Hawaiian monarchs might hope for British protection, but London had no intention of getting its fingers trapped in a closing door.

Looming larger than Hawaii on the map (though containing fewer people: perhaps 6000 against 60,000) is the United States' sole acquisition during this period, the territory of Alaska. The Russians had been looking to sell it for some time, on the grounds that "Russian America" was impossible to defend in the case of war and lost money in peacetime (its accumulated debt amounted to $500,000). In 1867, the American secretary of state, William Seward, agreed to a price of $7.2 million. It was a purchase that few were enthusiastic about at the time—for many years to come it was referred to as "Seward's folly"—but the more far-sighted reckoned it appropriate. In Canada it caused some perturbation. Would the British Columbians, now hemmed in by American territory, be tempted into an association with the United States? In the event, British Columbia signed up to join the new Dominion of Canada—created the same year as the purchase of Alaska—but only on condition that the Canadian government build a transcontinental railroad within ten years. The promise was made, and the Canadian Pacific duly tied the nation together, a bit behind schedule, in 1885.

While the Americans were focusing on America, the British, French, and Dutch were rounding out their colonial empires. The British annexed the Nicobars in 1869, strengthened their grip on the Malay peninsula by imposing resident advisers on the local sultans (from 1873), expanded their protectorate in Borneo to include the northern quarter of the country (1881), and took over the remainder of the Burmese kingdom (1885–1886). The Dutch absorbed Atjeh (in 1874, after clearing the move with the British). The French, the most vigorous empire builders at this time, expanded their foothold in Vietnam, annexing the southern provinces in 1862 and subsequently imposing a protectorate on the remainder of the country (1883). Making this effective proved troublesome. There was sharp fighting along the Red River in 1883, and things got worse the next year when Chinese regular forces appeared in support of the local "black flag" patriots. France responded by sending a fleet to burn the Chinese navy yard at Fuzhou (built by French engineers only a few years earlier) and, more significantly, to threaten Taiwan. The Chinese quickly decided that this particular war wasn't in their interest and agreed to back off (1885). Two years later the French shepherded their acquisitions in the region, which included Cambodia, a protectorate since 1863, into a *Union Indo-Chinoise*.

Other powers were building empires too: Germany joined the club in the 1880s. This was too late for anything very meaty in the way of conquests, and the German expeditions of 1884–1885 had to be content with bits of Melanesia and Micronesia that no one else had thought worth taking. The result was a German mini-empire consisting of northeast New Guinea (Kaiser Wilhelm Land in the new dispensation), New Britain, and New Ireland (together constituting the Bismarck archipelago), the northern Solomons, and the Marshalls. The Germans also made a play for Yap, but this aroused the Spanish authorities in the Philippines, and the pope, called in to arbitrate, awarded the island to Spain. The Spanish subsequently set up an administrative framework for the Carolines as a whole; they had earlier imposed a somewhat nominal suzerainty on the sultanate of Sulu (1870). Germany's advance into northeast New Guinea prompted the British to move into the southeast of the country, an

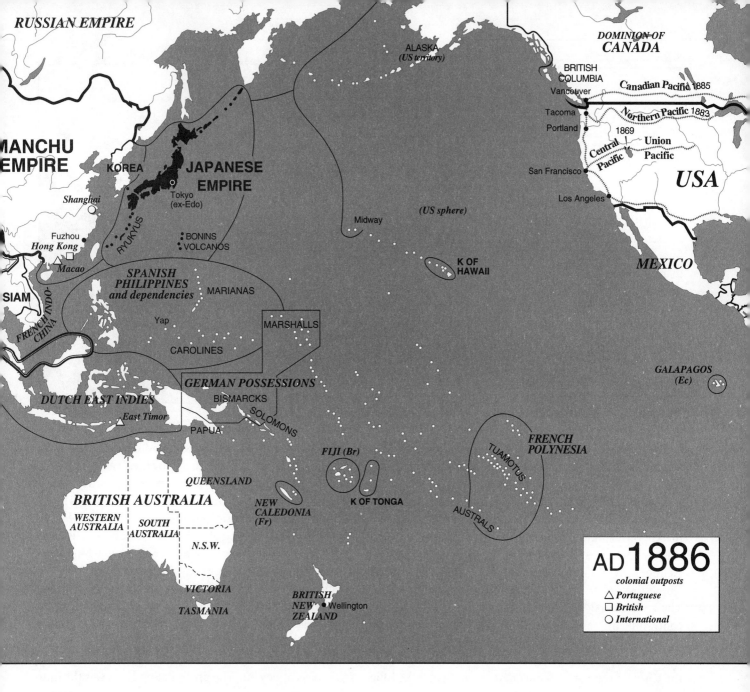

area known as Papua. In Australia, New South Wales relinquished its detached northern territories to Queensland and South Australia (1861–1863); New Zealand moved its capital from Auckland to Wellington (1865). In the South Pacific the British annexed Fiji (1874); the French added the Tuamotu archipelago and the eastern Australs to their holdings in Polynesia (1880).

Meanwhile Japan was taking the steps necessary to establish itself as a player rather than a pawn. First came a series of moves designed to create an internationally recognized perimeter for the empire. The Ryukyus, which had technically been tributary to China as well as Japan,

were absorbed into the Japanese provincial system; the Bonins and Volcanos were occupied; and the half-share in Sakhalin was traded off in return for the Russian stake in the Kurils (all in the course of the 1870s and 1880s). At the same time Korea was opened up, and China, which had been Korea's sole protecting power, was forced to concede equal standing to Japan. Unfortunately, the Japanese didn't manage to win any hearts and minds, and when, in early 1894, Korea's rulers had trouble with a peasant rebellion, it was to China that they turned. The Japanese weren't having this; they sank a Chinese troopship making for Inchon and built up their forces in the peninsula to the point where they were able to run the Chinese garrison out of the country. This brought China's northern fleet out of its base at Weihai, on the Shandong peninsula. The Chinese had two battleships and eight cruisers; the Japanese navy put forward its eight cruisers and, thanks to superior seamanship and more accurate gunnery, had much the better of the encounter. The Chinese limped back to Weihai and never put to sea again. The Japanese were able to land their Second Army on the Liaodong peninsula, and take Port Arthur on its tip, before the year was out.

The next year the Japanese pressed their advantage. The Second Army was transferred to the Shandong peninsula, where, in early February, it captured Weihai and the ships it contained. Then the army returned to Port Arthur to prepare for a landing at Shanhaiguang, and from there a march on Beijing. At the same time another expeditionary force was assembled for an invasion of Taiwan. Neither operation proved necessary, for the disheartened Chinese threw in the towel and accepted Japan's terms. These were harsh. China would have to recognize Japan's controlling interest in Korea, cede Taiwan, and pay a $155 million (£32 million) indemnity. The Japanese also wanted the Liaodong peninsula. However, in this instance the Chinese were able to outsmart them: they leaked the terms to the western powers, who they guessed wouldn't want to see Japan getting too big for its boots. They were right. The Russian, French, and German ambassadors in Tokyo "advised" the Japanese government to return Liaodong to China, advice backed up in Russia's case by partial mobilization in the eastern provinces. Reluctantly, the Japanese dropped the Liaodong clause in return for an extra $23 million (£4.8 million) on the indemnity.

All in all it was a disappointing victory. Japan had pushed China aside only to find, behind it, the menacing bulk of Russia. The role that Japan had coveted, as protector of Manchuria, seemed likely to go to the Russian bear, and that would put Korea under threat. Nor were these distant worries: the Russians had started work on the

Trans-Siberian Railway in 1891, and once this was completed, they would be able to deploy their vast resources of manpower to advance their interests. It is true that the Trans-Siberian was an immense project, three times longer than any of the American transcontinental lines, but the Russians were pressing ahead with it as fast as they could. And in 1896 they scored a major coup when China, eager to have Russian backup in any future conflict with Japan, decided to let the construction teams run the last section of the line across the north of Manchuria. This would cut 340 miles (550 kilometers) off the route and bring the completion date forward to the early 1900s.

Before then China had to endure another mugging by the colonial powers. The precipitating event was the murder of two German missionaries: in reprisal, the Germans forced the cession of the port of Qingdao. This meant that all the other powers had to have equivalent sweeteners, with the Russians asking for, and getting, Port Arthur, the British Weihai, and the French Guangzhouwan (1897–1898). These depredations so outraged the Chinese that many of them turned away from their halfhearted attempts to westernize and began to listen once more to the siren voices of the traditionalists. Among those who promised most were the Boxers, martial arts cultists who proposed to eject the foreign devils by using traditional techniques of hand-to-hand combat. Alas, life is not a Bruce Lee movie, and all the Boxers achieved by their attacks was more humiliation: another international inter-

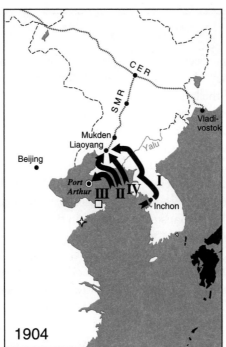

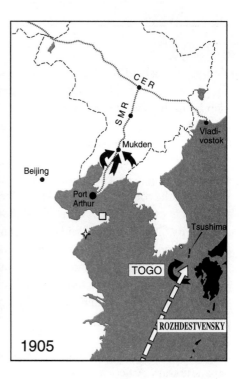

vention (to relieve the embassies in Beijing under siege by the Boxers), the imposition of a new set of indemnities (to pay for the intervention), and, most seriously, a significant loss of authority in Manchuria (where the Russians imposed an unofficial protectorate when it became clear that the Chinese administration could not or would not control the Boxers). In fact, by 1900 the Russians had a position in Manchuria beyond anything the Japanese had dreamed of. The next year they underscored their success by opening both the Chinese Eastern Railway (CER), the Manchurian shortcut that completed the Trans-Siberian) and the South Manchurian Railway (SMR, the branch line from the CER to Port Arthur). The infrastructure needed to maintain their Far Eastern empire was now in place.

The Japanese, sensible of Russian might, offered a deal: they would stay clear of Manchuria if the Russians would keep out of Korea. The Russians said they would, then changed their minds and began interfering in the peninsula. The Japanese cabinet decided it had to fight, and on the night of February 4, 1904, Japanese torpedo boats launched a surprise attack on Russia's Far Eastern fleet in Port Arthur. A formal declaration of war followed two days later.

The Japanese navy didn't do much damage with its torpedoes (the first wartime use of these weapons), but it did get the upper hand in terms of morale: the Russian warships stayed in port while the Japanese ferried their First Army across to Inchon and marched it up to the Yalu River, the frontier between Korea and Manchuria. Then, just as they had done in the war with China ten years earlier, the Japanese landed their Second Army on the Liaodong peninsula. Of course, the Russians provided stronger opposition than the Chinese, but the Japanese too had upped their strength: the Second Army was quickly followed by the Third and Fourth, and by the end of May the Japanese were astride the peninsula. The Third Army settled down to the siege of Port Arthur; the other two linked up with the First Army and, in a bitter battle in late August and early September, drove the main Russian force back from Liaoyang.

Strategically the Japanese now had a winning position: their only problem was that the Trans-Siberian was delivering the equivalent of a fresh Russian army every three months. The Japanese had actually been outnumbered at the battle of Liaoyang: they would have to scrape up all their reserves if they were to win the next round. By doing just that, and by taking Port Arthur on January 1, 1905, they managed to field five armies for the crucial Battle of Mukden (end of February and early March 1905). This was a convincing victory for the Japanese, but not a decisive one. For that the nation had to wait till May, when the Russian Baltic fleet, which had set out in October of the year before, arrived in Japanese waters. Admiral Heihachiro Togo, commanding a fleet of similar size but vastly superior speed and cohesion, brought the Russians to battle near the island of Tsushima. In the first fleet action fought since the battle of Trafalgar, all seven of the Russian battleships were sunk, as were most of the lesser vessels. The tsar was left with no more cards to play. At the peace treaty (brokered by the American president, Theodore Roosevelt, at Portsmouth, New Hampshire) the Japanese got Port Arthur, the SMR as far as Changchun, and the southern half of Sakhalin (seized in the closing phase of the war). What they didn't get was an indemnity. "Not a kopeck," said the tsar, and the exhausted Japanese had no way of making him change his mind. As had been the case in the Sino-Japanese war, the end result of a series of smashing victories was a letdown for the average Japanese and a bitter disappointment for the super-patriots.

IN THE INTERVAL BETWEEN the Sino-Japanese and Russo-Japanese wars, America too became involved in the business of empire building. The process had looked as if it would begin a few years earlier, when the sugar barons on Hawaii, provoked by the reactionary measures of Queen Liliuokalani, forced her to abdicate, declared a republic, and asked the United States government to take over (1893–1894). But President Cleveland wasn't at all keen, and the matter was left dangling for the next few years. Then in 1898 the Americans got into a confrontation with Spain, which was attempting to suppress an independence movement on Cuba, the most important of its remaining possessions in the New World. The small but very vocal imperialist faction in the United States did its best to stoke up anti-Spanish sentiment, but it is doubtful if feelings would have run high enough to produce a declaration of war if the USS *Maine*, a battleship making an ambiguous "courtesy call," hadn't blown up in Havana harbor. That did it. Convinced that the *Maine* had been mined (which wasn't true), the Americans swooped on Cuba and liberated it, along with neighboring Puerto Rico. More to the point as far as our map is concerned, the Asiatic squadron of the U.S. Navy, under the command of Commodore George Dewey, sortied from Hong Kong and made for the Philippines. Confident in the superiority of his ships ("You may fire when you are ready, Gridley"), Dewey engaged the Spanish flotilla defending Manila Bay and quickly reduced it to matchwood. The Philippines were there for the taking. What still remained to be decided was who would take them: the Americans, the Filipinos, or perhaps the Germans, who were shopping around for ad-

ditions to their empire. In the end the enthusiasm engendered by an almost bloodless series of victories proved just enough to overcome America's habitual scruples about overseas acquisitions. President McKinley, who earlier in the year hadn't known where the Philippines were, now decided that they were essential to the safety of the United States. The triumphant mood was also sufficient to swing Congress in favor of the annexation of Hawaii.

So, almost overnight, America acquired a considerable empire in the Pacific. The U.S. Army soon disposed of the Filipino independence movement (officially in 1902, though the suppression of the Muslims in the south took another decade); the navy raised the stars and stripes over Midway, Wake, and Guam, completing the chain of bases needed to support the army's effort. The Hawaiian islands (plus Johnston and Palmyra, two outliers worked by American-Hawaiian guano-mining companies) were given a United States territorial government in 1900.

In the South Pacific, Australia and New Zealand became independent dominions within the British empire. For Australia the change was of considerable moment, for it meant setting up a unitary commonwealth government (provisionally sited at Melbourne) for what had previously been six separate colonies. In New Zealand, the coming of age made less difference: it had been a single colony all along. The Australian commonwealth was established in 1901, when the population was approaching the 4 million mark; it took over responsibility for Papua the next year. New Zealand, which attained dominion status in 1907, had a population of just under 1 million at that time; it became responsible for Chatham Island, the Kermadecs, Niue, and the Northern and Southern Cooks. (Chatham had been in the British sphere since its discovery in 1791; the Kermadecs had been annexed by New Zealand in 1887, and Niue and the Cooks by Britain in 1900 and 1899.)

The Pacific Islands were the subject of a considerable amount of rivalry among the great powers at this time, the Germans in particular being keen to pick up as many as they could. The main contest was over Samoa, where American shipping interests had established a coaling station (for a shipping line from San Francisco to Sydney) back in 1878. Later the Germans moved in, then the British, always keen to keep the Germans in check. Eventually, in 1898, there was a relatively amicable division, with the Germans getting the western islands, the Americans the eastern ones, and the British, in compensation,

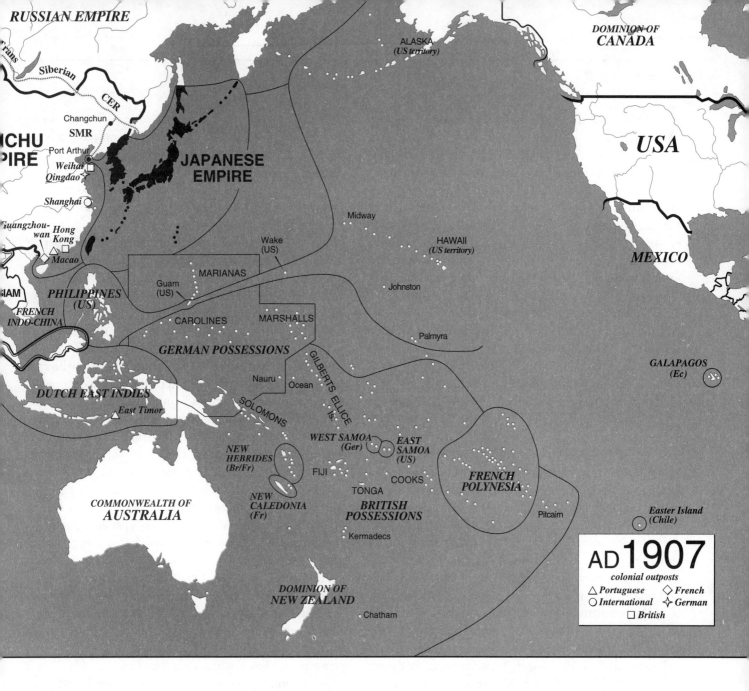

the kingdom of Tonga. The next year, the Germans bought the Spanish islands that the United States couldn't be bothered with, which amounted to the Marianas (except Guam), the Carolines, and the Palaus; they had taken Nauru in 1888. The French took the rest of the Societies (1887) and Australs (1889–1900), and got British agreement to a joint administration of the New Hebrides (1887). This eventually flowered into the extraordinary system of separate but equal governments referred to by officials as the "Condominium," and by everyone else as the "Pandemonium." Chile took Easter Island in 1888. Most of the remaining islands were collected by the British: the Gilbert and Ellice Islands in 1892, the southern Solomons in 1893, the central Solomons (ceded by Germany as part of the Samoa deal) in 1900, Ocean Island in 1901, and the Pitcairn group in 1898–1902.

In Southeast Asia, note that France has been squeezing Siam, forcing it to disgorge the provinces that now form the state of Laos, as well as some minor areas on the frontier with Cambodia. In the northeast, in 1907, the Japanese lost patience with the maneuverings of the Korean monarch and forced him to abdicate; Korea can be regarded as being under direct Japanese rule from that date, although it wasn't officially annexed till 1910.

In 1911–1912 China finally lurched into the modern world with an army revolt, the proclamation of a republic, and the formal abdication of the last Manchu emperor. Mongolia refused to acknowledge the authority of the republic, a secession that was immediately recognized by the Russians (who rewarded themselves with a slice of Mongolian territory west of Lake Baikal) and, after some hesitation, by the Chinese. The next empire to disappear was Germany's, the Pacific portion of which was forfeit as soon as the First World War began. The Japanese took Qingdao and the Central Pacific islands; the Australians took New Guinea, the Bismarcks, and Bougainville; the British took Nauru; and the New Zealanders took western Samoa (all 1914). These gains (except for Qingado, which was returned to China in 1922) were labeled "mandates" by the League of Nations after the war, the idea being that the occupying power was merely preparing the native peoples for self-government.

The return of Qingdao was the result of American pressure. The United States had emerged from the World War I as the world's first superpower and was trying to bring a bit of order, and some sense of fair play, into international affairs. In the Pacific this meant coming down particularly hard on the Japanese, and relations between the two nations quickly soured. It was quite a turnaround from the situation in the Russo-Japanese war, when American opinion had been solidly for the plucky little newcomer and against the big Russian bully. Alas, the Japanese had used the opportunities presented by the First World War in an unexpectedly brash and unprincipled way, first by trying to impose a protectorate on China—the famous "21 demands" of 1916—then by attempting to detach some of Russia's Far Eastern territories on the excuse of saving them from Bolshevism. No doubt about who was doing the bullying now.

Unfortunately, America soon tired of playing policeman, and the Japanese were able to resume their expansionist course. In 1931 an undercover team blew up a 4-meter section of the South Manchurian Railway, an economical bit of sabotage that gave the Japanese army based in Port Arthur the excuse it needed to fan out across Manchuria "restoring order." The next year Manchuria was declared an independent state under the name of Manchukuo, and Henry Pu Yi, the last Manchu emperor of China, was brought out of exile to be its puppet ruler. Jehol, the adjacent part of Inner Mongolia, was added to the Japanese-controlled area in 1933. China was too weak to contest these advances, and Russia, now the Soviet Union and under the iron rule of Joseph Stalin, chose not to. Stalin had inherited an all-Russian Trans-Siberian—the Amur section had been completed in 1916—and was prepared to let the CER go: Soviet and Japanese negotiators agreed on a price in 1935.[1]

While the Japanese labored to realize their imperial dream, the British empire was enjoying an Indian summer. Its bounds had never been set wider. Victory in the First World War had led to new areas being colored British, and if the gains in the Pacific were relatively few, all the trappings of power were in place. But the underpinnings were not. Britain's ranking among the industrial nations had been slipping for half a century, and the men who ran the empire were deeply worried by the increasing imbalance between resources and commitments. An alliance with Japan, made at a time when both were concerned to check tsarist Russia, had given Britain peace of mind as regards the Pacific during the First World War. Now Japan's clearly readable plans for dominion over China, and the disapproval these aroused in the United States, forced Britain to choose between Japan and America. This was no choice at all. When the Anglo-Japanese agreement expired in 1921, it was not renewed; instead, works were put in hand at Singapore, which the Royal Navy would need as its forward base if matters ever came to a head in the Far East. Of course, if there was another war in Europe it was unlikely that any ships could be spared for the Far East, in which case there was nothing to be done except pray that Uncle Sam would come to the rescue. The empire was a lot less glorious than it looked.

Minor points to note are British Malaya's acquisition of four small sultanates, previously tributary to Siam, in 1909; the return of Weihai to China (1930); and the inauguration of Canberra as the federal capital of Australia (1927). The United States declared the Philippines a commonwealth in 1934 and promised independence in ten years' time: it also took over Jarvis, one of the Line Islands previously claimed, but not occupied, by Britain (1935). A big event, but off the map, is the opening of the Panama Canal (1914).[2]

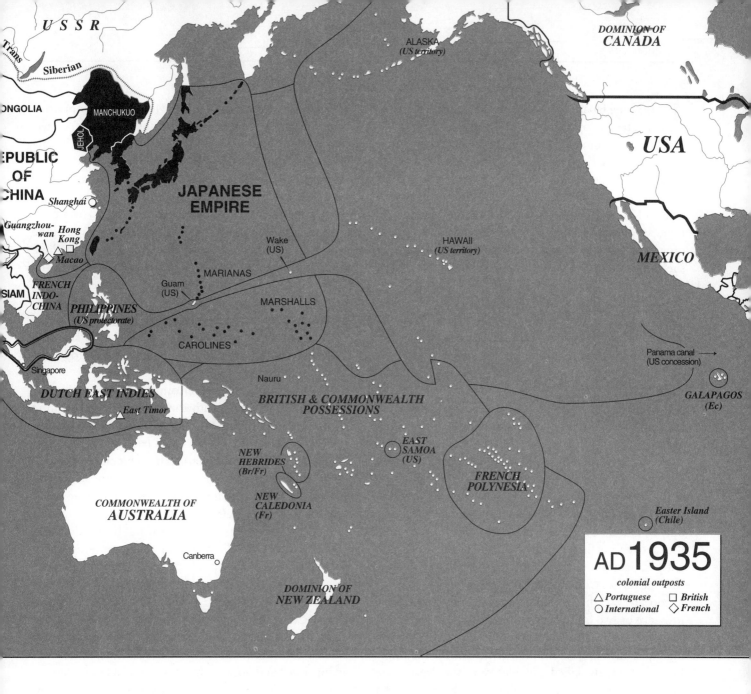

*1. Only Italy and El Salvador recognized the state of Manchukuo, whose creation was roundly condemned by the League of Nations. This rebuff led Japan to resign from the League, the first country to do so.

*2. The original plan for the Panama Canal had been French, but—despite the services of de Lesseps of Suez Canal fame—successive French efforts spread over a 20-year period failed to get the job done. In 1902 the United States took over and drove the project through, near enough on schedule and at cost, within 12 years. The United States also had to engineer the creation of a new country to get the political control it wanted: this was done by supporting the secession of the republic of Panama from Colombia in 1903.

In 1937 the Japanese army used a skirmish near Beijing as a pretext for a full-scale invasion of China. The Manchurian command had been sliding troops into north China for some time; now general headquarters in Tokyo organized an expeditionary force that quickly overran the entire northeast of the country. China's leader, General Chiang Kai-shek, tried to defend his capital, Nanjing, but to no avail: resistance merely provoked the attackers to an orgy of killing when the city fell. Undeterred, Chiang Kai-shek retreated up the Yangzi and reestablished his government at Chongqing on the far side of the Yangzi gorges. The Japanese made no attempt to follow him, but by occupying the ports on China's southern coast (together with the island of Hainan) they severed most of his links with the outside world: the only way supplies could get to him once these moves were completed (in 1938–1939) was via Indo-China or Burma.

Despite the pressure he was under, Chiang Kai-shek refused to consider any accommodation with the invaders, and the "China incident," which Japan's generals had assured the emperor would be over in a matter of months, settled down to a costly stalemate. This didn't lead to any rethinking by the generals, who remained convinced that to thrive the Japanese empire had to expand. For them the only question was where to make their next move. At first they looked north, for the rise of Adolf Hitler's belligerently anticommunist Nazi party in Germany suggested that the Soviet Union could soon be enmeshed in a new European war: that would give Japan a chance to lop a province or two off the eastern end of the Soviet empire. A clash on the Manchurian border in 1939 proved sobering—the Russians had much the better of the fighting—but what finally killed the idea was the Nazi-Soviet nonaggression pact, an ideological turnaround that temporarily bewildered the Japanese. Hitler soon made amends. By provoking a general war, his invasion of Poland in September 1939 ensured that the energies of the colonial powers would be concentrated on Europe. This had to be to Japan's advantage. What came next was even better. In the summer of 1940 the German army achieved the victory that had eluded it in 1914, rolling over the Low Countries and France in a six-week blitzkrieg. The German triumph left the French and Dutch empires in the Far East effectively defenseless and the British possessions in little better case—Britain hadn't gone under, but with the home islands under threat it had few thoughts or resources to spare for anywhere else.

Japan's generals moved quickly to exploit the opportunity. They forced the French to let them into north Vietnam and pressured the British into closing the Burma road, the tortuous route by which truck traffic passed from upper Burma to southern China. This completed Chiang Kai-shek's isolation. Japan also began the process of winning Thailand (as Siam now called itself) over to its side by making the French authorities return some of the border provinces annexed in the early 1900s. But these were small matters. The really exciting prospect was the extension of Japanese control over the Indonesian archipelago. This contained the resources necessary to give Japan the world-power status it had craved for so long: in particular, it contained the oil fields needed to keep the Japanese war machine functioning. And, thanks to Hitler, it was there for the taking.

Well, not quite. The Americans had been getting increasingly exasperated with the Japanese. As a warning gesture President Franklin Roosevelt had already moved the Pacific fleet from its West Coast bases to Pearl Harbor on Oahu Island in the Hawaiian archipelago. Now he made it clear that if there were any more aggressive moves, he would embargo Japan's oil supply. And when the Japanese made their next advance, into south Vietnam in July 1941, he was as good as his word. Unless the Japanese withdrew from Vietnam, and what is more, agreed to begin negotiations on a pullback in China too, they would be allowed to buy only a month's supply of oil at a time.

The embargo certainly worked. The Japanese leadership, deciding that war was inevitable, ordered planning to begin immediately. The objective, of course, was to gain control of the oil-rich "southern area" (the Indonesian archipelago) and do so as speedily as possible. Despite existing commitments, the army would have no problem finding ten divisions, and that was all that would be needed to deal with the poorly equipped British army in Malaya, the rather better equipped American-Filipino forces in the Philippines, and the puny Dutch detachments in the East Indies. The deadline was set for the first week in December.

The transports carrying the two divisions that were to spearhead the invasion of Malaya set out from Hainan island on December 4th. A British search plane picked up the convoy and correctly interpreted it as an invasion fleet. The news was passed on to Washington, causing a worried secretary of the navy to ask, "Are they going to hit us?" "No," replied the admiral at his elbow, "they are going to hit the British. They aren't ready for us yet."

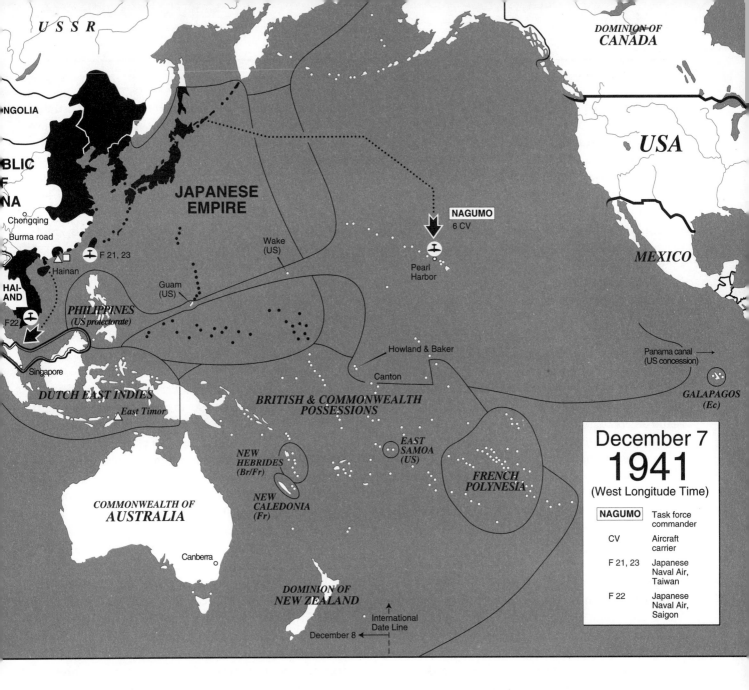

The first part of this assessment was entirely correct. In the early hours of the next day the Japanese convoy began landing its troops at sites on either side of the Thai-Malay border. The second part proved less happy. The Japanese navy had sent all six of its fleet carriers to Hawaiian waters, and at first light they began launching their planes for a strike against Pearl Harbor. As the American Pacific fleet was enjoying its regular sleepy Sunday morning, surprise was complete. The Japanese planes—356 in all, attacking in two waves—sank four of the eight battleships at anchor and disabled the others. They also destroyed some 200 aircraft, nearly all of them on the ground.

Japanese losses in the two-hour onslaught amounted to 29 planes, most of them in the second wave. The mercy was that none of the Pacific fleet's three carriers was in port.[1]

*1. The bisection of the Pacific by the international date line means that the events of this day took place on December 7th as regards the right half of the map, and December 8th as regards the left half. Clock time (as opposed to date) advances from left to right. As the attackers went in on Pearl Harbor, it was 1 A.M. in Malaya (where hostilities had also just begun), and 3:30 A.M. in Tokyo (both December 8th); it was 8 A.M. in Pearl, and 1:30 P.M. in Washington (both December 7th). The Japanese declaration of war was delivered in Washington at (footnote continued on page 111)

Once the Japanese had decided on war, the fate of the British and American forces in Malaya and the Philippines was sealed. There was no possibility of relieving, or even reinforcing, the Philippines, and—with or without Pearl Harbor—there never had been. Nor could the British get sufficient airpower or sea power to Malaya to affect the result. The Royal Navy had dispatched two battleships to the Far East as the war clouds were gathering: both were sunk by Saigon-based torpedo-bombers as soon as they put their noses out of Singapore harbor. On land the British position crumbled almost as quickly. The Japanese expeditionary force made short work of the two Indian divisions that were supposed to defend the frontier, and the remnants of these formations, even when reinforced by two fresh divisions (one British, diverted from the Middle East; one Australian) proved too weak to hold a final defense line across the tip of the peninsula. Crossing to Singapore, the Japanese forced the surrender of the island on February 15th. It wasn't a surprising result—the British had no armor, few planes, and no real hope of stabilizing the situation at any stage—but it was a staggering blow to the pretensions of the British empire and, with 140,000 prisoners taken, a notable triumph for Japan.

The opening moves in the Philippines went every bit as well for the Japanese. Two divisions landed on Luzon, swept aside the American-Filipino forces opposing them and, on February 2, 1942, captured Manila. A mopping-up operation seemed all that was required to bring the campaign to a conclusion, and, acting on this assessment, the Japanese high command decided to speed up its plans for the conquest of the "southern area" by withdrawing one division and redeploying it against Java. This made a lot of sense and in strategic terms was to work out well, but it left the Japanese troops on Luzon badly outnumbered: the single division that remained faced American-Filipino forces roughly four times as strong. The defending army had withdrawn to the Bataan peninsula (the northern lip of Manila Bay); it was in better shape than the Japanese realized, and what was being asked of it was within its capacity. After five weeks of fighting, the Bataan peninsula remained firmly in American-Filipino hands, and it was the attacking force, not the defending army, that had disintegrated. The successful defense of Bataan gave a tremendous fillip to American morale and made a hero of General Douglas MacArthur, the American commander in the Philippines. Considered too valuable to be left in jeopardy, MacArthur was spirited away by boat to Mindanao and from there by plane to Australia, where he was put in charge of the American and Australian forces being assembled for the defense of the southwest Pacific.

By this time the Dutch East Indies had been incorporated into the Japanese empire. Only small forces had been needed to take the nearly defenseless upper tier of islands: Borneo, Sulawesi, and the Moluccas. By mid-February the attack on the lower tier had begun, and at the end of that month landings in divisional strength were made at both ends of Java. A scratch Allied naval force of cruisers and destroyers made a hopeless attempt to disrupt the invasion, only to be defeated in the battle of the Java Sea (February 27th), and all but annihilated as it tried to escape (March 1st). Within a week all of Java was under Japanese control.

The conquest of the Dutch East Indies meant that the Japanese had achieved the main object of their southward drive. However, the overall plan also called for the subjugation of mainland Southeast Asia, i.e., Thailand and Burma as well as French Indochina. Thailand agreed to throw in its lot with Japan on the outbreak of war: a Japanese force of two divisions subsequently moved via Bangkok to the Thai-Burmese frontier. There they waited until it was clear that the Malayan operation was proceeding satisfactorily; then they moved on Yangon. The solitary Indian division guarding the frontier was outflanked and largely destroyed: Yangon fell in early March. The British withdrew up-country, where they established a defensive line with an army that was heterogeneous even by the relaxed standards of the British imperial twilight: an Indian division, a Burmese division, a British armored brigade, and a Chinese force amounting to the equivalent of another division. The Chinese had been persuaded to move into north Burma to protect their last link with the west, the Burma road, and it was this commitment that encouraged the allies to believe there was still a faint chance of saving something from the wreck.

While these major campaigns were in progress, minor Japanese forces picked off various American and British outposts: Guam, Wake Island, Makin, and Tarawa in the Gilberts, and Rabaul in the Bismarcks. Rabaul became the central stronghold for a forward line running from Lae in New Guinea to Bougainville at the north end of the Solomons.

The Japanese carriers put in an occasional appearance during this phase. Two were detached from the main body

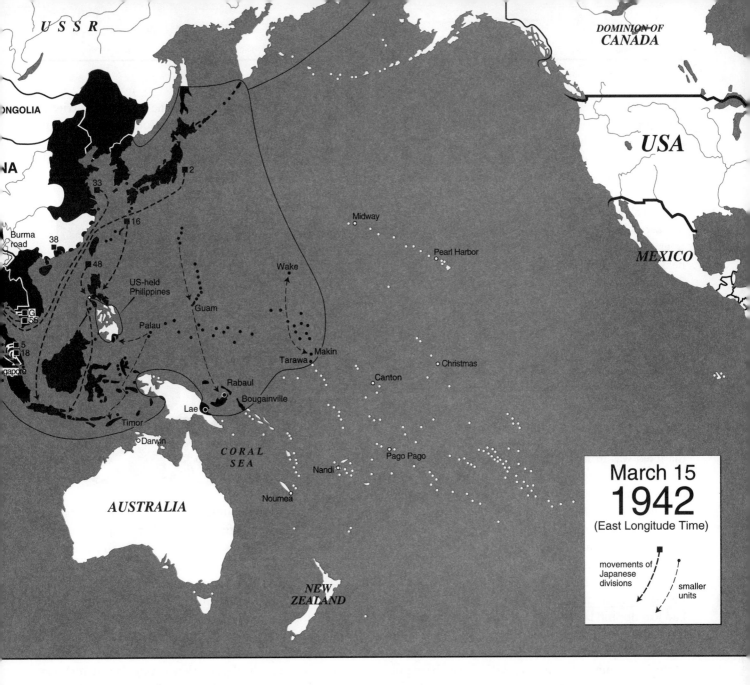

as it returned from Pearl Harbor to deal with Wake Island, which was putting up an unexpectedly spirited defense: they soon put a stop to that. In February four assembled at Palau to support the final push in the Indies. Passing east of Timor, the carriers launched their planes against Darwin in Australia's Northern Territory, which was being used as a supply point for the Allied forces in Java. The town was so shattered that for a while it was totally abandoned. The tide of war was now lapping at the shores of Australia.[1]

*1. The Australians could take some comfort from the fact that Admiral Chester Nimitz, the new commander-in-chief of the United States' Pacific operations, was giving top priority to strengthening his lines of communication with Australia and New Zealand. During this period garrisons were installed in the Line and Phoenix Islands (at Christmas Island and Canton), in American Samoa (Pago Pago), and in New Caledonia (Noumea). The sequence was completed by the New Zealand base at Nandi in the Fijis.

The political divisions of the South Pacific, which were effectively in abeyance during the war, are dropped from the maps covering it.

By late March the Philippine campaign was approaching its inevitable close. Hastily assembled reinforcements had brought the Japanese force on Luzon up to the equivalent of nearly three divisions, and a new offensive against the Bataan peninsula was scheduled for early April. The defenders had been cut off from all supply and all hope of relief for four months, and they were in no condition to resist: the fighting was over within a week. Corregidor, the fortified island off the tip of Bataan, held out till May 7th; three days later the American-Filipino forces on the other islands, previously ignored by the Japanese, surrendered too. The flag could be lowered with pride: the tenacious defense of Bataan had deprived the Japanese of the sort of walkover victory they had won at Singapore.

Japan's other unfinished business was in Burma. By this time the Japanese had built up their army there to four divisions (one redeployed from Malaya, one newly arrived from Japan), and neither the British nor the Chinese proved able to hold them up for long. All of Burma that mattered was in Japanese hands by early May. The Chinese pulled back to Yunnan; the surviving British and Indian troops escaped to India just ahead of the monsoon and the pursuing Japanese.

The gods of war had certainly smiled on Japan. Almost the entire set of movements involved in the conquest of the "southern area" had been achieved ahead of schedule and at far less than the expected cost. The army's casualties had been minimal, perhaps 25,000 all told. The navy had lost no ship larger than a destroyer. Only one operation had had to be postponed, the relatively small forward movement needed to complete the Japanese occupation of the New Guinea–Solomons area. This had been put on hold back in March, when an American carrier was found to be operating in the Coral Sea, and there was no Japanese carrier available to deal with it.

Plans for remedying this situation were not difficult to make. The Japanese carriers would be through with their current business—a foray into the Indian Ocean to keep the British off balance—by the middle of April, and two of them could then be sent to the South Pacific. The operation was then to go ahead as originally planned, but with a new timetable: Tulagi, a small island in the lower Solomons, would be occupied by May 3, 1942, and Port Moresby, on the underside of New Guinea, four days later. The invasion fleet, under the command of Admiral Aritomo Goto, included a light carrier, which would pro-

vide local air cover: however, if the American carrier reported earlier was still in the area, Goto would be looking to Admiral Takio Takagi's big fleet carriers to do the business. Takagi intended to sail down the north side of the Solomons during the opening phase of the operation,

then around their southern end to enter the Coral Sea, where, if he couldn't find anything better to do, he would make a series of strikes against the Australian bases on the York peninsula.[1]

The Americans, with two carriers operating in the Coral Sea, were stronger than the Japanese realized; they also had better intelligence, including accurate estimates of the composition and intentions of both Takagi's and Goto's forces. This enabled Admiral Frank Jack Fletcher, in command of the fleet carriers *Lexington* and *Yorktown,* to get the drop on the Japanese. Fletcher wasn't able to stop the Tulagi landing, but he picked up Goto's force as it was heading for Port Moresby and launched a full strike of 93 planes against its escorting carrier. Little *Shoho* was subjected to a cascade of bombs and torpedoes that sent it to the bottom in 30 minutes. Admiral Goto pulled back and waited to see how the battle would develop.

That afternoon it was the Americans who had the luck. Less than an hour's flying time to the east of them, Admiral Takagi's *Shokaku* and *Zuikaku* were putting a major strike together, but what they thought was an American carrier turned out to be an oiler. Sinking it was poor consolation for the loss of *Shoho.* The next day fortune changed sides. Fletcher and Takagi located each other

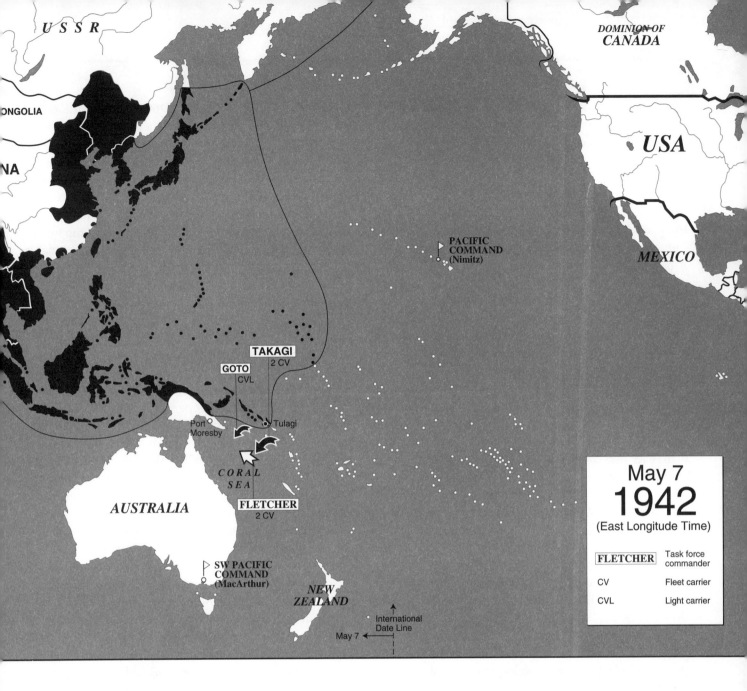

May 7
1942
(East Longitude Time)

FLETCHER	Task force commander
CV	Fleet carrier
CVL	Light carrier

early on and launched simultaneous strikes. The American dive-bombers got three hits on *Shokaku;* but *Zuikaku,* dodging into a timely squall, escaped unscathed. The Japanese, favored by better weather over their targets, hit *Yorktown* with a bomb and *Lexington* with two bombs and two torpedoes. This was more than *Lexington*'s damage control could handle, and five hours later it had to be abandoned. And there the matter rested. With only a single functioning carrier apiece, and their air groups exhausted, neither side felt like renewing the contest: the battle of the Coral Sea—the first naval encounter in which there had been no sighting of ship by ship—was over.

The Japanese had undeniably won a tactical victory. They had traded a light carrier for a fleet carrier—and fleet carriers, it was now clear, were the warships that mattered. But the Americans could also feel pleased with the result. The battle led the Japanese to postpone the move to Port Moresby again, and gaining time was an important American interest. Strategically the issue was in the United States' favor.

*1. For note see page 111

If the opening months of the war had gone well for Japan, this was no surprise to Admiral Isoroku Yamamoto, the man with overall responsibility for the operations on the Japanese fleet: he had never had any doubts about this phase of the struggle. What occupied his mind was the second and third years of the war, when the new ships already ordered for the United States' Navy began to appear on the scene. The sobering fact was that the imperial navy, which was roughly the same size as the American Pacific fleet in December 1941, would be outnumbered three to two by the end of 1943, and by more than two to one by the end of 1944. And this was assuming that the Germans continued to keep the United States busy in the Atlantic. Clearly something would have to be done to whittle down the American numbers before they got beyond Japan's ability to cope with.

The answer, as Yamamoto saw it, was to provoke a fleet action and win the sort of annihilating victory that his predecessor, Admiral Togo, had inflicted on the Russians at Tsushima. At the very least this would put American plans back by a couple of years; with a bit of luck it might fatally sap their will to continue the struggle. To bring out the American fleet, the Japanese would have to threaten an asset that the Americans considered vital, and exactly what asset best filled the bill was something about which Yamamoto had thought long and hard. He had come to the conclusion that only one target would do—Midway Island, at the near end of the Hawaiian archipelago. The naval staff didn't like this plan at all: they wanted the next thrust to be made to the southwest, against Samoa and Fiji. But Yamamoto thought the Americans might not be prepared to commit themselves fully in defense of such peripheral places. By threatening to resign if his plan wasn't accepted and, in a more compromising mode, by promising to take Samoa and Fiji once he had won his big battle, he got the naval staff's agreement to the Midway operation. The formal go-ahead was given on April 5th.

Almost the entire Japanese navy was to be committed to the new offensive, though not all of it was to sail against Midway: there was to be a sizable diversionary move in the North Pacific aimed at confusing the American high command. In fact, there were to be no less than eight separate task forces. The two northernmost carried troops for the conquest and occupation of the islands of Attu and Adak in the Aleutians. To the south of these two convoys, and a considerable distance in advance of them, was the Aleutians striking force of two light carriers. Its planes would

open the campaign by raiding Dutch Harbor, the only American base of significance in the islands, on June 3, 1942. At the southern end of the Japanese lineup were the two formations that would be responsible for the assault and capture of Midway, the provocation intended to bring the American fleet hurrying up from Pearl. The troops were in a slow-moving convoy that would allow itself to be sighted on June 3rd, close behind would be a backup force (two battleships, four cruisers, and a light carrier), which would provide close support for the landing. On a more northerly track, initially somewhat behind but closing up fast, would come the heavy mob, six fleet carriers and nine battleships. These had a variety of tasks. The six fleet carriers (plus two escorting battleships)—commanded, as at Pearl Harbor, by Admiral Chuichi Nagumo—constituted the main striking force: on June 4th their planes would hit Midway to soften up the island's defenses before the landings due the next day. This done, Nagumo would pull back to await the appearance of the American fleet. Meanwhile, the battleships would be closing up behind the various task forces, four in support of the Aleutians operation, the three latest and largest behind Nagumo's striking force. It was a concentration of naval power that the Americans would find hard to match.

In fact, the Americans weren't even going to try as regards battleships. Despite the losses at Pearl Harbor, they had seven fit for duty, but all were old and slow, and they seemed out of place in a world of fast-moving carrier actions. The sensible thing, Admiral Nimitz felt, was to keep them out of harm's way on the West Coast. Fleet carriers were a different matter, and here the Americans could expect to have five by midsummer: *Yorktown, Lexington, Enterprise,* and *Hornet,* plus *Saratoga,* which had taken a torpedo from a Japanese submarine in January but should be ready for action again sometime in June. But then came the battle of the Coral Sea, in which *Lexington* was sunk and *Yorktown* hit. Damage reports suggested that it would take three months to make *Yorktown* battleworthy again.

By this time Admiral Nimitz knew that he didn't have three weeks, let alone three months. Radio intercepts plus masterly work by the code-breakers had provided him with the essentials of the Japanese plan, including the dates of the first strikes on Dutch Harbor and Midway. If he was to take full advantage of this intelligence coup, Nimitz needed to get his carriers into a flanking position northeast of Midway by the beginning of June. *Saratoga* probably wasn't going to make it in time. *Yorktown* prob-

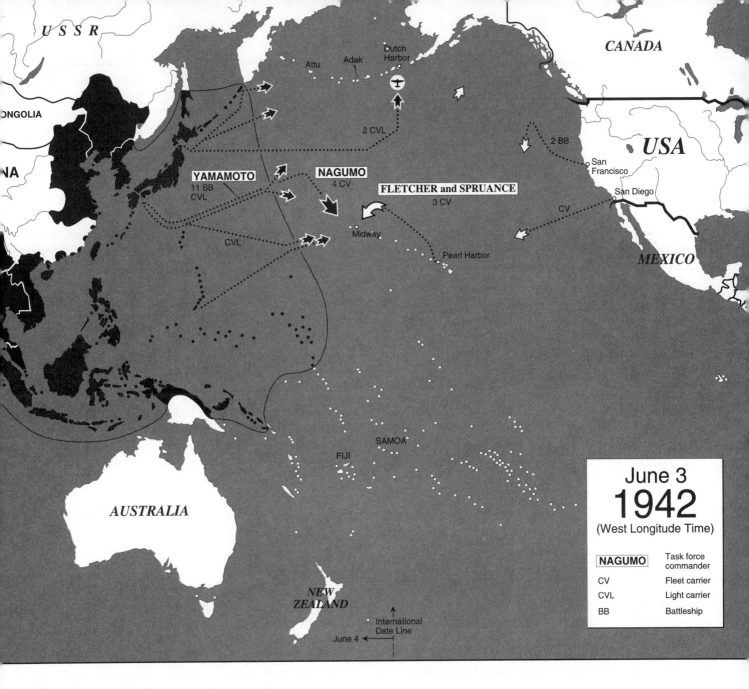

June 3
1942
(West Longitude Time)

NAGUMO	Task force commander
CV	Fleet carrier
CVL	Light carrier
BB	Battleship

ably would, provided that the repair teams limited themselves to what could be done in three days. And, thanks to round-the-clock working, a patched-up but battle-ready *Yorktown* did, in fact, make the rendezvous with the carriers *Enterprise* and *Hornet* on June 2nd.

The Japanese showed none of the same urgency. When their carriers *Shokaku* and *Zuikaku* returned from the Coral Sea, the assessment was that *Shokaku* needed a minimum of two months in the repair yards and undamaged *Zuikaku* much the same time, to rebuild its air groups. This assessment was accepted without demur by Admiral Nagumo, so Japan's tactical victory in the Coral Sea had actually reduced its advantage as regards the Midway

campaign: instead of six to four, the advantage was now four to three. Nagumo's view, shared by his staff, was that four to three would be quite sufficient: in fact, given the demonstrable superiority of the Japanese navy's air groups, he would probably have settled for an even match.

Apart from the two missing carriers, all Japanese units were in their allocated positions by the beginning of June. On June 3rd, planes from the light carriers *Ryujo* and *Junyo* made the diversionary raid on Dutch Harbor, which was supposed to confuse the Americans but which in fact merely told them that the information they had on the Japanese plan was correct. The same day, American planes operating from Midway found, and ineffectively bombed, the troop convoy headed for the island. The next day would see Admiral Nagumo's four-carrier striking force enter the battle zone and begin operations with a major raid on Midway.

Nagumo was right on time. At dawn on June 4th, the decks of all four carriers came alive as a first strike of 108 planes formed up. Two hours later these planes were closing on Midway, unworried by the few fighters that the island was able to put up in its defense. However, the results of the raid were disappointing. Forewarned, Midway had flown off its planes in good time, and the Japanese caught none on the ground. And the volume of antiaircraft fire proved formidable. If the landing was to go ahead, a lot more softening up was needed. The strike leader signaled Nagumo, "Need second wave."

Nagumo had been half expecting this. He had a second strike already armed in case any American carriers put in an appearance. Now he ordered these planes to be reequipped with bombs instead of torpedoes. This time-consuming work began as the ships were maneuvering to avoid a series of attacks by Midway-based planes—low-level torpedo bombers that were quickly cut to pieces by the Japanese fighter screen, and high-level bombers that suffered less but scored no hits either. Then, at 8:20 A.M., came a message that threw Nagumo's plans into reverse: a scout plane had spotted an American carrier two hours' flying time to the northeast. Midway immediately ceased to be the prime concern: the earlier order was rescinded and the armorers were told to put torpedoes back in place of bombs. While this was being done, the Midway strike was recovered. Then, with all his planes safely aboard and the torpedo bombers being readied for assembly on the carriers' decks, Nagumo turned away from Midway and toward the enemy.

The Americans, who knew when and where to look, had located Nagumo as early as 6 A.M., and Admiral Raymond Spruance, in command of *Enterprise* and *Hornet,* had begun launching full strikes from both carriers an hour later. Admiral Frank Jack Fletcher, his senior, and in direct command of *Yorktown,* held his hand till 8:30. Then he too put up every plane he could. In contrast to Spruance's squadrons, which fanned out over a 35-degree arc so as to be sure not to miss their mobile target, the *Yorktown* planes kept together, making a best guess as to where Nagumo would have gotten to by 10:30 A.M. This proved to be the better strategy. *Hornet*'s dive-bombers passed so far to the north that they missed the Japanese altogether,

while the carrier's torpedo bombers, which made a swing to the south, found their targets but, arriving on their own, had to face the undivided attention of the Japanese fighter screen. The result was a massacre. As the squadron's 15 planes made their slow run in toward the Japanese ships, the fighters picked them off one after another. A single plane got close enough to drop its torpedo, then it too was hacked down and spun into the sea. Nor did the *Enterprise*'s torpedo planes, which arrived shortly after, do much better: perhaps five or six got close enough to launch, but none scored, and only three escaped the pursuing fighters. When the third and last of the torpedo bomb squadrons arrived, the Japanese pilots must have felt they had the situation well in hand. If any of these lumbering aircraft were to penetrate the fighter screen, they would hardly be capable of making the sort of cool coordinated runs necessary to get hits.

In this they were entirely right. But what the Japanese failed to notice was that the near-suicidal attacks of the torpedo planes had pulled more and more of the defending fighters down to sea level. In fact, the skies above the carriers were wide open, and this at the very moment when the *Yorktown* dive-bombers were moving into position overhead. Even worse for the Japanese, the *Enterprise*'s dive-bomber squadrons, circling northward from their original flight path, arrived on the scene from the opposite direction at exactly the same moment. After a harrowing series of mischances, Spruance and Fletcher had achieved exactly the sort of focused air attack they had been looking for; a dozen torpedo bombers were in among the Japanese at sea level, and more than 40 dive-bombers stacked up above. As before, the unescorted torpedo bombers suffered terribly: perhaps five or six launched, but they scored no hits and only two survived. But there was nothing the Japanese could do to fend off the dive-bombers: indeed, they didn't even see them until, 20,000 feet overhead, the lead planes tipped over into their dives and their wings momentarily caught the sun.

The Americans went for the three nearest carriers: *Akagi, Kaga,* and *Soryu.* The carrier captains put their helms hard over to try and throw off the attackers' aim, but to no avail. Planes from the *Enterprise* scored two hits on *Akagi* and three on *Kaga;* planes from the *Yorktown* scored three on *Soryu.* As all three Japanese carriers were ready to launch—*Akagi*'s lead plane was actually taking off when the first bomb struck—they were little better than floating bombs themselves. The first hit on *Kaga* ignited the mass

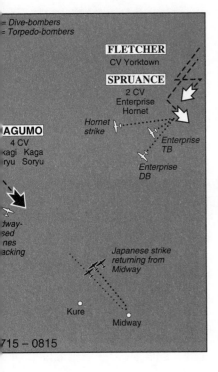

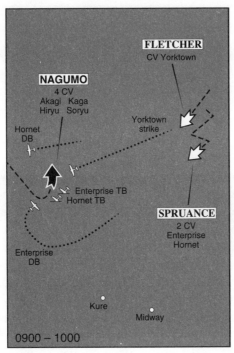

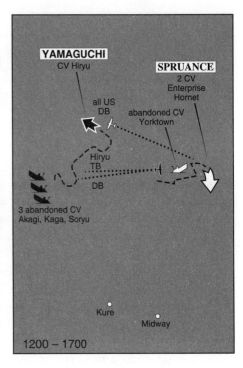

of fully armed and fueled planes crowded on its afterdeck, turning the deck into a sea of flames and the hangar below into an inferno. The next two hits spread the conflagration and doomed the ship. Even the off-loaded bombs originally intended for Midway played their part: there had been no time to return them to storage, and they were still on the hangar deck, ready to ignite in the blaze. On *Akagi* and *Soryu* the story was much the same: both were ripped apart, as much by the explosion of their own munitions as by American bombs. Five minutes earlier the battle had scarcely begun; now it was lost.

Not that the Japanese were prepared to admit it. They still had *Hiryu*, whose commander, Tamon Yamaguchi, was revered throughout the imperial navy for his fighting spirit. He immediately launched what he had—a squadron of dive-bombers followed, 2½ hours later, by a squadron of torpedo bombers. They did him proud. Boring in through *Yorktown*'s fighter screen, they made five hits on the carrier, two of them with torpedoes. It was enough to overwhelm *Yorktown*'s damage control and force its crew to abandon ship. Spruance handled the Americans' reply. By midafternoon he had 39 dive-bombers aloft—there were no flyable torpedo planes left—and at 5 P.M. they found *Hiryu*, made four hits, and reduced the last of Nagumo's carriers to an unsteerable wreck.

Admiral Yamamoto, aboard the newest and biggest of the battleships in the backup force, followed the day's events with mounting alarm. By evening he knew the

worst. His first thought was to try to force a night action, which would enable him to exploit his enormous preponderance in battleships (11 against none) and cruisers (10 to 5). But Spruance, who knew exactly how the Japanese commander's mind would be working, hauled off to the east, well out of harm's way. Early in the morning of June 5th, Yamamoto faced the fact that, without airpower, his position could not be sustained; abandoning any hope of retrieving the situation, he ordered all forces involved in the operations against Midway to turn about and set course for their home ports. Even in their retreat the Japanese were unlucky: two heavy cruisers collided and were unable to clear the area before they were picked up by American search planes. On June 6th Spruance found them, severely damaged one, and sank the other. They were the last Japanese casualties of the fleet action which Yamamoto had sought so eagerly, and which had turned out so differently from his expectations.

For the bitter truth was that the Japanese navy had fatally overreached itself. So far from cutting back the American navy to its roots, Midway had brought forward the day when American strength would become preponderant. Poor planning and abysmal security had thrown away an advantage that could never be retrieved. From now on there would be no more grandiose offensive schemes: the Japanese navy would have its work cut out to defend the empire's perimeter.[1]

1. For note see page 111

For the Japanese navy, defeat at Midway meant the automatic cancellation of the planned moves against Fiji and Samoa: there simply wasn't the carrier-based airpower left to support a major amphibious operation. But abandoning the initiative was anathema to the army, which regarded the navy as hesitant at the best of times and anyway put willpower above weaponry. Its answer was an offensive against Port Moresby by the overland route, across the Owen Stanley Mountains. The navy was shamed into making a small-scale supporting move, to Milne Bay at the tip of the New Guinea tail. Both moves failed, the land attack petering out because of the impossibility of getting sufficient supplies forward, the seaborne landing because the force involved was far too small. By November it was the Japanese who were on the defensive, attempting to hang on to Buna, at the northern end of the trail to Port Moresby, in the face of assaults by two air-supported divisions (one American, one Australian). At least the defenders did their job well: Buna didn't fall till January 1943.

During this period an equally fiercely contested and, as far as ships and planes were concerned, far more costly battle was being fought out in the Solomons. In July Admiral Nimitz had decided to make the islands the scene of America's first offensive by using the First Marine Division to take the Japanese seaplane base at Tulagi. Shortly after planning began, air reconnaissance found an airstrip under construction on the neighboring island of Guadalcanal; this immediately became the main target of the operation. The landing went off without a hitch on August 7th; the Marines established a perimeter defense around the captured airstrip (which they named Henderson Field), while a fighter screen supplied by the three carriers providing backup fended off most of the air attacks launched by the Japanese from Rabaul. So far, so good, but the Marines' position was going to be less happy when the carriers withdrew (which they did on the evening of August 8th) and the Japanese got their act together (which, in fact, they had already done). A Japanese cruiser force based on Rabaul sailed down the Slot (the channel between the two rows of Solomon Islands) and, late that night, surprised a similar-sized Australian-American flotilla posted to protect the beachhead. The subsequent battle of Savo Island was brief, bloody, and one-sided, the Japanese emerging almost unscathed while the Allied forces lost four of its five cruisers. The fact that the Japanese admiral failed to press on and shoot up the transports still unloading at the landing site was poor consolation for the Americans: they

had lost control of the waters around Guadalcanal, leaving the Japanese free to run nighttime convoys to the island, build up an army there, and try to recapture the airstrip. The Japanese couldn't operate by day because the Americans soon had Henderson operational, and aircraft based there made the lower Solomons a no-go area for Japanese shipping in the daytime. But if they set out at dusk, Japanese ships could run down the Slot, unload their supplies, and get back up to the northern Solomons and the protection of their own planes before dawn. If they were feeling particularly frisky, they could even find time to bombard the Marine bridgehead.

The American navy, of course, could contest these Japanese moves, and frequently did so. The Guadalcanal campaign consequently developed a pattern in which surface battles at night alternated with air and air-to-surface combats in daylight hours. Destroyers, cruisers, and, on occasion, battleships got to fire their guns at each other during the night actions, though the most effective weapon proved to be the torpedo. As the Japanese had the best torpedoes, their lavish use of these usually gave them the advantage. However, because the Americans could pick off stragglers during the daytime, there was not much difference in the final score: the Japanese lost 2 battleships, 4 cruisers, and 14 destroyers in the course of the campaign, as against the Americans' 8 cruisers and 10 destroyers.

There were also two carrier battles. The first, the battle of the eastern Solomons on August 24, 1943, saw the Japanese advancing a light carrier, the *Ryujo*, as bait, while *Zuikaku* and *Shokaku* lay further back ready to strike the American carriers when they revealed their position. The stratagem was clearly based on the successful combination achieved—more by luck than by foresight—in the battle of the Coral Sea. It half worked. The Americans duly sank the proffered *Ryujo;* but the Japanese, though they got in a major strike on the two American carriers responsible, *Enterprise* and *Saratoga,* managed only three hits on the *Enterprise,* not enough to sink it. As far as the Americans were concerned, this was a victory; in truth, it was a missed opportunity: they had four fleet carriers available but failed to concentrate them and failed to find the Japanese striking force. By the next battle they had lost their advantage (*Wasp* had been sunk by a submarine and *Saratoga* damaged by another), and the battle of Santa Cruz (October 26th) saw *Shokaku, Zuikaku,* and the light carrier *Zuiho* trading strikes with *Enterprise* and *Hornet* on equal terms. Once again *Enterprise* was hit three times

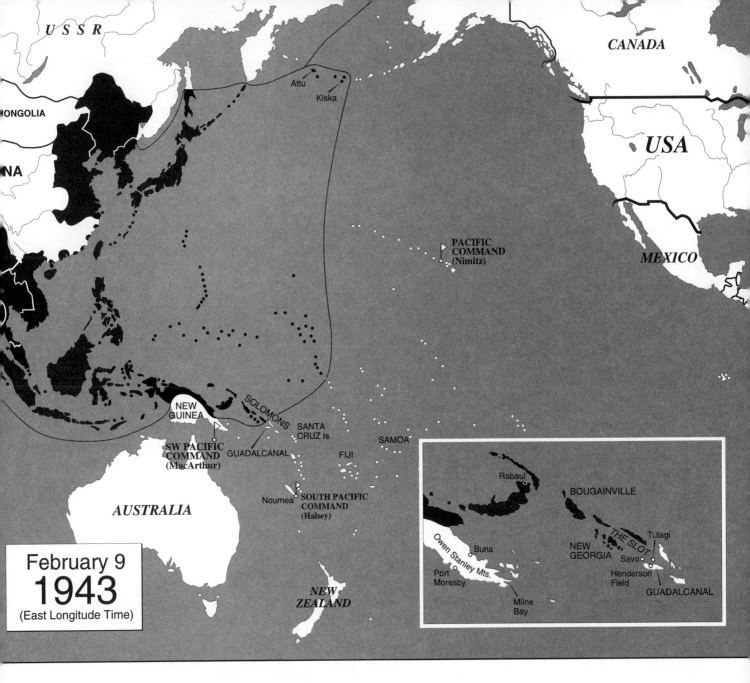

February 9
1943
(East Longitude Time)

but survived: *Hornet* was not so fortunate, taking torpedo and bomb hits that forced the crew to abandon it. The Americans could manage only nonfatal hits on *Shokaku* and *Zuiho.* As *Enterprise* withdrew, Japanese surface ships had the satisfaction of dispatching *Hornet,* bringing the tally of fleet carriers sunk to four a side.

If this was a morale-booster for the Japanese navy, the Japanese army had less to be pleased about: all its attacks on the Guadalcanal bridgehead had failed. At its best the force deployed on the island amounted to less than two divisions, nothing like enough to win against an American defense that eventually built up to three. In January 1943, headquarters at Rabaul made the decision to evacu-

ate the remaining troops, and this was duly done in early February. In both Papua and the southern Solomons, the battle had gone America's way.[1]

*1. All 10,000 surviving Japanese were successfully lifted from the island before the Americans realized what was happening; they represented about a third of the troops deployed during the campaign. American losses were much lighter, around 1600 out of 60,000.

The American effort in the Solomons was directed by a South Pacific command (headquarters at Noumea, New Caledonia) that reported to Admiral Nimitz. The New Guinea operation was run by General MacArthur's Southwest Pacific command. MacArthur moved his HQ up from Melbourne to Brisbane at the start of the campaign in July 1942, and from Brisbane to Port Moresby in November.

The Americans' success at Guadalcanal confirmed that they had seized the initiative; the next step, the rupture of the defensive perimeter established by Japan in the opening months of the war, was to take a year of equally hard fighting. The first task the Americans set themselves, the undermining of the New Guinea–Solomons angle, was slowed by the awesomely difficult terrain, the dig-in-and-die tactics adopted by the Japanese, and the necessity of building airfields to support each phase of the advance. In fact, by the beginning of November 1943, nine months after the end of the Buna and Guadalcanal campaigns, the Australian and American troops in New Guinea had gotten no further than the Huon peninsula, and the naval and marine forces making the climb up the Solomons ladder had only just reached Bougainville. Rabaul, the linchpin of the Japanese defense system in this sector, remained conspicuously intact.

At this point the pace quickened. America's naval construction program had yielded its first major dividends in the summer, when 3 *Essex*-class fleet carriers (out of 24 on order) and 5 *Independence*-class light carriers (out of 9) joined the Pacific fleet. Their arrival meant that Admiral Nimitz had at his disposal carrier-based airpower to the tune of 600 planes, enough to obliterate the land-based opposition on any of the smaller Pacific archipelagos. Nimitz used his new ships to open up a new axis of advance in the Central Pacific. The first step was to clear the Japanese out of the Gilberts. There were only two defended atolls in the group, Makin and Tarawa; Nimitz seized both in November. In the new year he moved against the Marshalls. Here there were six atolls with garrisons, but Nimitz decided to focus on just two, Kwajalein and Eniwetok. Both were secured at relatively low cost in February 1944, and their capture proved to be all that was necessary to establish control over the group. The Japanese on the four unconquered islands, lacking both air and sea power, simply became impotent spectators of the war. They had been bypassed.

The same concept, it had already been decided, could be applied to Rabaul, which had been hit so hard and so often by this time that the Japanese high command had pulled out its air and naval groups. In April, MacArthur simply moved past it—and past the main Japanese army in New Guinea as well—by shipping a corps to Hollandia in the Dutch half of the island. The Hollandia landing not only achieved complete surprise; it totally undid Japanese plans for the defense of this part of the perimeter. The

ability of Nimitz's carriers to project airpower as and where it was needed had enabled MacArthur to take a larger-than-expected stride on the road to Tokyo.

The question now was what the Americans would do next. The basic strategy was obvious, a westward drive that would split the Japanese empire in two and separate the homeland from the oil it needed to keep its war machine running. This could be achieved either by advancing from the Marshalls to the Marianas and then on to Taiwan (as Nimitz wanted to do), or (as MacArthur preferred) by moving up from New Guinea to the Philippines. Ultimately the chiefs of staff in Washington decided to combine both approaches, but from the Japanese point of view the exact line hardly mattered: any further advance would be fatal. The imperial navy, which had been dithering about when and where to fight its next battle, suddenly found itself with only one option: it had to block the next American advance. If it couldn't do that, the war was lost.

The crunch came in June, when Nimitz moved against the Marianas. His deputy, Admiral Spruance, had overall command of the two fleets involved. Of these the first had the task of transporting, landing, and supporting the five divisions earmarked for the conquest of the islands (starting with Saipan); it had seven escort carriers (merchant ship conversions) to provide the necessary local air cover. The second consisted of seven fleet carriers and eight light carriers, capable of putting up more than 800 planes between them; its function was to parry any blow that might be delivered by the commander of the Japanese Mobile Fleet, Admiral Jisaburo Ozawa.[1]

Ozawa couldn't muster as many ships or planes as Spruance: he had three fleet carriers and six light carriers, with 430 planes all told. But he did have some advantages. Planes in the Marianas—of which there were some 170—should be able to tell him where the Americans were and join in his attacks on them. And because his planes were capable of flying farther than their American equivalents, he should be able to get his strikes off first. In important ways this was the Midway situation in reverse, and Ozawa had high hopes of winning the victory that the empire needed so badly. On June 13th, the day Spruance began the bombardment of Saipan, he led the Mobile Fleet from its anchorage at Tawitawi in the Sulu archipelago and set course for the Marianas.

Ozawa achieved the tactical surprise he wanted. By the evening of June 18th, he knew exactly where Spruance

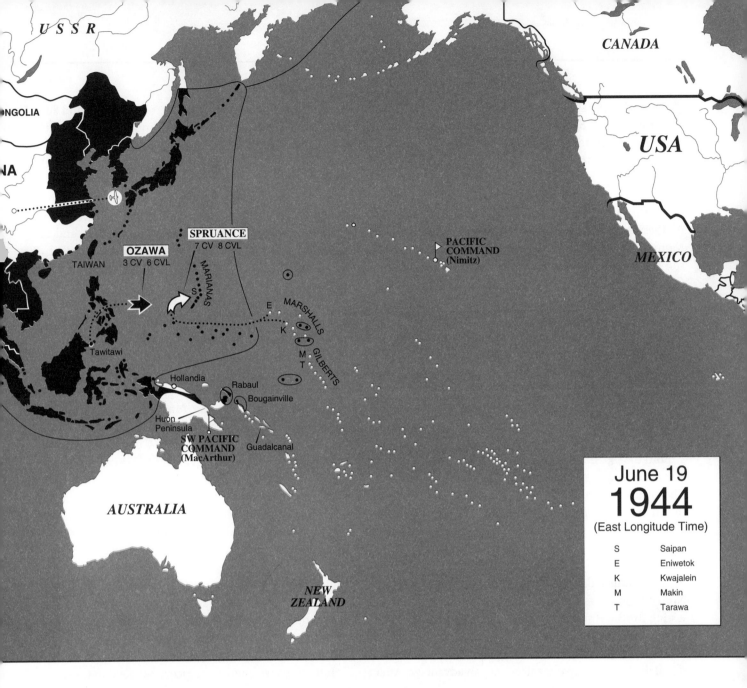

USSR

CANADA

NGOLIA

USA

SPRUANCE
7 CV 8 CVL

OZAWA
3 CV 6 CVL

TAIWAN

MEXICO

MARIANAS

S

E   MARSHALLS

K

Tawitawi

M

T   GILBERTS

Hollandia

Rabaul

Bougainville

Huon
Peninsula

**SW PACIFIC
COMMAND
(MacArthur)**   Guadalcanal

**PACIFIC
COMMAND
(Nimitz)**

AUSTRALIA

June 19
1944
(East Longitude Time)

S	Saipan
E	Eniwetok
K	Kwajalein
M	Makin
T	Tarawa

**NEW
ZEALAND**

was; and in the course of the next day he got off four strikes, totaling 328 aircraft, without the Americans' being able to locate him, let alone hit back. It was all to no avail. Since the last round of carrier encounters the Americans had upped the scale, the style, and the technology of this type of warfare in a manner that put them in a different class from the Japanese. They not only had more ships and planes, but their ships and planes were better and their crews were better trained. Radar-directed fighters intercepted the Japanese strikes at long range and cut them to pieces: only a few bombers managed to get through to the American carriers, and they scored no hits.

In what the Americans contemptuously termed the "great Marianas turkey shoot," Ozawa lost 230 of the 328 planes he had dispatched, for a zero result.[2]

The next day the battle petered out. At the time the Americans regarded it as a disappointment: in reality it was as crushing a victory as Midway. The Japanese were clearly incapable of preventing the Americans from extending their existing supremacy at sea into Japanese home waters. A month after the battle General Tojo, who as prime minister had led Japan to war, tendered his resignation to the emperor.[3]

*1. *2. *3. *For notes see pages 111–112*

Clearing the southern Marianas—Guam and Tinian as well as Saipan—took Admiral Nimitz's command till the end of August 1944, by which time it had been agreed that the Philippines would be the next major target and that Nimitz and MacArthur would combine forces for the operation. In September MacArthur established forward bases for his air squadrons with landings on the Vogelkop (the head of the New Guinea bird) and Morotai (off Halmahera, where a strong Japanese garrison was effectively sidelined); Nimitz took Ulithi atoll (a useful forward base for the fleet) and Peleliu (not worth its high cost). Finally, in mid-October, the armadas required for the invasion of the Philippines assembled—the frontline fleet under Admiral William Halsey and the transports and support ships under Admiral Thomas Kinkaid. The island chosen for the initial landing was Leyte, between Samar and Mindanao. By the end of A Day (October 20th) elements of four divisions were safely ashore, as was General MacArthur himself, announcing his return with understandable emotion.

Both the Japanese army and the Japanese navy had determined to give their all in defense of the Philippines. The army, with 13 divisions in the islands, was confident that it could stem the American tide. The navy had no such illusions: the plan it came up with was the equivalent of a banzai charge, the all-out suicidal onslaught that effectively conceded that the battle was lost and simply tried to do as much damage as possible on the way down. Nonetheless it was the navy's show that proved the more testing for the Americans. This was partly because of its sheer scale—just about every ship still afloat took part in it—and partly because of the way it turned a weakness, the division of the Japanese fleet, into an advantage. After the Marianas operation the Japanese battleships and cruisers had withdrawn to an anchorage near Singapore where there was still enough oil to keep them in business: the carriers had gone home in the vain hope of rebuilding their air groups. In consequence, there was now a striking force of big-gun ships to the west of the Philippines, and a set of completely useless carriers to the north. Well, not entirely useless, because they could make attractive targets for carrier-obsessed American airmen. So the navy planned to use the carriers (Admiral Ozawa in command, as at the Marianas) to draw the American battle fleet (Halsey) away from the Leyte bridgehead, allowing the battleships and cruisers (the bulk of them under the command of Admiral Takeo Kurita) to thread their way through the Philippines via the San Bernardino and Surigao Straits and pulp as many of Admiral Kinkaid's transports and support ships as possible.

By October 24th the Japanese fleets converging on the Philippines had all been sighted by the Americans: the sacrificial carriers, under Ozawa, moving down from Japan; the main force of battleships and cruisers, under Kurita, heading for the San Bernardino Strait and the northern approach to Leyte Gulf; and a detachment of two battleships and a cruiser, under Admiral Shoji Nishimura, making for the Surigao Strait and Leyte Gulf's southern end. Kurita's force had taken a bit of a battering, losing two cruisers to submarine attacks and a battleship to air strikes from Halsey's carriers. But it was far from being knocked out, as Halsey wanted to believe when he took his entire fleet—carriers and battleships—off north to deal with Ozawa. Astonishingly, Halsey had taken the proffered bait and left the San Bernardino Strait unguarded and Kurita free to sail through it. The outlook for the shipping milling about in Leyte Gulf was all the more grim because Kinkaid, believing that Halsey was protecting the northern flank of the gulf, had led such heavy ships as he possessed to Surigao Strait. Once there, he annihilated Nishimura's force in a perfectly coordinated night action, but come the morning, he was too far away to respond to the calls for help that began to come in from the gulf, and in particular from "Taffy 3." This highly vulnerable group of escort carriers had barely begun its roster of support missions for the troops on Leyte when its lookouts identified smudges on the horizon as Japanese warships. Kurita, with four battleships and six cruisers, had made it to the gulf.

Taffy 3, consisting of six escort carriers and a seven-strong destroyer screen, appeared doomed. In fact, it escaped with the loss of one carrier and three destroyers, while the rest of the "soft targets" in and around Leyte Gulf never came under fire at all. Kurita's force, constantly under air attack, was simply too exhausted to make use of its opportunity and, after losing three of its cruisers to destroyer and air strikes, broke off the action and withdrew the way it had come. At the last moment the will to suicide had failed.[1]

Not that the navy was short of individuals willing to give their lives for the emperor. The naval air arm got an enthusiastic response when it asked for volunteers for one-way kamikaze missions (named for the typhoons that wrecked Kublai's invasion fleets in the late thirteenth

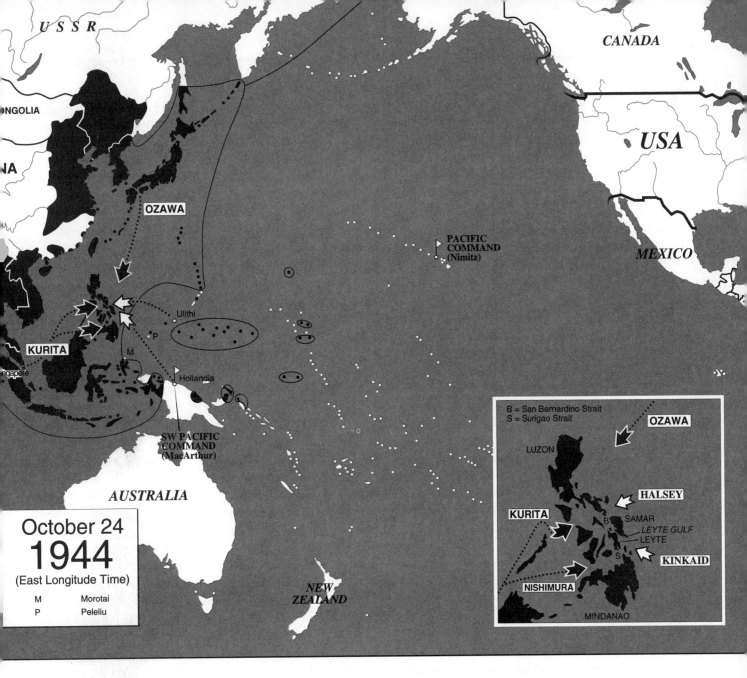

century), and the first squadrons specializing in such operations were activated on the eve of the Philippines campaign. During the battle of Leyte Gulf a kamikaze sank one of Taffy 3's carriers, which was as much as Kurita managed to do with four battleships in as many hours.[2]

In the course of 1944 the Japanese, stung by the air attacks the Americans were making from China, launched a series of offensives in the center and south of the country. Chiang Kai-shek's inability to cope with these completed America's disillusionment with his government: the B-29s were transferred to the Marianas, and plans to follow up on the Philippines campaign with a landing on the south

China coast were dropped. In India, Allied air superiority enabled British and Indian ground forces to defeat the Japanese invasion, but the Allied attempt to regain and reopen the Burma road stalled far short of its objective.

*1. Aside from exhaustion, Kurita must surely have been influenced by the feeble performance of his ships: his guns weren't able to inflict damage at the same rate as the swarm of aircraft put up by Taffys 1 to 3 (18 escort carriers in all), even though these were not equipped
(footnotes continued on page 112)

From Leyte, which took two months to conquer, MacArthur moved on to Mindoro (mid-December 1944) and then Luzon (early January 1945). Names that meant a lot to Americans—Manila, Bataan, Corregidor—reappeared in the communiqués, though as the Japanese fought with their usual tenacity it was early March before all were once more in American hands. Meanwhile, Nimitz's command had taken Iwo Jima in the Volcano Islands. Iwo Jima was to provide valuable support for the Marianas-based B-29 offensive but came at a high price: 25,000 casualties to eliminate the same number of Japanese.

The next stop proved even more costly. The army needed a forward base for the culminating operation of the war, the invasion of Japan. Early on in the planning, Amoy on the south China coast had been the favored option; later, Taiwan was preferred. Eventually the choice fell on Okinawa, the largest of the Ryukyus. The initial landing was unopposed, but there were well-prepared defenses in the southern half of the island, and it took an army of seven divisions three months (April to June) to dispose of the 100,000 Japanese manning them. The price paid was not limited to the 40,000 casualties suffered by the troops ashore; another 10,000 casualties were suffered by the navy, most of them as a result of kamikaze attacks. Although no major units were lost, the 1200-strong invasion fleet had 34 of its ships sunk and 368 damaged.

Losses on an even larger scale were bound to be incurred during the invasion of Japan. This was scheduled to begin in November with a landing on Kyushu by the Sixth Army (14 divisions). Five months later the Eighth and Tenth armies, totaling 25 divisions, would begin the reduction of Honshu. If the Japanese fought to the bitter end—and all the indications were that this was exactly what they intended to do—the invading forces were likely to suffer several hundred thousand casualties, perhaps half a million. How many Japanese would choose to immolate themselves was anybody's guess, but the total would certainly be in the millions.

Was there any way of avoiding this grim arithmetic? Was it possible to loosen the grip the military had on the Japanese mind? The B-29 bombing campaign had certainly brought the war home to the man in the street. After several false starts the bombers had found the tactics they needed, and a series of firebombings beginning in February had laid waste the centers of most of Japan's major cities. A single raid, on the night of March 9th, burned out 16 square miles of Tokyo, and killed, at a conservative estimate, more than 70,000 people. But there was no sign of any crack in civilians' morale: the Japanese people continued to obey the instructions of their totally unyielding leadership. Something truly extraordinary would be required to break open the iron front presented by this most disciplined and fatalistic of nations.

On July 16th Harry Truman, who had succeeded to the presidency on Roosevelt's death in April, learned that he had the weapon he needed: an atomic bomb with a destructive force equivalent to 20,000 tons of conventional explosive. The first example had just been successfully tested at Alamogordo, New Mexico. On August 6th, a B-29 carried another prototype bomb from Tinian in the Marianas to Hiroshima, Honshu, where its detonation killed some 60,000 people. A second bomb was dropped on Nagasaki to similar effect three days later. In between these two catastrophes came another, equally shattering to Japan's leadership: Russia had joined the circle of its enemies, and Soviet armored columns were thrusting deep into Manchuria. The cabinet was forced to consider the previously taboo question of surrender.

The civilian members of the cabinet had little doubt that immediate capitulation was the only practical course. The army held out for a chance to fight one last battle and continued to do so even after the emperor directed that America's terms be accepted. Four days later the army was still refusing to budge: this time the emperor spoke in the clearest terms, and the minister of the army reluctantly acquiesced. Messages were sent indicating Japan's willingness to surrender, the only proviso being the retention of the emperor's position as head of state. The next day, August 15th, the emperor, in his first broadcast, told his weeping subjects that they must "bear the unbearable." The war was over.[1]

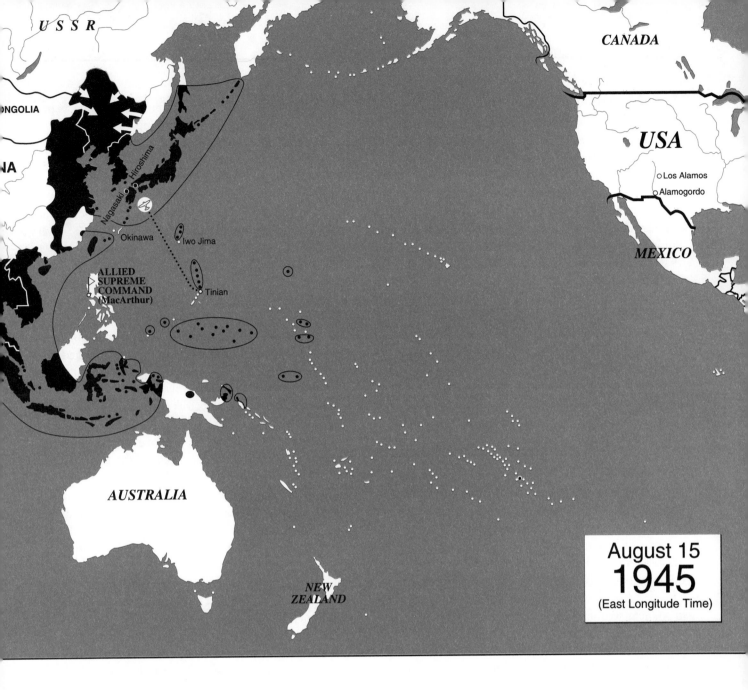

*1. MacArthur's forces had liberated the entire Philippine archipel-
ago by June: that same month saw the Australians move into North
Borneo. British and Indian forces recovered Burma in December
1944–May 1945 and were getting ready to go for Singapore when the
war ended. Japanese troops relinquished some of their gains in south
China during this period, and they lost Fuzhou and Wenzhou on the
coast.

MacArthur, who had moved his headquarters up to Manila when
the city was liberated (after great slaughter) in March 1945, was
nominated Allied supreme commander for the invasion of Japan
and, as such, received the Japanese surrender.

World War II brought the United States the superpower status that it had been toying with, but never fully accepted, since the beginning of the century. Nowhere was this more obvious than in the Pacific, where the U.S. Navy had carried all before it and now ran a string of bases extending across the ocean to the Philippines and Japan. But in neither the Philippines nor Japan did America intend to maintain an imperial role: the Philippines were given independence as promised in 1946, and the military administration in Japan was already beginning to wind down by early 1950. The only new long-term commitment was to the Central Pacific islands that had been mandated to Japan before the war: these were transferred to American trusteeship by the United Nations—the successor to the League of Nations—in 1947.

Russia also made gains at Japan's expense, quite considerable gains considering that it had been in the Pacific war for only a week. The southern half of Sakhalin, lost in 1905, was recovered, as were the Kurils, not only those renounced in 1875 but also the three nearest Japan, which had never been in Russian hands before. And in Manchuria the Soviets insisted on picking up where the tsars had left off, with a lease of Port Arthur and a stake in the railroads. Needless to say, these enforced concessions caused much resentment among the Chinese Nationalists, who had been hoping that postwar China would be free of all such blemishes on its sovereignty. However, Chiang Kai-shek's government had more to worry about in Manchuria than the question of Port Arthur and the railroads: under one pretext or another the Russians were preventing Nationalist troops from entering the country and were using the time gained, plus weaponry captured from the Japanese, to strengthen the local Communists. By the time Chiang did get his men in, the best they could do was occupy the major towns: the countryside was firmly in communist hands. In 1947 the situation seemed to stabilize along these lines, but in the course of the next year the communists brought the cities under siege and, one after another, snuffed out their garrisons. These had been some of the best units in Chiang's never very brilliant army, and their loss left the generalissimo with insufficient forces to suppress the insurgency in China proper. By late 1948, communist formations were astride the Beijing-Nanjing railway, and in early 1949 they started closing in on the capital. Chiang Kai-shek fled to Taiwan (surrendered by Japan at the war's end), abandoning the mainland to the new People's Republic of China as proclaimed by its chairman, Mao Zedong.

Communism had not made a more important gain since the Russian Revolution of 1917. The result was a surge of optimism about the prospects for further advance, with the Korean peninsula as its immediate focus. Korea had been divided into Russian and American zones in 1945, with the result that, when the occupying powers withdrew in 1948–1949, there were separate regimes in the two halves. Now the North invaded the South (June 1950) and had nearly conquered it when American troops landed on the west coast, recaptured the southern capital, Seoul, and forced the attackers to retreat (September). The drama was then replayed, with the Americans overrunning the North, only to be counterattacked and ejected by the Chinese (November). A busy year closed with the issue still unresolved.

Thanks to America's victory over Japan, the British were able to recover their prewar possessions in the Pacific (including Hong Kong, an enclave which, much to everyone's surprise, was respected by the communists). However, the British were sensible enough to realize that it was no longer possible to impose an empire where it wasn't wanted, and that this meant giving up India (in 1947) and Burma (in 1948). Less creditable was the way the British agreed to help the French and Dutch try to recover their colonial holdings. As far as the Dutch were concerned, it soon became apparent that the task was far beyond their strength, and in 1949 they recognized the republic of Indonesia as heir to the Indies, excepting only West New Guinea. They hung on there on the grounds that the inhabitants were not Malay, didn't want to be part of a Malay state, and weren't ready for self-rule. These propositions were all evident truths, but they didn't have much relevance in the existing political context and were seen by most outsiders as just an excuse for some residual Dutch obstinacy.

The resumption of French rule in Indochina got off to a smoother start: Cambodia, Laos, and the southern provinces of Vietnam were all occupied without significant fuss. However, in the north of Vietnam the communist leader Ho Chi Minh had established an independent state immediately following the Japanese surrender, and the French found that they needed his cooperation to facilitate their return. Negotiations as to the exact nature of this cooperation continued until the French felt strong enough to seize Hanoi, which they did in 1946. The

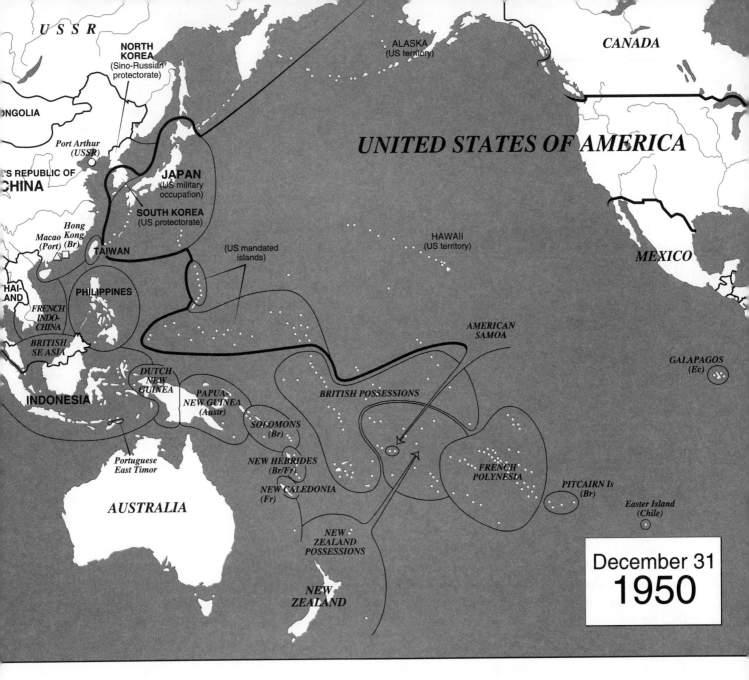

French army then won the opening round in the subsequent guerrilla war. So far, so good.

In 1946 Thailand was forced to disgorge the various Burmese, Malay, and Indo-Chinese provinces given to it by Japan: for a short time the country also went back to calling itself Siam (1946–1949).

The cold war—the confrontation between the communist bloc and the free world—was at its hottest during the Korean conflict. This ended in a grudging standoff—near enough on the basis of the *status quo ante*—in 1953. Over the next 40 years tensions gradually eased, and in 1991, when Russia officially repudiated both Marxism and the Soviet imperial system, the era of ill will came to an end. As its protagonists had always said it would, the idea of individual freedom had prevailed. Even in countries that retained a communist constitution, such as China, the state began to do less and let the people do more.

Before this happy state of affairs came about, the United States was to have some mortifying years attempting to keep Vietnam in the western camp. At Dien Bien Phu in 1954, Ho Chi Minh won a decisive victory over the French, who consequently decided to cut their losses and pull out. Rather than see the whole country go communist, America set up a new government for its southern half in the hope that the contrast between the two regimes—between the hard-line communism of Ho Chi Minh in Hanoi and the more liberal if not actually democratic administration in Saigon—would win local hearts and minds. After all, a similar program seemed to be working well in Korea. Alas, a better analogy would have been postwar China: the Saigon regime turned out to be, like Chiang Kai-shek's in the 1940s, hopelessly corrupt and totally ineffective as a belligerent. To keep it going the Americans had to commit first "military advisers" and then increasing numbers of ground troops, until by 1967 they had half a million men in the field. Even this didn't do the trick: in 1969 a disillusioned President Nixon began a reduction in the commitment, and by 1973 the Americans had gone. Saigon fell two years later, with the official reunification of Vietnam following in 1976.[1]

America's crisis of conscience over Vietnam was intensified by the fact that, whatever the war's origins, it ended up looking suspiciously like an old-style colonial venture—and that at a time when the traditional colonial powers were pulling out of the region. Russia gave China back its Manchurian railroads in 1952 and Port Arthur in 1954. The British withdrew from Malaya in 1957 and from most of North Borneo in 1963; these two areas were then combined under the name Malaysia. The predominantly Chinese island of Singapore first tried life as part of Malaya (1957–1959) and then as a component of Malaysia (1963–1965) before ending up as a sovereign

city-state. Oil-rich Brunei made another such enclave (1984). In Melanesia the Dutch relinquished West New Guinea to the Indonesians in 1963; the Australians withdrew from Papua–New Guinea in 1975; and the British withdrew from the Solomons in 1978. Fiji became independent in 1970, and the New Hebrides (which took the name of Vanuatu, meaning "Our Land Forever") in 1980.

Polynesia has proved more testing for the decolonizers, as many of the island groups are not really viable on their own. West Samoa received its independence in 1962, Nauru in 1968, and Tonga in 1970. The Ellice Islands became free (as Tuvalu) in 1978. The Gilberts were combined with Ocean Island (now Banaba), the Phoenix group, and the British Line Islands to form the state of Kiribati (pidgin for Gilberts, and pronounced Kiribass) in 1979.[2] The Tokelaus, the Northern and Southern Cooks, and Niue remain in voluntary association with New Zealand, the Pitcairn group with Britain. The French have hung on to all their islands as well as New Caledonia in Melanesia.

The United States has maintained its dominant role in the Pacific but has pulled its horns in somewhat. Japan had its sovereignty fully restored in 1951–1952: it got back the Bonins and Volcanos in 1968 and Okinawa and the other southern Ryukyus in 1972. Of the Central Pacific islands, the Palaus became independent (as the republic of Belau) in 1994; the other acquisitions—the northern Marianas, the Carolines (now the Federated States of Micronesia), and the Marshalls—continue in variously expressed forms of dependency. Alaska and Hawaii achieved statehood in 1959.

A few disputes remain, none too worrying. The Chinese, naturally enough, want Taiwan back but appear prepared to wait till this happens peaceably; as they were notably patient about Hong Kong (returned in 1997) and Macao (due back in 1999), it seems unlikely that they will take a chance on what would be a very difficult military option. The Japanese similarly hope for the voluntary return of the three nearest Kurils. North Korea still spits hatred at just about everyone, but it is so rundown after years of communist misrule that it probably isn't capable of causing any lasting mischief. That leaves Indonesia, which is having trouble coming to terms with the fact that the Christian people of East Timor, annexed shortly after declaring their independence from Portugal in 1974, don't want to be part of an Islamic state. Also Bougainville, which seems determined to secede from

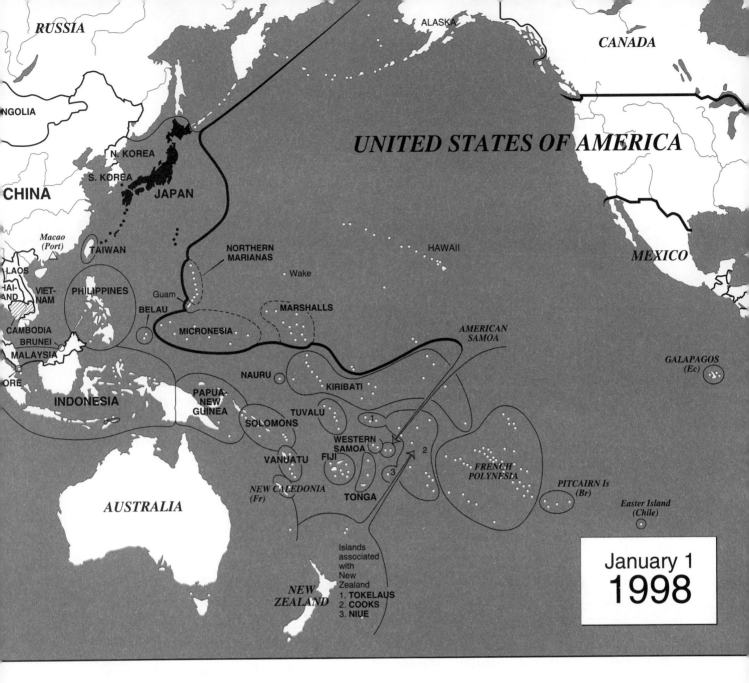

Papua–New Guinea. Not a long list for half the globe. Further reasons for optimism are to be found in the rising tide of prosperity observable at many points in the hemisphere. The original "tiger economies"—Japan, Taiwan, and Singapore—have recently been joined by others that looked as though they would never be able to move at the same sort of pace: South Korea, Thailand, Malaysia, the Philippines, and, most important of all, the vast, traditionally mismanaged, enigmatic monster that is China. The next millennium should be a lot more comfortable, if less exciting, than the last.

*1. Cambodia and Laos, which had been relinquished by the French in 1953, went communist in the aftermath of the American pullout. This was as far as the much feared "domino effect" went: Thailand remained firmly in the western camp. In fact, the next war in the region was between two communist states, Vietnam and Cambodia. Provoked by Cambodia's murderous Pol Pot, this war resulted in a Vietnamese occupation of Cambodia (1979–1989), followed by the reintroduction of a supposedly democratic regime, under the auspices of the United Nations, in 1993. During the reign of Pol Pot, Cambodia was known as Kampuchea; Burma has been calling itself Myanmar since 1988.

*2. Kiribati plans to capitalize on its position straddling the international date line and be the first nation to enter the year 2000. How-

(footnote continued on page 112)

Additional Notes

AD 1522

(continued from page 35)
*1. The total number of survivors of the circumnavigation was 35 (del Cano's 18 plus 13 left in the Cape Verde Islands and later repatriated, plus four of the *Trinidad*'s crew who eventually made it back to Spain). This was out of an initial complement of about 250, though the 50 or so who were aboard the vessel that defected in the strait have to be deducted from this total.

It is a measure of the high value attached to spices that despite all its losses, the expedition made a profit, the *Victoria*'s cargo of cloves more than paying the cost of fitting out all five of the ships. Pleased with the results, Charles V gave del Cano a coat of arms with the motto *Primus circumdedisti me* ("First to circumnavigate me"). Magellan, the architect of the voyage, was largely forgotten. The Portuguese regarded him as a traitor, and the Spanish as a foreign upstart who had almost wrecked the enterprise. It is only relatively recently that he has taken his rightful place among the makers of the modern world.

AD 1590

(continued from page 41)
Minor points: The Portuguese, expelled from Ternate in 1576, established a fort on the rival island of Tidore two years later. Sulu broke away from Brunei when the latter passed under Spanish control for a short spell (1578). Perak passed under the rule of Atjeh (1575).

AD 1741

(continued from page 57)
Soon after Roggeveen's visit the islanders began pulling the statues over—and doing so with the same enthusiasm that they had shown earlier in putting them up. The result was that by the early nineteenth century not a single one was left standing. This, and the later islanders' apparent lack of knowledge about the nature and purpose of the statues, led to the theory that they were the work of an earlier wave of colonists (perhaps from South America) who had succumbed to the current islanders (admitted by all to be Polynesians) not long before Roggeveen's arrival. The emotional pull of the "lost civilization" theory was enhanced by pictures of strange beetle-browed but eyeless colossi staring out to sea from the grassy slopes of Rano Raraku.

Recent studies have shown that most of Easter Island's questions have relatively straightforward answers and that there is no need to look outside Polynesia for any aspect of its culture. The statues are simply unusually large examples of a well-recognized type of Polynesian funerary figure. They were erected in rows on the seaside burial platforms used by the island's clans. Their backs were always to the sea to make it easy for ancestral spirits, whose afterlives were spent in islands over the horizon, to drop in and enjoy the offerings laid before them. The enigmatic-looking statues on Rano Raraku

were on their way to the burial grounds when the cult, which had grown to unsustainable proportions, was abandoned; their eye sockets were empty because the disappointingly garish eyes were added only when they reached their destination. On arrival they were presumably erected by rocking them up with levers, preserving the height gained by inserting stones underneath. The only mystery that remains is how they were moved from quarry to burial ground, a topic on which there is as yet no firm evidence.

AD 1782

(continued from page 65)
missed the Strait of Juan de Fuca. Heceta saw the mouth of the Columbia but didn't investigate.

This Spanish effort, intended to preempt British and Russian claims on the northwest, had no such effect. Alta California, on the other hand, filled out a bit with the foundation of San Francisco (1776) and Los Angeles (1781). Also worth noting is the northwest expansion of British North America. The impulse behind this was a widening search for beaver pelts; the organization was provided by the *voyageurs* of Montreal, who opened up a route from Lake Superior to Lake Athabasca.

Siam took Chiang Mai from Burma in 1775 and reduced the Laotian principalities to subordinate status in 1778.

AD 1790

(continued from page 67)
voyage the ship's second in command, Fletcher Christian, led a mutiny, which ended up with a protesting Bligh being bundled into the ship's launch along with 18 loyal members of the crew.

Bligh's task was both simple and arduous: to get himself back to civilization. The nearest European post he knew of was Kupang, in Dutch Timor, 4000 miles (6500 kilometers) to the west: it is a tribute to his seamanship that he completed the journey without significant mishap. He was back in England, bent on vengeance, by early 1790. Meanwhile the mutineers had split into two groups. The majority opted to stay in Tahiti despite the near-certainty of retribution: Christian, with eight mutineers and 19 Polynesians, looked for a safer haven and eventually found it in Pitcairn. The Tahitian contingent was duly rounded up by the Royal Navy, and of the ten who reached England, three were hanged. Christian's group remained undiscovered till 1807, when an American sealer, the *Topaz* of Boston, visited Pitcairn and was hailed by what appeared to be a couple of English-speaking Polynesians.

AD 1805

(continued from page 69)
Van Dieman's Land: by 1805 the total population had risen to 7000. Communications improved too: George Bass and Matthew Flinders's discovery of Bass Strait in 1802–1803 cut the sailing time

from London to Sydney by two weeks. Flinders then went on to circumnavigate Australia—a name that, thanks to his advocacy, soon became the generally accepted term for the country as a whole.

The inhabited islands of the Hawaiian archipelago were bought under one rule by King Kamehameha I—Hawaii itself in 1791; the others, except Kauai, in the later 1790s; and Kauai in 1810.

AD 1860

(continued from page 75)
*1. In 1855 the Russians also made a treaty with Japan: this confirmed the existing division of the Kurils and established joint sovereignty over Sakhalin. Elsewhere, existing colonial governments were rounding out their possessions. The British took lower Burma in 1852 and the Andamans in 1857. The Dutch absorbed Bali (1856) and Siak (1858) and confined the Portuguese to East Timor (1851). The Spanish conquered Mindanao (1860). The French, thwarted as regards Australia, established a penal colony on New Caledonia (1853); they also occupied Saigon, in southern Vietnam, following the massacre of a Catholic mission there (1859). In Australia the new colonies of Victoria and Queensland were set up with governments at Melbourne (1851) and Brisbane (1859); Van Dieman's land changed its name to Tasmania in 1853. In America the frontier between the United States and Mexico took its final form with the Gadsden Purchase of 1853.

Population in AD 1875

(continued from page 77)
deciphered, but it is clear that at least some of the boards record creation myths and that the signs are pictographs with no phonetic content. In other words, it isn't really a system of writing at all but a set of stylized pictures designed to look like writing. The stimulus for its invention seems to have been a visit by a Spanish ship in 1770, in the course of which the natives were shown an impressive-looking document imposing Spanish sovereignty.

December 7, 1941

(continued from page 89)
2:30 P.M., an hour after the start of the attack, and broadcast by Tokyo radio 2½ hours after that (7 A.M. Tokyo time).

The Japanese air fleets based on Saigon and Taiwan made their first strikes on Singapore and Manila just after 4 A.M. and just before 1 P.M. respectively: this means that the Philippine strike, which was delayed by bad weather, was delivered more than nine hours after the attack on Pearl Harbor and more than six hours after Tokyo had broadcast Japan's official declaration of war. Nonetheless it achieved complete tactical surprise, with more than 100 American planes being destroyed on the ground for a Japanese loss of seven. This suggests that an hour's advance warning of the attack on Pearl Harbor—all that would have been possible even if every clue had triggered an appropriate response—would have made little difference to the outcome.

Minor points to note in relation to this map include the opening of a Honolulu-to-Fiji air route, which prompted the United States to occupy the Central Pacific islands of Howland and Baker plus, by agreement with Britain, Canton in the Phoenix group. Also the reopening of the Burma road in October 1940, when the British, having beaten off the Luftwaffe in the battle of Britain, felt able to take a firmer line with the Japanese. As to the foreign enclaves in China, Guangzhouwan had passed into the Japanese orbit along with Vietnam, and Shanghai's international zone was occupied by Japanese troops on the outbreak of war. Hong Kong and Macao still appear on the map (as symbols only): Hong Kong, already under attack, managed to hold out till Christmas; Macao subsequently accepted Japanese direction.

May 7, 1942

(continued from page 93)
*1. World War II fleet carriers were battleship-sized vessels with a complement of around 75 aircraft; light carriers were smaller and carried only half as many planes. American light carriers (of which none were in service as yet) were built on cruiser hulls and could keep pace with the fleet. Japanese light carriers were typically converted from fleet auxiliaries and, because they were slower, usually operated independently.

June 3, 1942

(continued from page 97)
*1. The last victim of the battle was *Yorktown*. Abandoned on June 4th, the carrier was still afloat on June 5th, and a team was put aboard to try and salvage it. The work was going well when a Japanese submarine, sent to finish it off, did just that by hitting it with two torpedoes. *Yorktown* finally went down just before dawn on June 7th.

The Japanese did what they could to conceal the extent of the debacle. The Aleutian operation went ahead, with Attu and Kiska (the latter a last-minute substitution for Adak) being occupied on June 7th. This enabled the Japanese to claim that, in this area at least, the victory was theirs, and the fact that the islands were unimportant and undefended was glossed over: in this foggy, frozen backwater the rising sun had replaced the stars and stripes. As for the carrier battle, the Japanese genuinely believed that *Hiryu*'s two strikes had hit, and sunk, two different carriers. Accordingly, the naval staff decided to represent the contest as a hard-fought match in which two American carriers had been sunk at a cost of one Japanese carrier sunk and another seriously damaged. Japanese plane losses were put at 35. The gap between this figure and the true total—322—is a measure of the dismay the battle caused among Japan's leaders.

June 19, 1944

(continued from page 101)
*1. Admiral Yamamoto had been shot down and killed while on tour of the Solomons in April 1943: his route had been broadcast in advance using a variant of the code the Americans had broken the previous year, and the United States' South Pacific command was able to set up a successful ambush. Yamamoto's successor in command of the combined fleet, Admiral Koga, is mainly remembered for his decision to transfer the carrier air groups to Rabaul to bolster the defense of the northern Solomons; the disruption of their training schedules is considered to have contributed significantly to the subsequent debacle in the Marianas. After Koga's disappearance, on a flight to the Philippines in February 1944, the combined fleet became a shore command, like Admiral Nimitz's: most of the ships

were regrouped as the First Mobile Fleet and placed under the command of Admiral Ozawa.

*2. Total Japanese aircraft losses on the day of the "turkey shoot" were about 375 (all but 100 of the 430 planes in the carriers, 16 of the 43 floatplanes carried by the battleships and cruisers, and 30 or so of the 50 land-based planes still operational in the Marianas). The American loss was 29. The only hit the Japanese scored was on the battleship *South Dakota*.

On the second day of the battle, Spruance got off a strike, but it was far from full-strength and disposed of only a light carrier. Even when news came in that American submarines had sunk two major units—the fleet carriers *Taiho* (brand-new) and *Shokaku*—many American airmen still felt that an opportunity had been missed. But the Japanese had no illusions about the extent of the disaster. That some carriers had survived was irrelevant: their air groups had been destroyed, and there was no hope of rebuilding the carrier arm into an effective force.

*3. Elsewhere, the Japanese army tried to make positive use of an area where it still had the capacity to act offensively by launching a three-division invasion of India in March. Simultaneously the Allies were trying to reopen land communications with China via north Burma. Thailand received some Burmese and Malay border provinces as a reward for its continuing loyalty to Japan's "Greater East Asia Coprosperity Sphere." The Americans retook Attu and Kiska in the Aleutians and, using their new long-range bomber, the B-29, opened the air offensive against the Japanese homeland with a raid mounted from airfields in China.

October 24, 1944

(continued from page 103)

for operations against warships. He was, in effect, trying to fight a World War II battle with World War I technology.

This is no defense of Halsey. If Spruance had been in charge, not a single Japanese ship would have gotten through, and very few indeed would have gotten home.

*2. In addition to these two escort carriers the Americans lost one light carrier to conventional Luzon-based bombers. Japanese losses added up to one fleet carrier (*Zuikaku*, the last of the six that had struck Pearl Harbor), and three light carriers (all from Ozawa's force), plus three battleships and ten cruisers.

January 1, 1998

(continued from page 109)

ever—in terms of the first sunrise—the literal dawn of the new era—the Chatham islanders will win because of their higher latitude.

In this context it is perhaps worth mentioning that, despite its title, the international date line has no status in international law and wanders about to suit local convenience. Normal usage has the central section coinciding with the 180° meridian; in the north it makes a swing to the west (to put the Aleutians in with Alaska); and in the south it makes a rather smaller swing to the east (to put Tonga and Chatham in with New Zealand).

Acknowledgments

Part title illustrations: p. 1, "Kilauea in Eruption" from Samuel Kneeland, *Volcanoes and Earthquakes,* Boston: D. Lothrop Co. 1888; p. 33, Engraving of Dutch ships at Bantam, Java, 1597, courtesy National Maritime Museum London. Its caption reads (in translation), "Depiction of the great pepper-trading city of Bantam in the island of Java, to which the Dutch shipping came. And what happened to them with the inhabitants as will be explained in the text of this history"; p. 59, After James Cleveley, *View of Huahine, one of the Society Islands in the south seas,* courtesy National Maritime Museum London. The image is from Cook's third voyage: it shows *Resolution* and *Discovery* moored in Fare harbour on the west side of the island in 1777. James Cleveley was the *Resolution*'s carpenter; his sketches were worked up into finished pictures by his artist brother John after his return; p. 79, Detail of Japanese woodblock print showing a scene from the Sino-Japanese War, 1895. Copyright British Museum, London.

The Atlas's first map, showing the Pacific as it is believed to have looked 28 million years ago, draws heavily on the reconstruction proposed by Professor Robert Hall of the SE Asian Research Group, Department of Geology, Royal Holloway, University of London. An animated version of this can be downloaded from the Group's Web site at: http://www.gl.rhbnc.ac.uk/seasia/welcome.html

Index

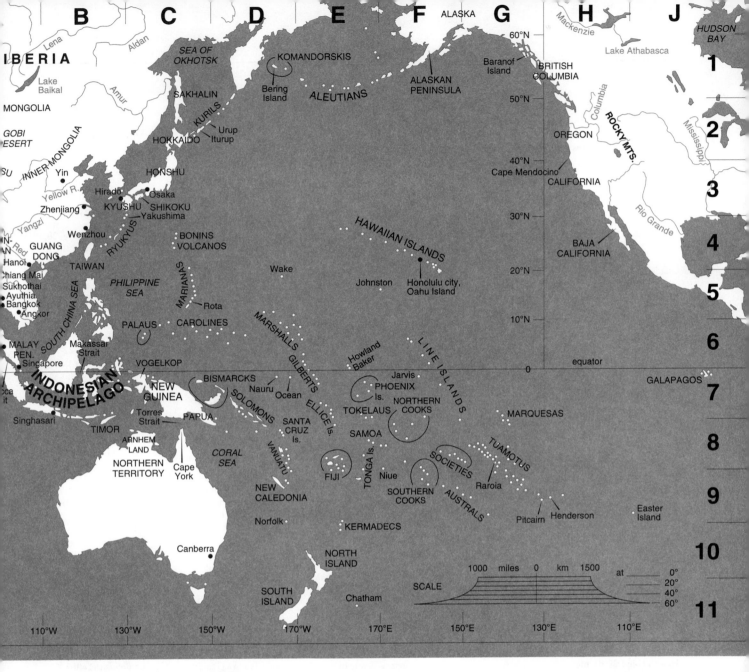